Also by Jane Kramer

OFF WASHINGTON SQUARE

ALLEN GINSBERG IN AMERICA

HONOR TO THE BRIDE

THE LAST COWBOY

UNSETTLING EUROPE

EUROPEANS

WHOSE ART IS IT?

THE POLITICS

OF

MEMORY

THE POLITICS

OF

MEMORY

LOOKING FOR GERMANY

IN THE NEW GERMANY

JANE KRAMER

RANDOM HOUSE   NEW YORK

Most of the names in the story "Peter Schmidt" were changed, and some details were disguised, at the request of Peter's mother, who, at the time it was written, feared reprisals from former members of the East German secret police.

All of the chapters in this book were originally published in *The New Yorker,*
two in somewhat shorter form.

Library of Congress Cataloging-in-Publication Data
Kramer, Jane.
The politics of memory / Jane Kramer. —1st ed.
p.   cm.
ISBN 0-679-44872-1
1. Historiography—Germany.   2. Political culture—Germany.
3. Holocaust, Jewish (1939–1945)—Germany—Influence.
4. Nationalism—Germany.   5. Germany—Ethnic relations.   I. Title.
DD290.24.K7   1996
907'.2043—dc20   95-49803

Random House website address: http://www.randomhouse.com/

Printed in the United States of America on acid-free paper
2   4   6   8   9   7   5   3
First Edition

for Vincent

Why should a man certain of immortality think of his life at all?

—JOSEPH CONRAD, *Under Western Eyes*

ACKNOWLEDGMENTS

Any list of acknowledgments has to begin with Ilse and Spiros Simitis, in Germany. They are my touchstones, the friends whose judgment and insight I value more than I can say. I turn to them on every trip, and I want to thank them now. This book could not have been written without them.

Many other people have helped me in Germany—too many to name them all. My thanks and gratitude go especially to Eike Geisel, Wiglaf Droste, Hans-Magnus Enzensberger, Hanns Zischler, Jürgen Habermas, Klaus Bittermann, and Esther Schapira; and also to Jurg Laederach, across the border in Basel, whose letters about Germany have kept me dazzled and informed through long absences. Tilo Kaiser, Lisa Harries, and Henrike Grohs have been intrepid assistants on my various trips. I want to thank them, too; and also Courtney Aison and Sheila Steeples, for their enormous help at my office in Paris; and Enrica Gadler, at Random House, for all *her* help over the past year.

I also want to thank the staff of *The New Yorker,* beginning with Tina Brown—and before her Bob Gottlieb—who sent me to find these stories and indulged me to the considerable time it took to research and write them; Pam McCarthy, whose sensitive common sense sustained me; John Bennet and Henry Finder, who edited the stories and advised me; Amy Tübke-Davidson, who checked the last story in the book; Bruce Diones, who solved the problems of my bicontinental reporter's life; Kate Kinast, who shook obscure articles out of the Internet for me; and Ann Goldstein, Elizabeth Pearson Griffiths, Liz Macklin, Eleanor Gould, Pat Keogh, and everyone else at the magazine who labored to save me from split infinitives, mixed metaphors and hyperbole as I nursed these stories from manuscript to the printed page.

There are two people to whom I am especially indebted. Liesl Schillinger is my checker at *The New Yorker,* and my third eye; I cannot imagine working without her. Jared Hohlt has been my research assistant, in Paris and New York, for the past two years, and he put together this book with me, copyedited it for me, and then worked his way through three hundred pages of proofs, checking for repeats, redundancies, and ramblings. By now, I think of him more as a partner than as an assistant. This book owes whatever rigor it has to Liesl and Jared.

Ann Godoff, my editor at Random House, is the person who, more than anyone else, understood that for me this collection of stories was in fact one story. I want to thank Ann for her support and encouragement.

And I want especially to thank my friend and agent Ed Victor, whose kindness, humor, and commitment have quite transformed my writing life.

Finally, I want to thank Aleksandra Crapanzano and John Burnham Schwartz, who are my first, best, and most patient readers, and my husband, Vincent Crapanzano, who has borne the brunt of being my best critic. It was Vincent who introduced me to Germany, nurtured my fascination with the country, read Hölderlin to me late at night to teach me the beauty of its language, left its philosophers on my pillow, and over the years argued me out of more received wisdom and fuzzy thoughts than I care to remember. This book is dedicated to him.

CONTENTS

INTRODUCTION   xv

MAXWELL   1

PETER SCHMIDT   51

BERLIN   101

STASI   153

SKINS   213

THE POLITICS OF MEMORY   255

INTRODUCTION

The Germany I got to know was two Germanys, but it was a relatively simple place, as far as reporting was concerned. Germans, in fact, were inventing it for us—which is to say that having lost "Germany," Germans on either side of the Cold War divide were still busy claiming the few fragile remaining virtues of Germanness for their own and placing the considerably more durable vices of Germanness squarely within the other system. East Germans had appropriated the myth of a German resistance, locating it, as it were, in the German Democratic Republic; the official truth was that anyone born east of the Elbe was by definition an anti-fascist, and thus anyone born west of the river was a Nazi. West Germans, for their part, had appropriated the myth of a German public culture, a democratic culture, locating *it* in the Federal Republic and turning "Communist East Germany" into another way of saying "Nazi East Germany"—since in the new mythology of the West, both words stood for the same "bad German."

And so it had gone—the evasions of history, the (literally, if one thinks of Ulrike Meinhof) maddening silences—for more than forty years. The Cold War replaced the real war when it came to that peculiarly German obsession with identity that the natives tend to regard as the highest expression of their *Innerlichkeit* (which means their "innerness" and is, I suspect, the most overused, overvalued, and wantonly exculpatory word in the German language). It buried the past—to Germans, the past means very specifically the Hitler years—without a reckoning, without committing the past to history. Inventing Germany had been anybody's game and everybody's game since the war ended, in 1945, and nothing about that changed until the night of November 9, 1989, when Helmut Kohl bought East Germany from Mikhail Gorbachev, and the Wall started coming down, and the two Germanys became "Germany"—became, again, the real country that had started two world wars and caused the death of nearly fifty million people, the country with a history that was specifically Germany's history, and not the East's history or the West's history. After forty-four years of distraction, Germans began the excruciating process of connecting the kind of people they thought they were to the people they had been and the people they wanted to be. They discovered that it was hard to be ordinary folks—ordinary European folks—when you had a Holocaust in your history.

∾

A young German anthropologist named Henrike Grohs, who helped me in Berlin when I was researching the last chapter of this book, talked a great deal about the problem of being "German" when you were twenty-nine and wanted simply to be German. She said that whenever she went abroad, the first thing people asked her about was the Holocaust. She was bewildered, and often angry, about always having to answer to other people's notions of collective guilt. She was tired of being ashamed of a past that was not *her* past. It was a feeling she shared with a lot of other young Germans. They did not know how to *be* German. They did not know what to think about a place that everyone else in the world referred to as—you can almost hear the quotation marks—"Germany."

Some young Germans refer to themselves today as "the generation of 1989," to distinguish themselves from their parents, in the generation of 1968, who were close enough to the Nazi past to suffer it and fear it. They are not averse to patriotism. They search history for what Henrike called "another way of being German," which means, of course, for the examples of Germans who fought *against* Hitler. May of 1995 was the fiftieth anniversary of the German defeat—or "the liberation," as the government now calls it. It was the first major commemoration involving the war in what was now a united Germany, and most of my own German friends were alarmed by the official enthusiasm for that commemoration, because it seemed to them that Helmut Kohl was turning the idea of "liberation" into an idea called "Victim Germany"—into an easy slogan of absolution. ("Fifty years of freedom in Germany," the posters said, although this was not a phrase that many people in the east of Germany would have chosen.) But Henrike and *her* friends were relieved, and even proud.

The Germany they would like to invent now is a kind of America—guilty, forgiven, and absolved. They make analogies with America. They talk about Hiroshima. One of the editors of the newspaper *Junge Welt*—a young East German of appealing unworldliness, who quotes Abe Rosenthal and Henry Kissinger as "Germany's friends on the American left"—told me the other day that Germany's "guilt problem" with the Holocaust was "just like America's anguish over Hiroshima." He was stunned when I asked him, "What anguish?" He found it hard to believe that Americans, on the whole, were neither particularly guilty—anguishingly, personally guilty—for the crimes of their parents' or grandparents' generation, the way some Germans are, nor were they in denial, the way other Germans seem, increasingly, to be. Like a lot of Germans, young *and* old, he thought of African-Americans and Native Americans as "America's Jews."

A few days ago, going through my German files, I came across a piece from *Der Spiegel* about (the Germans say this) "the Shoah business," written by the Berlin journalist Henryk Broder. Broder is Jewish. He was born in Poland, and he used to live in Israel, but he lives in Germany now and is, in fact, a German citizen, so it interested me, as I read the piece, to discover that it included an attack on the Holocaust Museum in Washington. Broder was boycotting the museum. He thought that Americans would do better to confront the corpses in their own closets than to lecture Germans about the Holocaust; he wondered why Americans bothered to spend a fortune teaching their kids about murder in Germany when they could just as easily send those kids to the streets of Chicago and teach them something about murder at home. Broder's confusion of Germany and America reminded me of the work of a German friend named Lothar Baumgarten, a Düsseldorf artist who used to collect Native American artifacts and display them, like death camp relics, to evoke what he called "the American genocide." Not long ago, he was asked to mount an installation at the Guggenheim; he covered the walls of the museum with the names of American Indian tribes from Patagonia to the Arctic

Circle. He turned the Guggenheim into a kind of minimalist holocaust memorial—and wondered why the critics were cold.

∞

All this is really to say that any outsider writing about Germany over the past few years has had the doubly difficult job of weighing his or her Germany against the Germany that Germans are now reinventing for themselves. It started not just when the Wall fell but, I would say, a year or two *before* it fell—as if Germans were acting in anticipation of events that nobody really knew would happen. So, at least, it seems to me now. There was a sea change, and all of us covering Germany felt it (though most of us would have been hard put to it to describe it). It was a feeling that after years of writing variations on the same story we were close to a new story, lurking somewhere inside all that *Innerlichkeit,* and that that story was going to be found not in the two official Germanys but in the readings and misreadings of "Germanness" on the part of ordinary people looking at themselves and trying to stake a claim to the truth of what "being German" meant. I felt it first in 1988, when I went to Berlin to write a piece—the kind of piece that's known in the trade as a "Whither Germany?"—and filed, instead, the story of a filmmaker named Hartmut Bitomsky and a kid called Strumpf, the story that begins this book. I remember arriving at Tegelhof, checking into my hotel, and calling a lawyer I knew, Otto Schilly—a lawyer who had represented Meinhof, and who at the time was a Green deputy in the Bundestag. We met for a drink at a Charlottenburg hangout called Fofi's, and I dutifully asked him what had been happening in Berlin since my last visit. He replied, "Hartmut Bitomsky's restaurant." I thought he meant a new hangout. I said, "I mean happening *politically.*" And he said, "I *mean* politically." The next morning, I was knocking on doors in Kreuzberg, trying to put together the pieces of what indeed had happened when a documentary filmmaker and semiologist, a child of 1968 who had spent the past twenty years looking at the images of Germanness—the forests and the autobahns and the golden pigtails—that the Nazis had appropriated as propaganda, opened a restaurant for his wife in a neighborhood of squatters and dropouts and latchkey children in heavy metal who were claiming the turf, and *its* images as, you could say, *Lebens-raum*. I found myself in the middle of a Western without a show-down to resolve it: a story about a middle-aged man who had misread the signs of the new Germany and a younger man who understood them all too well. I didn't know it then, but looking back, I would say that it was really a story about a new fascism, about the first stirrings of that fascism, in people whom we would now call skinheads but who were posing then, even to themselves, as something radical and revolutionary and free. What I did know then was that I was not *in* Germany—not in the way I had been *in* Germany on earlier visits, writing earlier stories. Running around Kreuzberg, trying to piece together the story of Hartmut and Strumpf, I began to understand that what I was really doing was looking *for* Germany. It was an accidental, trial-and-error, painfully inaccurate exercise. Almost a German exercise. It reminded me of something the novelist Walter Abish—who had written a wonderful book about an imagined Germany and had called it *How German Is It?*—once told me about actually going to Germany for the first time. He said that the Germans he met were agreeable and would drive him around, trying to "find" his Germany, but it was always they who asked "How German is it?" when they saw or heard something disturbing. I thought about stopping in Kreuzberg, and writing a book myself, but then the Wall fell, and I knew that looking for Germany now was a process that would take me years.

So I kept returning. My next German story was another accident. I was heading back to Berlin, a few months after the Wall fell, having assured *The New Yorker* that I was finally going to produce a "Whither Germany?" And that, in fact, was what I intended until I stopped in Hamburg to pick up a student—the daughter of friends—named Lisa Harries, who was going to help me. Lisa was American, but her father, Karsten, who taught philosophy at Yale, was German, and Lisa herself was in Hamburg doing a doctorate in German history. We had dinner that night, and were catching up on family gossip, when she happened to mention the roommate of a boy she knew in Hamburg—a strange, lost, East German boy who had tried to leave East Germany years earlier and had ended up in a political prison until the West German government bought him "out" in an exchange of Eastern prisoners for Western cash. I never got to Berlin. I stayed in Hamburg, getting to know "Peter Schmidt," and then I went to Mecklenburg with Peter on his first trip home since the East German secret police had deposited him across the West German border. And in the process I learned something about East Germany. I learned that "East Germany, trying to teach Peter *what* he was—trying to produce a worker for a workers' state, someone not too smart, not too skeptical, someone cooperative—had neglected to teach him anything about *who* he was or how to get to be himself." His story turned out to be a story about that deep passivity which was perhaps the East's most troubling legacy to the "new" Germany. Peter was really a boy without history. He was waiting for "history" to turn him into something appropriately "German."

By the time I did get back to Berlin, a year later, the Bundestag had voted to declare it, once again, the German capital. And so the story I filed from Berlin in 1991 was, perhaps inevitably, about what it meant, symbolically, psychologically, when you took what Auden would have called the "moral landscape" of postwar Germany, which was a western landscape, a Bonn landscape, and tried to transplant it, so to speak, in a city that was once the capital of Hitler's Reich—and hoped that it would take. It was about the psychology of that move, the ideology of that move. Very specifically, it was about what "being German" was going to mean in a united Germany where, as Walter Abish had suspected, everyone German was looking for Germany too.

That, I suppose, was as close as I got to a "Whither Germany?" because my next German story was another kind of accident. I was in Paris, thinking about a trip to Berlin and reading everything I could about Germany, when I opened that week's *Die Zeit* to the news that Wolf Biermann—the East German folksinger-poet who had had his citizenship "canceled" in 1976 and was now living a comfortable literary life in Hamburg—had just received the Georg Büchner Prize, the country's most important literary prize. The paper reprinted Biermann's acceptance speech. It was an angry speech, all about the "dark times" in Germany, but what interested *Die Zeit,* and in fact most of Germany, was that Biermann had used it as the occasion to "out" another East German poet, a not-very-good poet by the name of Sascha Anderson, as having been a paid informer for the Stasi—which is to say for the East German secret police—and, very likely, as the informer who once had spied on him. So I was back to "How German is it?" The story I wrote then was about the Prenzlauer Berg painters and poets, about freedom and betrayal in the German Democratic Republic. But you could say that it was really about the continuity of a culture of betrayal in Germany. I wondered how different, in the end, a Sascha Anderson—an artist who sold his friends to the state for cash, status, and "protection"—was from the thugs who had managed to shut down Hartmut Bitomsky's restaurant and, of course, from the spies and agents and informers who served the terror of National Socialism. I wanted to look at the specifically German conditions for setting oneself beyond morality, or decency, or friendship. They were really the old conditions, resurfacing even, and maybe especially, now.

It isn't surprising that by then I also wanted to look at the extent to which those conditions had resurfaced. I knew that I was on my way to a book, and the next time I went to Germany, I stopped in Frankfurt, to see two old friends whose advice I always rely on when it comes to "How German is it?"—Spiros Simitis, who teaches constitutional law at the University of Frankfurt, and his wife, Ilse, who is a psychoanalyst and writer. We met at the new museum of contemporary art for lunch and a look around, and Ilse asked me if I had happened to catch the morning news on the radio at my hotel. I said no. (I had in fact been having a very good time watching an old Steve McQueen movie on television.) And Ilse replied that, in that case, maybe I'd be interested in driving down to Ludwigshafen, in Rheinland-Pfalz, because a Turkish grocery had just been bombed in Ludwigshafen, and the assumption was that neo-Nazi skinheads were responsible. The next morning I was at the Ludwigshafen police station, talking to a big, bearded cop with boots and blue jeans and a stud in his ear—Detective Hans Jürgen Ladinek of the Ludwigshafen criminal police. I would describe *that* piece as a story about racist fantasies of a new "old" Germany; about Turks and skins and decent cops in a country where *jus sanguinis* is still practiced. It wasn't necessarily

"Whither Germany?" but it was certainly part of the Germany that was being reinvented.

By the time I got back to Berlin, it was 1995 and the fiftieth anniversary of the German defeat—and, clearly, the moment for "Whither Germany?" I had planned to write something about the million or more ethnic Germans who were "resettling" in Germany—about what Germans call, without a trace of irony, "the return of the German diaspora." In other words, about new stirrings of German nationalism. But something haunted me—something I had heard in Washington early that winter, when I was giving a talk at the Goethe Institute. The director of the institute, knowing that I was planning a trip, had talked to me then about a kind of ultimate revisionism that was taking place in Germany under the aegis of the German chancellor: an end-of-the-past project that was turning the twelve dark years of Hitler into twelve years of resistance *to* Hitler and occupation *by* Hitler; an abandonment, for the sake of settling the past into "history," of the very plain historical truth that Germany had *chosen* Hitler. So, in Berlin, I started asking questions about memory, and discovered that the politics of memory were arguably the most loaded politics of the new, united German state. I discovered that fifty years after the war, the most interesting story (at least, to me) in the capital was a story about Germans and Jews—about who "owned" the memory of the Holocaust and who had a right to that memory, the perpetrator or the victim. It was a story about Germany's plans to build a Holocaust memorial in the shadow of the Brandenburg Gate, a memorial, as the television talk-show hostess promoting the project (and herself with it), called it, "as big as the crime." It became the last chapter in this book.

∞

It may be that in the end "Whither Germany?" is really another way of saying "Whence Germany?" because Germany's particular hell is that for Germans reinventing Germany, looking for Germany, asking themselves how German is it, the past is undeniably as German as it gets. This is why Germany watchers like myself—people who like Germany, people who like Germans—have to watch *themselves* when they take on Germany as a subject. The experience of "Germany" is almost by definition voyeuristic, and we can never really be sure about our fascination—the "whence" and "whither" of that fascination. Jonathan Randal, who writes for *The Washington Post* and covered Germany for the first time last year, told me when he came home that maybe we were asking too much of Germans, putting too much of a burden on Germans. He said that we don't demand that Russians, say, account eternally for their genocides, or Cambodians or Rwandans, or even Serbs, who were commiting them now—not, at least, the way we demand it of Germans. It may be simply that we identify with Germans. Germans, insofar as they are part of what we like to call civilization, are us—and they have been the unimaginable *in* us. But it may also be that we demand it because Germans demand it of themselves. "How German is it?" is a national obsession—a letter I got from a professor at Amherst, after the last chapter of this book appeared in *The New Yorker,* called the Berlin Holocaust Memorial project an example of "the German genius for turning morbidly earnest self-examination into an exercise of grotesque narcissism and . . . self-parody"—but Germans themselves tend to see it as a condition of national salvation. Ten years ago, working on another book, I wrote that Germany "may be the only country in the world where people check up on reality with such persistence, anxiety, and desire," and I believe this more than ever now. The danger for Germans today is that they get caught in the double bind of a kind of pietistic historicism. They have embraced not so much "destiny" as *their* destiny, Germany's destiny, and they continue to embrace it, despite the best efforts of liberal German intellectuals like Jürgen Habermas, who have tried to pry them loose from that embrace and return them to a world where who they are is up to them, and not simply something terrible that happened to them. Habermas would say that any belief in a special German destiny— even a negative destiny—is really another kind of nationalism. All this, of course, is what makes Germany irresistible to writers: Germany is where you get to address the Big Issues; Germany is where you get to talk about good and evil, and your story runs. The danger for a writer, is that the *Innerlichkeit*—the narcissism and the self-parody—is catching.

Last year, I gave a reading at the Hamburg Literaturhaus. The subject was Germany. I was supposed to read selections from this book in English, but my friend Hanns Zischler—he is a Berlin writer and actor, and he had kindly offered to come to Hamburg and read parts of it in German—suggested that we "lighten" the evening with something from France, something from Italy, something "not so heavy and German." So I added passages from a story about a Calabrian con man, a self-styled Lacanian shrink named Armando Verdiglione, who had bilked his patients out of tens of millions of dollars, and a story about France's invention of the *le peuple*—the people. They were funny stories, and after I read them, a nice man raised his hand and asked, in a rather discouraged voice, "Why don't you ever write something funny, something like that, about Germany?" It's a question I have been asking myself since then, but I can't pretend to have the answer.

Jane Kramer
Paris, June 1996

MAXWELL

(NOVEMBER 1988)

One night last year, a punk working the Oranienstrasse—the main street in Kreuzberg—stopped with some neighborhood news at the back door of a restaurant called Maxwell. The punk worked the Oranienstrasse for scraps, and inasmuch as there were always plenty of good scraps at Maxwell, something like an arrangement, if not precisely a relationship, had established itself between the punk and the Bitomskys, Hartmut and Brigitte, who owned the restaurant. People in Kreuzberg make their own arrangements. They call their neighborhood Berlin's Berlin. They inhabit the most freewheeling and anarchic quarter of a city not noted for conformity to begin with, and many of them consider themselves outsiders to bourgeois life. "It was the atmosphere I liked, the people who were not 'arranged,' who were out of society a bit," Brigitte Bitomsky says now.

Wolfgang Krüger, the Kreuzberg mayor (every neighborhood in West Berlin has a mayor), likes to point out that unarranged people are not "ordinary Kreuzbergers." The mayor considers himself an ordinary Kreuzberger. He says that there are thousands of other ordinary Kreuzbergers just like him—by which he means thousands of middle-aged citizens from solid, conservative Berlin worker stock who vote for the Christian Democrats (or, at worst, the Social Democrats) and have never "squatted" an abandoned house or shaved their heads or smoked a joint or worn safety pins in their ears or made a punk-rock video or got teargassed at the barricades during a May Day demonstration. They are not what most Germans think of when they hear "Kreuzberg." Most Germans think of the street gangs and the outlaw communes that, taken together, are known to the country as the Autonomen. They think of an entirely exotic mix of sixties leftists, seventies squatters, Turkish workers, art people, craft people, and various other apostles of what Berliners call "alternative culture," punks, pimps, skinheads, addicts, architects, intellectuals, and runaway children trading the dreary certainties of an apprenticed life in the Federal Republic for the spacey possibilities of a "scene" in the shadow of the Berlin Wall. Those are the Kreuzbergers who have "chosen" Kreuzberg. Choosing Kreuzberg is a point of pride among them, though Kreuzbergers like the mayor tend to think of them as foreigners—even when they have come from no farther away than Schöneberg or Charlottenburg or some other West Berlin neighborhood. The feeling among ordinary Kreuzbergers these days is that the only good foreigners here are the Turkish workers. The Turks arrived in Kreuzberg after the Wall went up—cheap labor to replace the Poles and the East Germans in West Berlin's factories. They came when Kreuzberg was, properly speaking, more bombed out than spaced out, and their immigrants' fear of being sent away has turned them into model citizens.

Twenty years ago, these Kreuzberg Turks were herding sheep in Anatolia. Twenty years ago, the punk begging on the Oranienstrasse was flunking elementary school in a West German village. And twenty years ago Hartmut Bitomsky and seventeen friends at Berlin's new film school, the German Film and Television Academy, had occupied the school and renamed it the Dziga Vertov Academy, in honor of an old Soviet documentary filmmaker—and got expelled. Hartmut himself turned into one of Germany's best documentary filmmakers, although he never made the kind of money his old classmates made by "going over" to the Federal Republic and producing slick programs for West German television. Hartmut was known for a kind of dogged purity of purpose. He edited the magazine *Filmkritik,* which was as important to young German filmmakers in the sixties and seventies as *Cahiers du Cinéma* was to young French filmmakers. He wrote a book—a "Marxist aesthetics"—about film and politics. (It was called *Die Röte des Rots von Technicolor,* which means "The Redness of the Red in Technicolor.") And he settled down in Berlin and started working, slowly and painstakingly, on his movies. He was obsessed by what he calls "German images"—images of identity, images like forests and blond braids and superhighways, which the Nazis had appropriated or invented and postwar Germans had had to reinvent, purged of their associations, and Germans were still inventing as a country now. He considered himself an expert on images. When he talks about Kreuzberg, he sometimes says how much he liked "the images that Kreuzberg presented to me"— images of tolerance and eccentricity and community. He thought he understood those images, and he certainly thought he understood the image *he* presented to Kreuzberg when he fixed up a little restaurant on the Oranienstrasse so that Brigitte, who loved to cook, could practice her "refined bourgeois cooking"—her puréed borscht and her rabbit with tarragon and her flourless sauces—for the neighborhood. He felt at home in Kreuzberg. He was not prepared for the news that the punk, making a small exchange for some old baguettes and a bowl of Brigitte's soup, brought that night to the Oranienstrasse—the news that Hartmut and Brigitte Bitomsky were on a hit list.

The list was posted down the street, off the Heinrichplatz, in an Autonomen bar called SO 36 (after Südost 36, one of the two Kreuzberg postal codes), and the punk had seen it when he went to the bar for a Sunday soup kitchen. There were fifty names on the hit list, and some fifty pictures, representing what the Autonomen at SO 36 called *Kiezfremde*—the "enemies" who were threatening Kreuzberg. There was a picture of Maxwell. There was a picture of a shop with ten-speed bicycles and a shop with handmade silk underwear and a shop specializing in Italian books and a bar the Autonomen considered Schicki-Micki—which means "Mickey Mouse chic," and which people in Kreuzberg use to mean anything that offends them, anything affected or pretentious or expensive or simply out of place, like a nouvelle-cuisine restaurant with an English name on a street claimed by freaks and punks and runaways and dropouts whose own affectation it is to pretend to have more in common with a Turkish sheepherder doing piecework in a Berlin factory than with neighbors like Brigitte and Hartmut Bitomsky. The Autonomen had decided that the Bitomskys were part of the enemy culture that was gentrifying Kreuzberg—the culture that was driving up prices, bringing in rich, chic people from Charlottenburg and the other expensive Berlin neighborhoods, ruining a scene that had made Kreuzberg the fantasy of half the teenagers in West (and East) Germany and on the European backpack circuit, and forcing "the people" out. The message was that Brigitte and Hartmut Bitomsky had to go.

∞

There are nearly two million people living inside the Wall in West Berlin, and some of them think of the city as a prison and some of them think of it as a playpen and some think of it as a place to collect their pensions and die and some as a place to dodge the army, and some as a place they are simply passing through on their way to a sober grown-up life a couple of hundred miles away in the prosperous *Länder* of the Federal Republic. Some West Germans have not been to Berlin since the obligatory grade-school trip they took at eleven. The trip is intended as a history lesson, but most of those Germans cannot even remember if their Berlin lesson had to do with the city's history as the real capital of a disastrously united Germany or the symbolic capital of a peacefully divided one—if it was a lesson in shame or pride or in the contradictions of tainted nationality. They do not know what their memories of Berlin should be, or what kind of "German" the city is supposed to awaken in them. A lot of people think that Berlin is the only "real" city in West Germany—that its schizy, provisional character is a much more authentic "Germany" than the sleek, successful cities of the Federal Republic, where bluff and politics and money have groomed the past, like silver rinse on the thick gray hair of a Düsseldorf industrialist.

It is impossible to groom Berlin, to make it look like a normal city. This is not just a question of the Wall—although there is no escaping the fact that the Wall is there, at the end of every road. It is not even a question of the lugubrious restorations of the Third Reich that various postwar governments have inflicted on the city. It has to do with the fact that Berlin never recovered in the way that West Germany claims to have recovered. Beyond the trees and lakes of its lovely parks—a third of West Berlin is parks and forests—Berlin is a profoundly scarred city. It manages to look razed in its busiest, most built-up sectors—as if the past were scattering rubble in your eyes, like magic dust. Architects come from all over the world and build libraries and museums and modish and inventive housing, and instead of transforming Berlin, they manage to accentuate its ugliness. That ugliness is Berlin's distinction. It is a city under punishment, and there is nothing covert about it, nothing easy or soothing about *its* images. It wears its past like mise-en-scènes—which may be why people who make movies are so fascinated by it. The director Margarethe von Trotta, who is Bitomsky's age, once said that Berlin is the only city in Germany that looks the way Germany *should* look—the way Germany deserves to look in what is, after all, less than a half century since Hitler.

Berlin is provocative. It raises questions, by being there, which give it its vividness and its unnerving license. People who go to Berlin, like von Trotta, say that as Germans they *need* Berlin, that stopping every now and then in Berlin is a sort of reality check for them—but "reality" is precisely why other Germans hate the city, and never visit, and say that they could never live here. Those Germans mean something very different by "reality." They mean the relations and responsibilities of postwar German life, and Berlin, for them, is in every way disconnected from that life—a hundred and eighty-five square miles bounded by a hundred miles of barbed wire and white concrete and financed almost entirely by subsidies (by eleven and a half billion Deutsche marks a year directly from Bonn, and another eight billion in tax breaks and business credits and salary bonuses and hardship pensions that Bonn calls "indirect subsidies" and Berlin prefers to call "promotions"). They hate Berlin because Berlin is not accountable, because nothing is asked of Berlin beyond its own complicity in surviving. The city as such is a legal fiction. Officially, Berlin is still occupied. Officially, the mayor of West Berlin receives his permission to govern every morning from the commander of the Allied Occupation Forces. Officially, the law is still Occupation law, and Bonn's jurisdiction over its half of the city is still "temporarily suspended" by the Allies, but, then, officially, Berlin is still the four sectors of an unresolved war zone (and, officially, is intended to stay that way until Germany is united). Bonn, of course, does not know what to do about Berlin, except support it. The closest Bonn has come to a Berlin policy is to fill it with people and pay it to import enough culture and enough conventioneers to keep those people busy while the real Germany grits its teeth and "does" Berlin as a kind of civic duty, like military service—and in the end resents it.

The problem is that West Berlin is not responsible, even to itself.

It is a frontier, a way of going west by going east, a place for land grabs and easy money and summary justice like hit lists in soup kitchens, and also a place to experiment, and even fail, beyond the punishing scrutiny of the Germany of economic miracles and bulldozer recovery. Berlin is under another kind of scrutiny. People who like Berlin and try to describe it use words like "stage" and "laboratory" and "social theater." Foreigners tend to think of it as the stage where the Good West and the Bad East have been having their showdown for twenty-seven years. But for Germans it is a different kind of stage—a radical-workshop stage where the ideas and attitudes of West Germany are improvised. Germany's 1968 began in West Berlin. So did German revisionism and Ostpolitik and the Green movement (the West Berlin Greens call themselves the Alternativen, or Alternative List, and get 25 percent of the vote in neighborhoods like Kreuzberg). Politicians from every party use Berlin to practice their performance. Willy Brandt was the mayor of West Berlin when the Wall went up (and when John Kennedy said, "*Ich bin ein Berliner*"). Richard von Weizsäcker was the mayor here twenty years later—and is the president of Germany now.

There is a big difference between Berlin politicians and the politicians who are passing through on their way to power in the Federal Republic. The Berliners—wherever they come from—belong to a kind of local mafia. They are here for the cruder, material satisfactions of influence in a city where notions of conflict of interest have yet to be developed—where people describe corruption with the word for felt, *Filz,* because in Berlin the threads of power, politics, and profit are pressed together so tightly that no one can tell them apart. Everyone who has anything to do with Berlin is part of *der Filz.* The Cologne dentist who invests in a construction scheme—construction is the liveliest business in Berlin, though a lot of old buildings here are empty, held by West Germans for speculation—gets so many tax credits and subsidies for investing in Berlin that he ends up paying nothing for his property. The business that opens a branch factory in Berlin gets so many credits and subsidies that it can cancel its costs and write off whatever profits it is taking somewhere else. Officially, West Berlin is the first industrial city of West Germany, but that is really another way of saying there are more workers in Berlin than in, say, Hamburg or Düsseldorf. A shirt woven in the Ruhr may pass through Berlin to have its buttons sewn on by a machine in a local branch factory, but it goes back to the Ruhr for its finishing stitches.

The real business of Berlin is Berlin. Nearly a quarter of the people who work here work for the city—which means, in effect, that they are paid by West Germany—and probably more work in subsidized or "guaranteed" jobs. A lot of those jobs have to do with importing culture. (Kreuzbergers say "official culture.") Artists and writers and performers come to Berlin as guests of the city every year, and so do hundreds of scholars, because Berlin has a hundred and eighty-five think tanks and *Wissenschaft* institutes to invite them. They settle into free apartments and cash their grant money and get their table at the Paris Bar and are fussed over, like heads of state, for what they are told is their creative presence—and provide the "Berlin culture" for the West Germans who arrive as tourists, book into the Kempinski or the Schweitzerhof, buy their tickets, attend the city, and go home. One of the things they attend is Kreuzberg. This is why, when kids arrive in Kreuzberg with no money and no jobs, Berlin takes care of them, too—and why by way of assurance and insurance the mayor of Berlin writes the foreword to a guide to Kreuzberg and gives the Oranienstrasse his official imprimatur as a cultural happening, another one of Berlin's amazing tourist attractions, like the restored Reichstag or Herbert von Karajan or the Wall.

∞

When Hartmut Bitomsky arrived in West Berlin to study, it was 1962 and the Wall had just gone up and the city was digging in for a siege that would last for the next ten years, until the agreement establishing contact between the two Berlins was finally signed, and life in West Berlin was officially declared "back to normal." In 1962, life in West Berlin was exciting, exhausting, and entirely abnormal—and students like Hartmut, who was an architect's son in Bremen, and restless, he says, and full of art and politics, longed to go there. Hartmut started out at the Free University, studying philology and theater, but as soon as the film school opened he enrolled. There were only two film schools in West Germany in 1968, the Berlin school and a school in Munich, and for a young radical like Hartmut the Film and Television Academy in Berlin was the serious one, the one where people talked about Marx and Mao and about why socialism worked and capitalism didn't work, the one where people practiced making difficult, provocative movies for friends who already had the right high political standards, the one where May 1968 was being invented for the rest of Germany. Hartmut was famous, at twenty-six, for occupying the film school and getting expelled—much more famous, he says, than he would have been if the rector had let him stay once the sit-ins and demonstrations and occupations were over.

It never occurred to Hartmut to go home to Bremen. He liked the temper of Berlin. He subscribed to the Berlin maxim that within its Wall, Berlin was the freest city in the world. He liked the fact that Berliners were judged, by definition, to be a little crazy. It made them tolerant and gave them a kind of family solidarity, and, more important, it freed them from the pressures of the economic miracle—from the clothes and cars and the ostentatious proprieties of a successful West German life. One of the editors who worked with Hartmut on *Filmkritik* (which was a collective, with nine or ten editors, each with his own politics and his own theories and his own ideas about making movies) says that Hartmut was a natural Berliner. He was by disposition an outsider. He didn't belong to any of the groups or schools that were preaching a "new German cinema." He was not much interested in fame or money. He was not chic. He lived simply, and—in a city where half the people are in cashmere and the other half are in costumes—he dressed simply, something like a lumberjack, in mud boots and jeans and an old plaid or denim work shirt. He favored the kind of places that people the Autonomen call "the people" frequent. Brigitte, who was a policeman's daughter from Stuttgart, met Hartmut in a bar, at the pinball machine.

Brigitte Bitomsky was another natural Berliner—a dark, fragile, pretty girl who arrived at the age of twenty-one "in black and sunglasses," enrolled in teachers' college, and showed up once, on the first day. Her friends, she says, were dropouts and drifters. Or they were "lazybones"—which is how she likes to describe herself. They were always broke and often stoned, and some of them died,

she says, and all of them made a point of being *Verweigerer*, of re-
jecting the conventions of bourgeois German life. Brigitte says that
even then she could not imagine living in any other German city.
The longest she has been away since she moved here was six
months in 1971, when she went to Ibiza. The longest Hartmut has
been away was six months in 1980, when he crossed America on
Highway 40 West to make a three-hour documentary that Germans refer to as Hartmut Bitomsky's "road movie." After that, the
Bitomskys moved to Kreuzberg.

Brigitte was as much at home in Kreuzberg as Hartmut. "I liked
everything about it—everything that turned against us," she says
now. It was different from Schöneberg, where she and Hartmut
had lived before, and from the other neighborhoods they knew,
which were either for working or for sleeping and had none of the
texture of Kreuzberg, with its mixture of workers and Turks and
artists and students and freaky people from the Oranienstrasse
scene. They found an apartment on the Ritterstrasse, one block
south of the Oranienstrasse. It was in an old and fairly dilapidated
building, but there was a room free on the ground floor where
Hartmut could store his film and do his editing—an address for Big
Sky Film, which was the name he brought home from America for
a production company. "It seemed like a paradise," he says. "We
knew there was pressure, that there was 'money' invading, but
we had no money. We were not chic Charlottenburg people. We
didn't know that we were, maybe, part of this invasion—at least,
this has been the reproach to us, that we were part of the invasion.
For us, it was like a dream. It was like living an idea of cities—an
idea we had inherited from writers of the nineteenth century.
Kreuzberg, for us, was life lived in the street. It was people talking
and hawking. It was children playing."

The year the Bitomskys moved to Kreuzberg, the Copenhagen
Filmmuseet sent the West Berlin Kinemathek some twenty reels of
old Nazi propaganda film from its archives, and Hartmut started
going through them, and then through hundreds of others that he
dug out of the Bundesarchiv in Koblenz. He says there were literally rooms of uncatalogued Nazi propaganda films in Koblenz. It
was not military propaganda or political propaganda (which Hartmut thinks is the reason everyone had ignored it), but it was the

kind of propaganda that interested him. It had to do with the creation of what could be called an *Asphaltlyrik* of Nazi Germany—a poetry of highways and cars and engineering which Germans would somehow identify with National Socialism and with the triumph of National Socialism. It had to do with the idea of a collective German will expressing itself in industrial culture—in culture at the service of construction and construction at the service of the Third Reich. It was a treasure, Hartmut says, if "treasure" was a word you could use when you were talking about Nazis. He could not get over the energy and intelligence and expense that had gone into making these movies that on the surface looked like ordinary, and even boring, documentaries about things like building a road between two German cities. He had been thinking a lot about cities now that he was living in Kreuzberg. He was reading Roland Barthes and the French semiologists, and he was also reading Baudelaire, who in his own time and his own way had written an *Asphaltlyrik* of Paris—of a poet's life on Baron Haussmann's new boulevards. Hartmut says that sitting at his editing table at the Kinemathek, going over those reels of film, he saw that this was not so different from what Nazi artists had tried to do for Germany, using the image of Hitler's Reichsautobahn, the superhighway of the Third Reich, to create what Hartmut thinks of as a "Reichsautobahn genre." There were Reichsautobahn painters and Reichsautobahn poets and Reichsautobahn printers putting out Reichsautobahn stamps and Reichsautobahn posters, and mainly there were Reichsautobahn movies—movies about how the man who took the highway always got the prettiest girl, the girl who knew what she wanted and liked a fellow who could take over and drive fast and get where he was going before the others.

Hartmut wanted to do something of his own with the footage. He wanted to find a form—something between documentary and essay—that would re-create the experience of those Nazi images. He wanted to give Germans a sense of how images had worked on them in the past and maybe were working now. He says he did not want to "touch" those images—to intrude on them or explain them. He was not interested in making obvious comments about manipulation or duplicity (the Reichsautobahn was, after all, a highway for moving tanks and troops, a highway for conquering

Europe, and not just for handsome men and pretty girls in convertibles) or in censoring his treasure from the perspective of a 1968 Berlin radical turning forty. He wanted the people who saw his movies—he ended up planning a trilogy on the propaganda footage—to come to some sort of appropriate respect for the power of images in the hands of experts like those Nazi filmmakers. He wanted them to feel how susceptible they were. He wanted to make them vigilant. His critics said later that he was very austere and very demanding, but Hartmut says that he was simply working in his own way, and that it helped a lot—given such chilling material—to be living in such a lively, humane, tolerant place as Kreuzberg. It seemed to him then that Kreuzberg was the only place in Germany that fit what he calls "my politics and semiology." He spent the next seven years working in his room at home. He figures that after seven years, everybody in the neighborhood knew him.

∞

It is hard to miss Hartmut, even (or especially) in a place like Kreuzberg. He is a big, serious, slow-moving, cumbersome man. He has mild blue eyes and light brown hair and a droopy brown mustache that seems to be his major vanity, and he still dresses like a lumberjack, in his jeans and his work shirts. There is something laborious about Hartmut, like his movies—a diffidence, an awkwardness, as if he were thinking or watching or making up his mind or simply not wanting to intrude. People who were pro-Maxwell put it down to modesty or gentleness and people who were anti-Maxwell say that Hartmut is stubborn and that it comes from pigheadedness. But everyone agrees he is a kind man. He wanted Brigitte to have her restaurant. She had taught herself to cook from a copy of Escoffier, and while she is a nervous person, and shy, she was always confident about her cooking. She likes to say that after Escoffier all the cookbooks in the world are only pictures. She went out to apprentice at a big restaurant called Tessinerstube, near the Kurfürstendamm and the big stores, and sat through a couple of obligatory lessons in accounting and hygiene and nutrition at a commercial cooking school. She wanted to see how the pros did it, but the pros in a big Berlin kitchen work a kind of culinary assembly line, like pieceworkers in a factory, and according to Brigitte the ones at Tessinerstube were all "split and stressed"—doing the kind of work you go to Kreuzberg to avoid. So she decided to serve "the right sort of food" in Kreuzberg. She meant crisp vegetables and fresh fish and fine spices and meat that was neither breaded and deep-fried nor soaked in *Schlag*. She meant clear, delicate food—and in Kreuzberg this was something exotic. In Kreuzberg, any food that didn't settle like a weight in your stomach was called nouvelle cuisine, and was definitely Schicki-Micki, but, then, people from the scene ate junk food, and the Turks ate kebabs, dripping fat, and a worker's lunch was wurst, curried ketchup, and as much beer as he could get down.

Hartmut puts it this way. "You see, it was our neighborhood, and part of the impetus for Maxwell was the feeling we had that everything here was going in the direction of junk food. Everything was full of chemicals, and we thought—maybe in a missionary way—that a good restaurant would be uncommon *and* useful. We didn't intend a restaurant for upper-class people. Mainly, for us, Maxwell had to do with a principle of aesthetics. It was like my films, or my house—they share a principle of aesthetics. You know, you see a room, you have your own aesthetic *idea* of that room, and, well, our idea for Maxwell was the concept of minimal art. There would only be a few things, but they would be solid, authentic things, not plastic or shiny or flashy or synthetic. We didn't have the money for being flashy, anyway. I did a lot of the work myself. I had some practice from films, because you have to improvise—you discover you can install your own electricity, you can lay tiles, you can build anything. So I could build Maxwell the way we wanted it. We had one room. We had a wooden bar and seven wooden tables and thirty wooden chairs, and we had white linen tablecloths and white linen napkins. They said later that we had 'gastronomic custom plates,' but we had plain white plates, and our 'silver' was plain Spaten stainless flatware that I bought in a restaurant-supply house when I was in Paris, filming. But they were well chosen, with a certain idea—that nothing should look ordinary. Even the menu—well, the cooking wasn't really simple. It was modern French and fairly refined, but we tried to make the menu simple, to make it an *understatement,* and not use flowery

French language. It was the same with the name, Maxwell. We wanted a name that began with 'M,' because 'mmmm' means 'good,' and then because saying 'M' is like eating good food—you open your mouth and right away you have to close it. So we looked up all the 'M's in the phone book, and discovered Maxwell. There was one Maxwell in West Berlin. It sounded nice, it sounded different. You know, you have a certain illusion. You like something now, and then in six months time you know how stupid you were."

No one in Kreuzberg thought Hartmut Bitomsky or his wife were stupid. The Autonomen who wanted to force them out called them "imperialists" and accused them of being rich, fast movie people, like the movie people in Munich, and the Autonomen who wanted to let them "do their own thing" said that they were just naïve, and to leave them alone. Brigitte says that she certainly was naïve. She was a small-town girl, she says, like most of the kids in Kreuzberg who turned against Maxwell, and she was not very sophisticated, despite the fact that she looks sophisticated, with her fragile, fine-boned face and her straight black bangs and simple black clothes and big black sunglasses. She believed in Maxwell. She believed in bringing *beurre blanc à l'estragon* to Kreuzberg, and she believed that the plain pale walls and plain white dinner plates and plain stemmed wineglasses—seen from the street through plain plate glass by Turkish workers and punks with orange hair—looked solid and authentic. She believed she was giving object lessons in simplicity to people whose idea of authentically "simple" was Formica tables, mismatched jelly-jar glasses, a stacked sink, and bags of garbage separated from the customers by a beaded curtain. She believed that the neighbors would love and respect what she was doing for Kreuzberg, because she loved and respected the neighbors. She believed in the Kreuzberg scene and in the famous Kreuzberg freedom—she believed that Berlin Südost 36 was indeed the freest corner of the freest city in the world.

There are people here—old friends of the Bitomskys—who say that Hartmut should have warned Brigitte, that Hartmut must have known better, that a man who had spent his career thinking about how cultural images are created and manipulated and communicated, a man who read Barthes and talked about "politics and semiology," should have known that a place like Maxwell would stand out on the Oranienstrasse *because* of simplicity—that Maxwell wouldn't have looked much stranger painted gold with a footman at the door. Somebody all dressed up, like a footman, is in the Kreuzberg spirit; it is the dressing down that is ostentatious. But Hartmut believed in his principles the way Brigitte believed in the neighbors. He walked around Kreuzberg and found the space he wanted, at 170 Oranienstrasse, and the fact that the space happened to be halfway between Heinrichplatz and Moritzplatz, in the heart of the Kreuzberg scene, didn't trouble him at all. It was a wide storefront, and at the time Hartmut saw it, it was divided right down the middle into two thrift shops—providing two rents instead of one to the speculators who owned the building. Once the leases were free, Hartmut took over the storefront. He got a good rent—five hundred marks a month to start, doubling after five years—because, whatever Hartmut may have felt about Maxwell, his landlords thought of Maxwell as part of the gentrification of Kreuzberg, a good thing for the neighborhood, the sort of place that would attract the right people and raise the value of everybody's Kreuzberg property. Hartmut figures that opening Maxwell cost him two hundred and fifty thousand marks, including the cost of his own time and his own work. The Deutsche Bank Berlin loaned him fifty thousand, and a couple of friends invested ninety thousand, but the rest of the money was Hartmut and Brigitte's savings. It was all the money the Bitomskys had.

Maxwell opened for Christmas of 1985. The Bitomskys' friends came, and the friends brought their friends, and then the restaurant critics started coming. A magazine called *Zitty* sent someone who said that Maxwell was terrific, though maybe "a little fine for Kreuzberg," and even *The New York Times* sent a reporter—after which the artists and intellectuals who were spending their year in Berlin as the city's guests began driving out to Kreuzberg to taste Brigitte's good white wines and sample her five first courses and her four main courses and her cheese of the day and her three desserts. Maxwell was rarely full (and barely making money), but it was celebrated. It was a bright (some said aggressively bright) patch of light on a dark (some said aggressively dark) street where most of the eating and drinking took place behind blackened windows or at the back of courtyards, so no one would have to worry when the hash or the coke came out. Brigitte liked to cook and Hartmut liked to help her, and after a busy night they would sit down at the table in Maxwell's kitchen and Brigitte would cook them something soothing and familial—spinach and soft-boiled eggs, mashed together. Hartmut says that at first he had no idea of the "signs" that Maxwell was giving off in Kreuzberg, that he had no way to evaluate its glamour—not with Brigitte working fifteen hours a day, six days a week, with only two people to serve and two people to help her in the kitchen. He discovered just how chic Maxwell was when a group of Americans booked a table and one of them dropped his notebook on the way out—and it was Robert Wilson.

∞

Hardt-Waltherr Hämer is an old Berlin architect who has been working in Kreuzberg (he says "in Kreuzberg *for* Kreuzberg") over the past ten years, and for people in the scene he is probably the most important man in Südost 36, because he has put together a team of architects, sociologists, city planners, and economists, and taken on the enormous and exasperating job of restoring the neighborhood to the specifications of the people who live here. Hämer himself doesn't live in Kreuzberg. He says if he moved to Kreuzberg he would be taking someone else's place. Giving people a sense of place—a sense of confidence and tranquillity about where they live and the way it looks and the money it costs—is what Hämer means by architecture, and what he seems to be trying to do in Kreuzberg. Hämer was one of three directors of the architectural project IBA—the Internationale Bauausstellung Berlin—which managed to produce eighty new apartment blocks in West Berlin for the city's seven-hundred-and-fiftieth-birthday celebration, in 1987. IBA was sponsored by the Berlin Senat, and the idea behind it—at least at first—was a competition, with the Senat inviting famous architects from all over the world to join. It was "a very Berlin idea," Hämer says, "the idea of importing culture and creativity from the outside." He himself was not much interested in what he likes to describe as "imported aesthetics at the service of German real-estate interests." He was interested in

Kreuzberg, and in what would happen to poor Kreuzberg people—immigrants and kids and retired workers living on pensions—who were forced out of the neighborhood by the construction, and who could not afford to come home when the construction was over. Hämer is an old radical, and as far as he is concerned the important dates in his curriculum vitae are the dates he was fired from various Berlin projects for his architectural politics. He was never fired from IBA, but he fought from the beginning and led a kind of alternative IBA that got to be known as Old IBA, because it had mainly to do with restoring old houses instead of building new ones. Hämer's job was to restore six thousand apartments for fifteen thousand people in Hartmut Bitomsky's neighborhood.

Kreuzberg houses are a prototype of Mitteleuropa workers' housing, grimy memorials to the industrial revolution and to Berlin's place in that revolution. Hämer would say that "Germany" began in Kreuzberg with those houses—that it began a hundred and sixty years ago, when the city of Berlin began recruiting peasants to work in its new factories, and the peasants settled here. Kreuzberg village, southeast across the Spree from the Alexanderplatz and the old city, was the first working-class neighborhood in a chain of neighborhoods that eventually ringed the city and housed some 90 percent of its tenant population, and Hämer says it was a developer's paradise. The real-estate speculators of the eighteen-fifties bought up the land in Kreuzberg and started building for the new workers, and their buildings were known as *Mietskasernen*—rent barracks. Actually, a *Mietskaserne* was not so much a building as a peculiar kind of building complex. In Kreuzberg, it was five floors high and sometimes three rows of houses deep. (The houses ran back from the street, flanked by outbuildings and separated by dark, smelly courtyards—and got darker and smellier the farther back they were.) It was part barnyard, because the peasants brought their animals to Kreuzberg with them; part atelier, because the peasants' wives took in piecework; part factory, because the peasants' bosses found that they could rent loft space much more cheaply in Kreuzberg than in the old city; and, of course, part barracks. People in Kreuzberg's *Mietskasernen* shared their kitchens and their outhouses and their water, if they were lucky enough to have water—and lived the way thousands of foreign workers live in Germany's *Gastarbeiter* dormitories now.

Most of the buildings in Südost 36 were once *Mietskasernen.* The Bitomskys' flat was part of an old rent barracks, and so was Maxwell and the Turkish shops and Autonomen bars along the Oranienstrasse; Hardt-Waltherr Hämer's huge project offices and drafting rooms are in a building near the Spree that used to house a skirt factory and a machine shop. Hämer says that one of the many ironies of the neighborhood is that these barracks survived the war, whereas "good" Berlin was ravaged by the bombings. Südost 36 was probably the least damaged section of the city. It was full of people in the nineteen-fifties, and probably it would have stayed full if the Wall had cut through some other neighborhood. It was literally up against the Wall. And once the Wall went up it began to be abandoned. Nobody wanted to live in Kreuzberg until the Turks got here. At first it was frightening to live in Kreuzberg. Later it was boring. For years, there was nothing to do in Kreuzberg, and nowhere to go *from* Kreuzberg. It had always looked east, as a neighborhood. Its natural focus, its *point de repère,* was the old industrial city, and never the new city, to the west, that had been such a large part of Hitler's *Asphaltlyrik*—and that the Americans were busy rebuilding as a city center.

The actor and critic Hanns Zischler, who was a colleague of Hartmut's on *Filmkritik,* once said that West Berlin has a kind of amputation neurosis—that it feels its missing part and overcompensates by turning in on itself, by a kind of implosion. He said that West Berliners have "inskirts" instead of outskirts, that psychologically they have trouble tolerating their outlying quarters like Kreuzberg or Neukölln, south of Kreuzberg (and even poorer). With the Wall, Kreuzberg became the easternmost corner of the city, the outpost of the outpost, Berlin's Berlin in the most surreal way. There are Turks who remember arriving in 1962 and finding all the buildings on their streets boarded up and deserted. Those buildings—they were mainly in Südost 36, although a few were in the neighborhood Südost 61, which runs along the Paul-Lincke Ufer and is farther into town and is considered the "good" Kreuzberg—were held by the city or by speculators who had bought in Kreuzberg believing that the city was going to revive old plans for a traffic system that would make the Oranienplatz, halfway down the Oranienstrasse, the crossroads of two important tangential highways. They were delighted to rent to Turks until the highways came and made them rich, and the Turks were also delighted—because no other landlords wanted Turkish workers in their neighborhoods. There were a hundred and twenty thousand Turkish workers in West Berlin by the nineteen-seventies, and more than thirty thousand of them lived in *Mietskasernen* in Kreuzberg, each barracks, with its yards and its outhouse and its communal tap, creating a closed world, a village world, that was not so different from the world they left behind in Anatolia. If Berlin was imploding, Kreuzberg practiced implosion as a lifestyle. It suited the Turks, who could keep their wives and daughters in what was known as Kreuzberg purdah—away from family counselors and truant officers and the bad example of Berlin women in tight black leather and lacy stockings. It gave them a way to turn their backs on a city that did not find Turks the model citizens it does now, a city that liked to complain that in getting Turks, instead of Yugoslavs or Spaniards or Italians, it was getting the bottom of the *Gastarbeiter* barrel.

And Kreuzberg suited the squatters, who were the next Südost 36 settlers. The squatters arrived in the seventies and simply moved into the *Mietskasernen* that were still abandoned. They came in waves. (People in the scene say "generations.") There were the West German runaways coming over for their Berlin experience and discovering that they had nowhere to live, and no money for the rent anyway. There were the artists and performers who thought that in Kreuzberg they were going to turn daily life into street theater. There were the rich radicals, like the nurse who inherited a million marks and used it to put up a big tent near the Wall and start a circus, and there were the university radicals, who saw in the squatters' movement a commentary on the corruption here, on a system that subsidized speculators to hold empty houses (or to force the tenants out of full houses) while thousands of people were homeless. The radicals said that if Berlin was literally giving away its houses to speculators it was reasonable to assume that the houses were also theirs for the taking. They encouraged everyone to squat. They said it was obscene for *anyone* to be homeless in a city where more than eight hundred buildings were boarded up. They called themselves *Instandbesetzer*—"house restorers." Their rhetoric gave squatting a politics (which all the squatters took on, as common currency) and inspired a movement all over West Germany. By the beginning of 1981, there were a hundred and sixty-nine squatted houses in West Berlin, and ninety of those houses were in Kreuzberg. Everybody knew somebody who was squatting in Kreuzberg, or whose children were squatting in Kreuzberg, and there was nothing the police could do about them, because the son of the chief of police was squatting in Kreuzberg too. For a while, the city tried making peace with the squatters. The Social Democrats, who were running Berlin then, offered purchase contracts to various squatter households, offered easy terms and renovation subsidies to the successful squats—squats that were doing something useful, like taking in runaways, or were starting to support themselves as cottage industries or arts centers. But then the Christian Democrats took over, and *their* mayor—it was Richard von Weizsäcker, doing his obligatory Berlin service—was advised to start evicting squatters. Two thousand riot policemen entered Kreuzberg on orders from the new interior minister (a right-wing local politician named Heinrich Lummer) and shut down the squats, and there were a few bad weeks of street fighting and demonstrations all over town. In the course of one demonstration, a bus drove into the crowd and killed a boy of fifteen—and the squatters, in protest, called a strike that brought thousands of Berliners into the streets. It was the biggest political demonstration in Berlin since the 1968 student riots.

It was the squatters who gave Kreuzberg its radical cachet. Kreuzberg had been dark and dirty, and now, as a reporter named Renée Zucker, who lives in Kreuzberg, puts it, it was dark and dirty, and it had flair. Renée Zucker works for the *Tageszeitung*. Berliners say *Taz*. It is the city's "alternative" paper, and it documents the Kreuzberg scene, and in many ways was responsible for establishing Kreuzberg as a scene to begin with. It drew the artisans here, the printmakers and bookbinders and the serious young men who publish Derrida on handpressed paper, and then some young painters from a group the city was promoting under the name Neuen Wilden—the New Savages—bought studios around the Moritzplatz, and *they* drew the art-gallery people, and the trendy young lawyers and stockbrokers and businessmen who were their clients. Kreuzberg became a way of buying into bohemia, a way for the children of the economic miracle to live next door to a bar that charged double for the beer—and apologized with a sign saying "Our beer is expensive so you won't drink it and get drunk and give the imperialists power over you." Those children were instinctive investors. They used the services and the subsidies of the Old IBA to rebuild their houses, and the streets changed with them, and the rents went up around them. Hämer says that when the cleaning up of Kreuzberg started, people were renting in the *Mietskasernen* for two marks, three marks at the most, a square meter, and that now the price is six or seven—more than *his* young Kreuzbergers can possibly afford.

Hämer's young Kreuzbergers are the children raised on stories of a squatters' paradise in Südost 36. They get confused when they arrive here. They begin to associate the density and the poverty in Kreuzberg with their own freedom. The things that make the Kreuzberg natives leave when they have children—the lack of parks, of what Berliners call "green spaces," the lack of kindergartens, and even schools—are precisely the things that Hämer's Kreuzbergers cherish as what *they* call the "authentic infrastructure." They like using the word "infrastructure." They see in parks and kindergartens and central heating, and even in an advocate like Hardt-Waltherr Hämer, what they see in the new Kreuzberg rich and what they saw in Maxwell—a challenge to themselves, and to the scene, and to the infrastructure of the scene. They mean, by infrastructure, everything that keeps it cheap to live here.

Hämer says that sometimes he is very ambivalent about Kreuzberg, and about his mission in Kreuzberg—despite his ten years of defending Kreuzberg to the Berlin Senat, despite the five thousand apartments he has managed to return to Kreuzberg without having to send away a single family, despite the long nights sitting up with "the people" while the people argued the pros and cons of indoor plumbing or changed their minds for the tenth time about having heat. He is ambivalent because every time he makes Kreuzberg a little more livable, a little more attractive, the more expensive it gets. "The people—the *young* people—look at me and at this office, and they see the head of a bourgeois institution. And all they know is that they are against bourgeois institutions. Especially bourgeois institutions so close to them. I don't welcome being the enemy, but I welcome the conflict. I want to know what's on their minds—to know what's going on in Kreuzberg. The fact is, these Autonomen people change when you build together with them. They are very unformed, you see. They are not political like the squatters were. It was easy to help the squatters because they had a politics, but these young Autonomen have no concept of politics, just a lot of words they inherited. Either they grew up here, in the slums, with no possibility of finding their way, or they grew up in beautiful, clean West Germany, with no possibility of finding their way. Their only identity is to be against something—and how can a human being get self-confidence being against something all the time, and never *for* something? It's a chaotic situation for them. For one thing, they are always provoked. The politicians provoke them. The interior minister shuts down the U-Bahn here and says he is researching 'demonstration potential' or he is 'determining the potential for violence.' And the mayor—well, I go to the mayor of Berlin and I ask if he could find another street for something he wants to build, or maybe have a discussion of what the people there want, and he says something equally stupid. He says, 'No, not possible. We cannot discuss. To discuss is to accept the Wall!' So these Autonomen try to provoke back. They look for things to criticize. They say the Schicki-Micki people are coming. They say that if Kreuzberg changes too fast the Schicki-Micki people will take over—and to a certain point I agree with them. But what happens to the Autonomen is not the Schicki-Micki people taking over. What happens is their own fear taking over. They have no resources, they have no knowledge, and, remember, they have no real politics. They react with violence. They call themselves Commandos or Redskins or Indians. They talk about 'actions.' Their politics is knocking people down. They threaten me. They threaten my assistants. They beat up my assistants. They knock out my assistants' teeth. So everybody is scared, and the good things here, the special intimacy and the great tolerance and freedom—all this disappears the moment the violence starts."

∞

Hartmut Bitomsky began to feel afraid after May Day last year. There are May Day demonstrations every year in Kreuzberg. People from the Autonomen meet at SO 36 and in a bar called Pinox, down the street at 45 Oranienstrasse, to plan their actions and talk about liberating Berlin from the imperialists and the Schicki-Micki professors, and then they cover the scene, handing out flyers and distributing posters with the year's themes and the year's instructions and the year's quotes. (*"Die Revolution ist grossartig, alles andere ist Quark"* was this year's quote. Rosa Luxemburg said it: "Revolution is magnificent, all the rest is rubbish.") But mainly what people in Kreuzberg do on May Day is go to the little park in Lausitzer Platz, across from the Lutheran church, with their children and buy ice cream and popcorn and kebabs and drink beer and listen to speeches and have a party. Celebrating May Day in the park at Lausitzer Platz is an old tradition among Kreuzberg workers, and it has not changed much now that the workers are Turkish and half the children have green hair.

No one can explain exactly what happened last year in the park on May Day, except to say that early that afternoon a couple of policemen who claimed to be making a census count (they were in fact counting heads at Autonomen hangouts) parked their patrol car around the corner from the Lausitzer Platz and walked off looking for ice-cream cones, and that while they were gone some Autonomen trashed the car—which everyone agreed later was just what you would expect to happen to an empty police car parked in Kreuzberg. Minutes later, there were two hundred riot policemen in the Lausitzer Platz. They arrived with water cannons and tear gas, and they gassed everybody at the party. They gassed women and babies and old Kreuzberg pensioners who were out mainly for the sun, and people panicked because of the gas, and because children were crying and girls were fainting and Autonomen were starting to throw up barricades—and then, suddenly, the police pulled back. Hartmut says that for a while the neighborhood was quiet. He and Brigitte opened Maxwell, and customers came, and for a couple of eerie hours the only noise anybody heard was the sirens on some police cars cruising the Oranienstrasse. Then the police invaded Kreuzberg. At eleven that night, eight hundred policemen arrived in armored vans, and the rioting began in earnest.

Brigitte says that the night was like a terrible dream—that the Oranienstrasse seemed to burst, like a dam bursting, and thousands of people came pouring down it. She was so astonished, she says, that it took a few minutes to see that people were running for their lives. There were about twelve customers left in Maxwell, and they spent the night there. Outside, people were getting crushed by the crowds, beaten by the police, hit by rocks and stones. People would knock at the door, injured, and Brigitte would take them in and she and Hartmut and the customers would nurse them. One man's leg was badly broken. He was from the scene, and frightened about getting arrested if he went to the hospital, so Hartmut braved the riot to find a doctor who would come back to Maxwell and treat him there. Hartmut says it was the worst night in Kreuzberg since the squatters rioted. He says that the police were brutal and the neighborhood went wild. By all accounts, *everyone* went wild. It was not just that the police were attacking everyone, Hartmut says, it was that everyone fought back, everyone reacted. People went up to their roofs and started hurling bricks at the police vans. They started burning cars. They set fire to the police barricades. By the middle of the night, old Kreuzberg *Frauen* were robbing thrift shops and Turkish elders and Oranienstrasse punks were out together looting candy stores. By morning, the biggest supermarket in Kreuzberg was on fire.

Hartmut says that the trouble in Kreuzberg never really stopped that spring and summer. There was more rioting in May, and serious rioting in June, when Ronald Reagan visited Berlin and a new Christian Democratic interior minister decided to protect the president from Kreuzberg by stopping the subway in and out of Kreuzberg and literally sealing the neighborhood. The new minister is a law professor from Cologne named Wilhelm Kewenig—a smooth conservative who looks and talks like William Buckley. He arrived in 1981 to campaign for the Christian Democrats, and seems to have been kept around to remind the rest of the country that there is a "new right" in German politics, that the fractious caricatures of the German right like Franz Josef Strauss (who died this year) and Friedrich Zimmermann and Alfred Dregger are being replaced by civilized, attractive men who can talk about art and books while dispatching police with water cannons to a May Day picnic or sealing a neighborhood so that no one can leave to demonstrate against an American president. Kewenig claims that in June last year twenty or thirty thousand "contemptible people" arrived in West Berlin from the "outside" with the clear intention of setting fire to the city during Reagan's visit, and that there was nothing a responsible interior minister could do but lock them up, so to speak, in Kreuzberg, where they were being sheltered. He would happily seal off Kreuzberg permanently if he had the chance. He likes to say that security is a very complicated business, and that security decisions are very complicated decisions—and not the ordinary sort of Berlin decision, which he describes as deciding whether or not to hire Herbert von Karajan for a concert. He does not believe in waiting around for the worst to happen. When the International Monetary Fund and the World Bank met in Berlin this fall for their yearly conference, he borrowed twenty-seven hundred riot policemen from West Germany to add to the six thousand who were in the city already. He said he wanted to protect the delegates. He protected them so well that when a couple of hundred masked Autonomen (they said they were the "Black Commandos") joined a protest march against the I.M.F., every Autonomer had a riot policeman of his own marching beside him.

Wilhelm Kewenig is not the most popular man in Kreuzberg. The only Kreuzbergers who can be said actually to admire him are Wolfgang Krüger, the mayor, who dotes on him, and the Turkish elders he is trying to woo to compliance by telling them what hardworking, upscale people Turks are—"like the Irish in New York." He takes a long view of what he calls his Kreuzberg policy. There were three or four streets, at most, involved in the Kreuzberg riots, and as far as Kewenig is concerned it was simply Hartmut and Brigitte Bitomsky's "misfortune" to have been on one of those streets instead of on some quiet little street around the corner. This is the one conviction Kewenig shares with people from the scene in Kreuzberg—the conviction that if Maxwell had been one block away from the Oranienstrasse the terrible things that happened would have been avoided.

∞

Hartmut figures that at some time during the riots that summer he and Brigitte became "the enemy"—that something happening in Kreuzberg was turning them into outsiders. People rioting or running away from rioting would pass Maxwell and spit at the windows or stick their heads in the door and shout something like "You're next" or "We're going to get you." Or people would stop Hartmut on the street and ask him about the "infrastructure" at Maxwell, or the working conditions there, or the ratio between the salaries and profits. Then the Autonomen had their "exhibition of enemy culture" at SO 36. After that, people (as Brigitte puts it) started "visiting." Four or five men in black leather regalia—they were boys, really—would arrive at night and claim an empty table. They would order the most expensive food on the menu and sit around for a couple of hours, staring down the customers, making everybody nervous, and in the end walk out without paying. The visiting went on like this for a few weeks. Then, one day—it was July 19, a month after the police sealed Kreuzberg—the punk who always brought them news appeared with a warning. He told the Bitomskys to lock their door that night, because the visitors were coming back. The visitors were going to tear Maxwell apart.

"They came late," Brigitte said one day this summer. She and Hartmut were at home, and they were talking about what happened at Maxwell. Hartmut is used to talking—he has been a kind of family spokesman since the first visitors—but it is still hard for Brigitte to talk about Maxwell. It was a year before she could talk about Maxwell at all. Even now she tells the story slowly, detail by detail, date by date, stopping as she tells it, repeating, reflecting, straining for something—some hidden meaning or forgotten fact—that will make sense of the experience. "It was about twelve-thirty, and there were four people left in the restaurant, and suddenly twenty people—I counted nineteen men and one woman—ran in. I remember thinking they must be skinheads, right-wing skinheads, because they were dressed like the British skinheads, in jeans and bomber jackets and fighting boots. And I got hysterical. I said, 'We're closed, go away.' But they were drinking beer and shouting, and they wouldn't go. Some of them threw beer cans at the lights, and the others started throwing furniture. They threw everything. Tables, chairs, lamps, glasses, even jars of mayonnaise. And then, just like that, they left. They took some brandy and left, and I saw that there were people standing around outside, watching. That was the worst of it. The people watching. There was a gallery—the Endart Gallery—across the street from Maxwell, and it was open, and even the people from the gallery, people we knew, just watched and did nothing. Hartmut went over to them. He said, 'Please, you must know these people who attacked us. Please put us in contact with them.' But they denied knowing anybody. They were a little ashamed, and reticent, and I know they had a bad conscience. But they wouldn't help us, so the next day Hartmut went to see the people at SO 36, the people who had the soup kitchen. They wouldn't give us any names either, but they said there were about fifty people involved, very militant, very radical people from the gang called Redskins, and that maybe we would have to give them a little money, that maybe they would leave us alone if we contributed some money to help the May Day prisoners—you know, the people who were arrested during the May Day riots. So all week Hartmut ran around, trying to make contact, leaving messages. He said we were willing to talk about anything, even money. It was our neighborhood, and we were *solidaire* with the prisoners. But we wanted to make sure that the money was really for the prisoners and not for beer, because, you know, there's a lot of protection money paid in Kreuzberg, a lot of blackmailing. The people are threatened, and afterward they say they are paying their 'rent' to the Autonomen.

"Well, they came back on Sunday, when Hartmut was at home, working on his movie. They were all West Germans. There wasn't a Berlin kid among them. They came in and sat down and told me that I was on trial. It was a *Volksgericht*, they said. A people's trial. Well, you can imagine! There I was, alone with fifteen guests—they were like stone, my guests—and the cook and two girls serving. I had called the police this time. As soon as I saw them coming, I ran to a phone, next door, and called, but it was twenty minutes before the police came, and during those twenty minutes they had their 'trial.' One guy did the talking. He said stupid things. He said, 'What are you doing in Kreuzberg? You're destroying the infrastructure of Kreuzberg.' And then another guy asked for *Schutzgeld*—for protection money. But when the police came they didn't really take it seriously. Three policemen walked in, and one of them said, 'Ach, what's happening here?' and another said, 'Little lady, don't take it seriously,' and it was absurd theater, with the policemen smiling and patronizing, and the gang leaving and calling, 'Yoo hoo, till next time!,' while out on the street, for the whole neighborhood to see, there were these big police vans and dozens of riot troops waiting.

"You know, we are not friends of the police. That made it difficult. That, and the fact that we would go out and see the people who attacked us. Once, I saw some of them eating in Exil. The people from the Paris Bar used to own Exil, and Exil is an institution. So they wouldn't attack Exil. But they attacked us. Why us? We kept asking the neighbors—Why us? And the neighbors— there is a word in German, '*Schadenfroh.*' It means 'malicious.' It is used to describe people who enjoy the damage done to others. Well, there was a lot of that in Kreuzberg, and, you know, you get fed up, you don't want to see that every day. I thought that maybe if we went away it would get better. So we closed up. We went to an island in the North Sea called Sylt. We were going to try to forget everything, have a vacation, but we were too nervous. It was not right—our 'vacation.' We stayed a week and came home, and re-opened Maxwell.

"We opened on a Tuesday, and waited for our first Sunday. We figured there would be trouble on Sunday. It was hot, and August, and we had only four customers—plus Hartmut, sitting by the door, waiting, and, of course, the whole street watching. But they took us by surprise when they came. You see, we were watching for twenty Redskins. We were watching for motorcycles and boots and bomber jackets, and this time it was different. There were only three of them, to begin with. Three men with dark sunglasses and woollen caps pulled low on their foreheads—and carrying buckets. Three men carrying three buckets full of shit. They ran in with their buckets of shit and emptied the shit in my restaurant and then they vanished. At that moment, it was all over. We cleaned up and closed the restaurant for good. Who would ever want to eat in Maxwell again?"

∞

By all accounts, there are no more than a few hundred active, organized Autonomen in Kreuzberg, and no more than a few thousand *Sympathisanten*—which is what Kreuzbergers call the people who form an Autonomen community, a community in which Autonomen can operate and flourish. The Autonomen do not run Kreuzberg. Not even the Alternativen run Kreuzberg. The mayor of Kreuzberg is a backslapping Christian Democrat, and his idea of the proper Kreuzberg Zeitgeist is best expressed by the collection of toy Berlin bears in his office at the town hall. But the Autonomen dominate Kreuzberg. They maintain its dark, dirty flair and its disquieting tone and they make the rules—or, rather, the taboos—for the neighborhood. Don't have jobs. Don't make money. Don't deal with any institution. No matter what happens, don't call the police.

People in the scene say there are probably ten active Autonomen *Gruppen,* but no one can be sure, because as people move in and out of Kreuzberg the gangs keep changing, and because one of the Kreuzberg taboos is Don't belong to anything—which makes it a point of pride among Autonomen to deny being Autonomen in the first place. Most Autonomen prefer to describe themselves as revolutionaries. They get their slogans from bookshops off the Oranienstrasse that have not moved or even dusted their stock since the seventies—bookshops with stacks of mimeographs about Albanian Leninist factions and Armenian Maoist factions—and they talk endlessly about capitalists and imperialists, but when they get violent they deal in what Hartmut Bitomsky would call fascist images. They practice persuasion. They enforce a kind of neighborhood "volunteerism" that people anywhere else would say was neighborhood terrorism. They are (if political categories apply) the vigilantes of a local left-wing moral majority. They punish their neighbors, to set an example.

The "action" against Maxwell was known in Autonomen circles as the *Kübelaktion*—the bucket action. It was widely discussed in the scene, and a number of groups took credit for it. Hartmut himself has no proof of who was really responsible. He can identify the first visitors they had—the kids who arrived on motorcycles and threw beer cans at the lights and put his wife on people's trial. It was accepted in the scene that they were Redskins, and Hartmut thinks they probably were Redskins. But the three men with the buckets didn't look like Redskins. Their bucket action was not what Hartmut would call a Redskin sort of action, the way Brigitte's trial was a Redskin action, or collecting money for "political prisoners" was something Redskins would do. Hartmut tried to explain this when the police showed up at Maxwell. He hadn't called the police, or intended to call them. The police had read in *Taz* about the *Kübelaktion.* Someone at headquarters had put together a dossier of pictures called "known Redskins" and had come to Hartmut with the pictures, and—as Hartmut suspected—none of the pictures fit the three men who had visited Maxwell on August 23. Hartmut says that, at the time, it crossed his mind that the Redskins might have recruited people for the *Kübelaktion.* He knew that some of the most violent Autonomen in Kreuzberg—the police say fifty Autonomen—were not, properly speaking, part of any gang but rented themselves out for actions, like hit men in the movies, and were known in the neighborhood as *Kiezpolizei,* Kreuzberg policemen, and did the dirty work that other Autonomen opposed.

On the other hand, there were people in the scene who swore to Hartmut that it was not *Kiezpolizei,* and *they* said it was the gang called Hönkel. The Hönkel were the self-appointed clowns of the Autonomen movement. They were around in Kreuzberg for a year or so (and then, for all practical purposes, disappeared), and they did things like crash Berlin's official seven-hundred-and-fiftieth-birthday parties and drink up all the champagne, knowing that no one would throw them out in front of the foreign celebrities, or they wrote open letters on the mayor's stationery, which a friend at the Rathaus stole for them. They were a kind of poltergeist gang. People "saw" them everywhere, practicing "humor as revolution." Hartmut does not think that depositing three buckets of human excrement in the middle of his wife's restaurant is either humor or revolution, but he can see that the Hönkel might have considered it very funny and very political.

The trouble with identifying a Kreuzberg action is that whenever anything bad happens there so many people take the credit. For instance, there was the action against the Eiszeit Kino. The Eiszeit is a little theater on the Zeughofstrasse that shows underground movies, and last spring it was showing a movie called *Fingered,* directed by a Miss Lydia Lunch, which some Kreuzbergers considered pornographic and some sexist and some violent—although apparently not too pornographic or sexist or violent to have been shown a few weeks earlier at a theater in town. Twelve masked men and women broke into the Eiszeit during the movie's run to deal with *Fingered.* They destroyed the projector and the film in the projector (which turned out to be some other movie), and then they emptied the cash register and fled. The action was called Por No. The bulletins that circulate in the scene described it as an action against the pornography industry and said that the stolen money was now in the hands of an "international women's project," but no one knew for sure *whose* action Por No was because so many Kreuzbergers claimed it. First a radical lesbian group claimed it, and then a couple of anti-imperialist groups said no, it was *their* action, and after that it seemed as if half the Autonomen in Kreuzberg were involved.

People, of course, assumed that Autonomen were responsible. When anything happens in Kreuzberg that is not obviously the work of the Italian mafia or the Turkish mafia or the construction mafia or the local political mafia, people blame it on the Autonomen. A year and a half ago, a new and undeniably ugly kindergarten burned down here, and everyone, including the Autonomen, called it an "Autonomen fire." (The kindergarten was on a dead-end street where some Autonomen had a "children's farm," consisting of a little log barn and a couple of goats and turkeys; the city had put the kindergarten there under considerable protest from the Autonomen, and the Autonomen, for their part, had threatened to burn it, and had even sent out invitations to a bonfire.) The fact is that there are fires all the time in Kreuzberg, and that some of the Autonomen set some of those fires. Last year, Autonomen set fire to the cellar of a house that Kreuzberg's deputy in the West Berlin parliament, a jeans-and-buckskin Alternativer by the name of Volker Härtig, shares with a *Taz* reporter called Gerd Nowakowski. Autonomen had already stoned Nowakowski's car, because they didn't like his columns, and beaten up Härtig, because they didn't like his politics—Härtig is considered by Autonomen to be pro-kindergarten and anti-squat and, like all Alternativen, to have sold out to the government. There was a lot of talk about the actions against Härtig, and about Härtig's reaction to the actions. It was suspected that he and Nowakowski had gone to the police and asked for an investigation (which they had), and Härtig himself admitted "carrying a gun in self-defense" (he meant a gas pistol) for the next six months. This was considered a very "un-Kreuzberg" thing to do.

There is, in Kreuzberg, what could be called an etiquette of retaliation. Wiglaf Droste, the arts critic at *Taz,* says that when people pay you a visit, the way the Autonomen paid Volker Härtig a visit, you make a few phone calls, get your friends together, and visit them. This, in Kreuzberg, is called having a discussion. Droste himself has been visited. He came home one afternoon to find his door smeared with blood (the blood said "666" and "Heil Satan") and twenty pounds of dead fish and rotted meat on his doormat, and the people who did it bragged in the scene that they were Autonomen, but Droste knew that they were just disgruntled musicians who didn't like what he had to say about their rock group, so he never "visited back." Droste is one of the most measured and astute chroniclers of the Kreuzberg scene (though strangers would find it hard to distinguish him from that scene, dressing, as he does, in baggy striped circus trousers, a black dinner jacket, a torn T-shirt, a piece of red string for a belt, and ancient sneakers with the laces untied). He arrived in Kreuzberg five years ago, at the age of twenty-one, after touring West Germany with a rock band, looking for what he calls "a city of big dreams."

"There is one unwritten law in Kreuzberg," Droste says. "If there is a quarrel, we don't need the state, the Senat, or the police. We are artists and Turks and normal people and people from the street, and for ten or fifteen years the balance between us has worked and it's very special. It's not something you see in Hamburg. For instance, I'm interested—that's a stupid word, 'interested,' but I'm interested in avant-garde music. Well, the music here in Berlin is quite disappointing. It sounds like the wet cellars where the bands practice. But the point is, year after year so many musicians come to Kreuzberg and carry all their inspiration with them, and it makes a special atmosphere of creativity. Many of them fail, but to me it's not important what comes out of Kreuzberg, it's that atmosphere of creativity, of work in progress, that's important. I think this has something to do with what happened to Maxwell. The Oranienstrasse is holy territory for some of the people here. I never cared about the Oranienstrasse, but they do. They say it has to be dirty, like we are. When they say keep Kreuzberg clean, no Schicki-Micki, no rich people, that's what they're really saying—keep it dirty, like we are. Keep the atmosphere, keep the balance. The kids who come over from provincial villages in West Germany to 'protect' May Day, or to protect the Oranienstrasse, or to protect what they call the infrastructure— they've grown up on the myth of that holy territory. It's their identity. You ask them, 'Who are you? What do you do?' And they say, 'We come from Kreuzberg. It's dirty, like us.' So they take on Maxwell. They think they're fighting against capitalism, against imperialism, against blah-blah-blah, but—and this is only what I think—it's not a fight against capitalism, it's a fight against symbols, and it's easier to fight symbols than the things behind them.

"To the kids, Maxwell was this fishbowl that was trying to teach them a lifestyle. You know, you weren't allowed to sit around and have a couple of drinks, you had to have a meal—which in Kreuzberg is very pretentious. Having a meal is something you do at home, in your parents' house, in *Germany*. So to them Hartmut Bitomsky was like a tourist from Germany, even though he lived in Kreuzberg. To them, he was like the guy from the magazine *Wiener* who showed up for the discussions at Pinox—there were a lot of discussions at Pinox about what happened to Bitomsky— and was scared of the punks and tried to borrow a bad leather jacket so nobody would spot him. Don't forget, these kids are pretty stupid. It was stupid—it was absolutely idiotic—to destroy a restaurant where Hartmut Bitomsky was working. But I don't think the guys who did it knew who Hartmut Bitomsky was—that this was the man who made *Highway 40 West*. All they knew was that Bitomsky broke the Kreuzberg taboo with a restaurant about lifestyle and good manners and *behavior* on the Oranienstrasse.

"There was a lot of hysteria, on both sides, after the *Kübelaktion*. The people on the list, the people with the stores and the restaurants—some of them were very scared. After the action, a lot of journalists came and said, 'Aren't you scared?' and they said, 'Yes, we're scared'—and then they *got* scared, whether or not they were before. And on the other side, the people who made the list were not necessarily supported by the rest of the scene. You'd go to Pinox—Pinox is a collective, and it's the place the political scene meets, every day the same people talking about the same thing. They were against the Maxwell action at Pinox, and they put out a leaflet about it. Anyway, you'd go to Pinox and everybody would be arguing: Should we throw them out? Shouldn't we throw them out? But nobody really knew who *they* were. Some of the Autonomen said, 'Well, *they* need to pay to be here, because we need to raise money for the political prisoners.' And the fact is that there are still May Day people in prison in Berlin"—Droste was arrested himself, covering the May Day demonstrations this year, and spent ten days in prison—"and I know two guys, one in Dortmund and one here in Berlin, who are in on twenty-two-month sentences. So some people from the scene said that because of the prisoners the action against Maxwell was a 'justified aggression.' And it was generally agreed that *those* people were stupid. You read that in Kreuzberg a few hundred people are potentially violent. That's what the politicians like to say, 'potentially violent.' Well, it depends. Maybe there are others who are violent against the police, but not against a theater or a restaurant. I know that the violent groups try to control their members, and lately there's been this development—I mean that more and more people refuse to be controlled by any group, and nobody really knows those people. Not even the potentially violent groups know them."

∞

There are people who think that West Berlin is dividing into two cities—"Kreuzberg and the rest," Hartmut's friend Hanns Zischler calls it—the way Berlin is divided and Germany itself is divided. They think of Germany as a kind of hologram, an endlessly refracting set of images, with Kreuzberg as the fragment that carries all the information in a couple of streets, leading nowhere. They are interested in Kreuzberg because in Kreuzberg, with its symbols of enemies and its cycles of retribution, they can see the historical claustrophobia of Germany being reenacted. It may be that all bohemias are symptoms of claustrophobia—Zischler thinks so—but Kreuzberg is Germany's particular symptom, because the Wall is there, around it, and because there is something clearly familiar about the ease with which the neighborhood slips from claustrophobia into panic, and about how fast the language slips with it and becomes a language about enemies, a mob language, undiscerning and provocative.

Karl Schlögel, the East European social historian, lives in Kreuzberg and has started writing about the neighborhood—he says he was driven to write about it—from the point of view of someone who spends his professional life thinking about what he calls "the history of urban culture." He has come to the conclusion that Kreuzberg has nothing to do with urban culture anymore. Schlögel spent five years here as a student, and then went over to West Germany and dreamed about coming back to live in Kreuzberg because it had such a symbolic significance for him—because it was close to the old historical center of the city and was all, really, that was left of Mitteleuropa Berlin in the western sector. He says that looking down the Köpenicker Strasse toward the Wall from his living-room window, he could feel a "postwar spirit" that he missed in the cities of the Federal Republic. The problem now is that he can feel the same spirit looking out of his back window, into his courtyard, because the courtyard looks as if it had not been cleared since the bombings. It is filled with rubble, and the back buildings of his *Mietskaserne* are skeletons of buildings—there are no windows or moldings or doors or even staircases. The owners stripped them when they were trying to clear the place for speculation, and then some Autonomen moved in and "claimed" the courtyard for making rock videos, and they stole everything that was left.

Schlögel's own building is due for restoration—it was one of the buildings earmarked by the Old IBA, and now it is under the protection of Hardt-Waltherr Hämer's Kreuzberg project—and he is determined to stay there, though he does not know how the tenants are going to agree on anything when the only people in the building who seem to respect what he calls "the rules of close urban space" are he and his wife, who comes from Moscow, and a Turkish family on the third floor. The rest of the tenants are drifters out of the Autonomen scene, and they do not live what Schlögel would call neighborly urban lives. They play soccer in the rubble at two in the morning. They weld their "found objects" at three in the morning. At four, they turn their amplifiers up and get stoned and have a disco party. Schlögel says that he tried to talk to them at first. He told them about his daughter, who is four years old and awake all night with the noise, and about his wife's frayed nerves and his own problem, trying to finish his book on Russian intellectual history on two or three hours of sleep a night, but his neighbors told him he was a crazy professor and ought to live in Dahlem, where there were big private houses with plenty of space around them, and after that—to "discipline" him, they said—they gathered in the courtyard with pots and pans and tin boxes and garbage pails and radios and record players and subjected the Schlögels to what they called a "noise concert." The scene refers to it as the *Professoraktion.* Schlögel says that it was "terrible but interesting." It was a breakdown of all the arrangements and understandings that make life in cities possible, and it came down to something very simple. It was a matter of people demanding for themselves more rights than they were willing to concede to anybody else.

Schlögel likes to say that, as an old radical from a Maoist faction of one of West Germany's wilder communist parties, he was not much fazed by what his neighbors called their ideology. (It had to do with claiming Kreuzberg for "the new proletarian class.") What troubled Schlögel was that in his Kreuzberg building the usual forms of communication between neighbors seemed to have stopped working, and people existed side by side with no reference to one another. It was the neighbors, he says, who really belonged in Dahlem. It was the neighbors who lived as if they were all alone in a big villa in the suburbs—where no one cared about the volume on their Yamahas, or the bass vibrations that felt like a minor earthquake. "A lot of young people come here, the way I came in the sixties," Schlögel says. "They come to the metropole. They have a specific if naïve ideology—which is that the city is a place where you can shake the provincial regulations of your old life. But they are wrong in this case. One of the achievements of

Kreuzberg—and it's not a positive achievement—has been a deur-banization of city life. Kreuzberg today is a village world, and this rebirth of the village in Kreuzberg means that the urban culture is being destroyed. It's more like Turkey here than Germany—except that it's the Germans and not the Turks who are responsible. It's the Germans who make this cultivation of provincialism into an ideological demonstration. You see it in the way the German kids try to speak in dialect. Schwäbisch dialect. Bayrisch dialect. It used to be 'Speak Schwäbisch, you don't have to hide your roots.' Now it's 'Speak Schwäbisch, you don't have to communicate.' "

Schlögel says that most of the intellectuals he knows are leaving Kreuzberg, that the friends who moved here with the same enthu-siasm he had—the friends who borrowed a room in the Schlesi-sches Tor, the last Kreuzberg subway stop before East Germany, and held "evenings" about Lvov and Vilnius and Budapest—are moving to Schöneberg or Charlottenburg. They are moving into the "real" world of West Berlin the way other Berliners go over to the Federal Republic—to get on with their lives and their careers and families, to settle down to plumbing and heating and good kindergartens and parks for the children, and all the other things that people in the Kreuzberg scene find alarming. The problem of schools is critical in Kreuzberg. The Autonomen want their own schools, and Autonomen ideals of scholarship are not apt to appeal to people like Dr. Schlögel, with four languages and a doctorate in sociology and a new book out called *Beyond the October Revolu-tion*—or, indeed, like Frau Schlögel, a biologist who spends her spare time writing about Osip Mandelstam's poetry. Sonja Mar-golina Schlögel used to like Kreuzberg. She was shocked by the poverty, but she felt at home here. She thought that the neighbor-hood—with what she took for shortages in the stores, with its grimy kaleidoscope of people from so many places—was some-thing like Moscow. But now she worries about things like kinder-gartens. She does not think that a children's farm with a couple of goats and turkeys is a substitute for schools where her daughter could learn to read and write, let alone prepare for *Gymnasium* and university.

Intellectuals, of course, have the privilege of leaving Kreuzberg. So do the more prosperous children of old Kreuzberg workers who want to raise their own families in respectable neighborhoods—in neighborhoods where there are no punks, and no foreigners living in the house next door. According to the mayor, a third of the Kreuzberg population changes every three or four years, and that figure is an understatement. Gustav Roth, who was the Lutheran suffragan bishop here, says that every three years a third of *his* old congregation leaves Kreuzberg. He says that they have their fun in what he calls "the Free Republic of Kreuzberg" and head back to the Federal Republic. "The strong leave" is how Roth puts it. "The young, powerful, interesting people" leave, and surface in a few years in powerful, interesting jobs somewhere else, and the scene people who are "not so strong" stay on—which means that there is now a generation of Kreuzbergers who have lived their whole lives without working, who have no chance of working now, and who are getting desperate. They are cut off—by the politicians, by their own poverty, and by the Wall. They may live at the Wall, but most of them have never been to East Berlin or even tried to cross a checkpoint. They do not have the twenty-five marks they need to cross. They hear about Prenzlauer Berg, which is considered the Kreuzberg of East Berlin, the scene across the Wall, but not from one another. They get their information from the kids who are passing through, the ones who know when it is time to leave Kreuzberg, like the student who lived a couple of blocks from Maxwell and went to the Pinox discussions and said, "Look, I know if I were to go very seriously into something—into *any-thing*—I'd have to leave Kreuzberg. There is a certain avant-garde here, but it always moves out. You have *fun* here, but you don't get anywhere." They are left with the Turks, whom they claim to defend when they reject kindergartens and parks and plumbing in the name of the infrastructure. But the Turks want kindergartens and parks and plumbing as much as the Kreuzberg professors do. There were fifteen hundred Turkish children on the waiting list for the kindergarten that was burned down.

∽

The Bitomskys sold Maxwell—sold the lease and everything in the restaurant—last December, and in July they moved to Schöneberg and Brigitte opened a new Maxwell and Hartmut began to work on the last movie in his trilogy about fascist images. He wants to call the movie *Volkswagen*. It tells the story of how Hitler opened a factory called Volkswagen to produce "people's cars" for his great German highway, and how the cars, like the highway, entered the ideology of Nazi Germany and are now part of the ideology of a democratic West Germany. Hartmut is already thinking about his next movie. He says that some people expect him to make a movie about Kreuzberg, but he thinks that maybe it is too soon for Kreuzberg, that maybe Kreuzberg would be dangerous for him—and, besides, most of the time he wants to forget Kreuzberg. After more than a year, he is still incredulous about his neighbors' behavior. His neighbors said they were sorry but they just didn't want to get involved in Hartmut Bitomsky's problems. In the end, they talked about Maxwell to everybody but him. They went on television in hoods and masks, as if they were Baader-Meinhof informers putting their lives at risk by talking. "They sat in their masks and acted as if we had been serving oysters and caviar while people on the streets were starving," Hartmut says. "They said we should have known better, or should never have come, or should have opened around the corner, or should have served worse food. They said our reputation was 'too good'—these people we thought were just like us said this. They seemed to think *we* should apologize to the neighborhood. So you see, nobody was very disgusted, and the Autonomen got what they wanted."

In the end, it was a question of morale. It was that everyone was a little embarrassed by the Bitomskys. Even the articles in *Taz* (which had had its share of Autonomen actions, and had nearly lost its printing presses during one of them) implied that somehow Maxwell had been at fault for being there, and being itself, in the first place; they seemed to be saying that if Maxwell stayed closed for a year or so, everything would be forgotten, but that if Hartmut Bitomsky got stubborn and tried to reopen, he was asking for trouble, he was upsetting the famous Kreuzberg balance, he was being insensitive. This is what the mayor seemed to be saying, too. Wolfgang Krüger was very nervous after the *Kübelaktion*. He had lived through May Day and Ronald Reagan's visit, and now here was Hartmut Bitomsky's restaurant calling more attention to Kreuzberg, making the mayor look bad (or weak or stupid). Television crews would move their cameras into his paneled office, and the mayor would sit in front of his Berlin bears, looking jovial and a little sick, and saying that it was all a big fuss over nothing—that Maxwell wasn't really in the Kreuzberg spirit anyway, that Maxwell was one of those fancy *liberal* restaurants selling dishes, he had heard, at sixty marks—and then he would apologize to the Bitomskys and a week later he would go on television and say the same thing.

The Bitomskys never really expected much of Krüger, but they did expect the local Alternativer to help them. They thought that surely an important Alternativer like Volker Härtig would be able to do something. Hartmut called Härtig, and Härtig agreed that, yes, the *Kübelaktion* was a terrible thing to have happened. He went on record saying that the *Kübelaktion* was certainly against the liberal atmosphere so dear to Kreuzberg and Kreuzbergers. He told the newspapers and the magazines and anybody else who asked him. But he didn't really *help* the Bitomskys. He didn't rally the Kreuzberg Greens to the Bitomskys' cause (giving some weight to Daniel Cohn-Bendit's statement about Germans being more passionate about saving trees than saving people). He said he understood that Hartmut Bitomsky might have had it with Kreuzberg—he himself had nearly had it, which was why he was walking around with a gas pistol in his pocket—but, politically speaking, it made no sense to take the *Kübelaktion* as a symbol. Kreuzberg was against violence, and everybody knew it.

Hartmut says it is hard for someone who is making his third movie about fascist images not to be sensitive when it comes to neighbors like his old neighbors. In the end, he says, there was probably as much concern among Autonomen about what had happened to Maxwell as there was among most of the respectable Kreuzbergers. A lot of Autonomen told him they were disgusted by the *Kübelaktion*. They were disgusted by the propaganda that went around defending the action—the flyers that said, "Throw the liberals out, throw the artists out, throw IBA and the architects out" and "We warned Maxwell, we asked them to pay and they said no." They did not much like the fact that people were working the Oranienstrasse, in the name of the scene, demanding money—that people were hitting galleries and shops and bars, saying, "Here's our collection box. If you don't have money, raise your prices." One of the rules of the scene has always been discussion. You plan your actions. You get the scene together and talk things over and find out what the scene thinks about what you plan to do. But nobody discussed the *Kübelaktion,* and when it was over some of the Autonomen got together and publicly denounced the violence, saying that trashing Maxwell was not "political"— that the people who had trashed Maxwell had not reflected properly on the political implications of what they were doing to the neighborhood. Those Autonomen put out their own propaganda. Some of them—the Pinox collective among them—called the *Kübelaktion* a fascist action and said that maybe the Kreuzberg scene should be less militant and more "constructive." They said that the scene should spend its time taking peaceful actions against real enemies. They wanted to know what good it did to take on Hartmut Bitomsky when there were things like the International Monetary Fund for Kreuzberg to worry about.

∞

At first, and from the street, nothing looks much different at 170 Oranienstrasse. From the street, there is the same "minimalist aesthetic." The four big windows look just as severe as they did when the Bitomskys were there (and maybe more severe, now that Brigitte's dark-green woolen curtains, hung low on the windows from thick brass rods, are gone). It takes a while to see the changes, to notice, say, this year's May Day poster in the window—the one about revolution being magnificent and everything else being rubbish—or the posters for a Turkish variety act called Putsch in Bonn and an evening with the Three Tornados at one of the Autonomen factories. It takes a while to notice that the name, discreetly painted in the bottom corner of one window, has been changed from Maxwell to Anton.

Anton is ten. His mother is Gabi Loher and his mother's boyfriend is Karl-Heinz Kraus—known in the scene as Strumpf— and Gabi and Strumpf are the people who bought out Maxwell from Brigitte and Hartmut Bitomsky. Occasionally, Anton comes to the restaurant. He sits at a table with his comic book, and sometimes he is joined by an old wino who spends the mornings there, dressed in rags, reading the paper and nursing a cup of coffee and generally keeping warm, and sometimes by a large Rottweiler that wanders over to the restaurant from Strumpf's house whenever it wants company or food. Strumpf's house is an old squat on the Leuschnerdamm, near the Wall, which was turned over to the squatters while the Social Democrats were in power. The rules of the scene are the rules at Strumpf's, and now they are the restaurant's rules, too. The place is still a fishbowl (which was one of the accusations against it), but now the people looking in and the people looking out are pretty much the same people, and they come and go as they are hungry or thirsty or simply spot a friend inside and feel like talking. Anton is open all day long. You can go in in the morning and have a "Day After"—two aspirin and a cup of coffee—or, if you want a Gitane, an "Existentialist." For hard-core Kreuzberg drunks, there is the beer-and-vodka breakfast at six marks, and for the Kreuzberg bodybuilders—the leather crowd—there is juice, fruit, pot cheese, toast, and Ovaltine at eight marks. This is not exactly a people's breakfast. Six marks is over three dollars, and eight marks is nearly four dollars and fifty cents, and it is doubtful that Brigitte Bitomsky would have charged much more. But Brigitte wasn't open mornings. The people who came to Maxwell came for dinner. They did not come to sit around and plan a squat or discuss an action or spend a couple of hours with a cup of weak coffee listening to the reggae and the American rock that now blare from the stereo speakers Strumpf and Gabi installed to make the restaurant "friendly."

It is generally agreed in the scene that the restaurant "looks the same, but different, because the freaks are there now." It is more of a piece, people say, with the other places on the block—the junk shop specializing in Coca-Cola signs and fast-food menus, the Turkish merchant with the net bridal gowns and the strippers' feathers, the underground T-shirt shop, the old beer hall draped, whatever the season, with dusty Christmas decorations—and with the freaks who use them. The freak style is androgynous—hair sliced short and spiky and bleached pale yellow in the front, leather jeans, leather jackets, black T-shirts, white socks. And the transportation is motorcycles. (The Mercedeses parked up and down the Oranienstrasse belong to Turkish merchants and not food lovers from Charlottenburg.) There is one terrible painting on Anton's wall—giving the finger to art, and to thinking about art, and to choosing art—and the white linen has been replaced by paper napkins and brown laminated tabletops. "Why not brown?" is Strumpf's position. The Anton banquettes have all been covered with wrinkled Naugahyde. Strumpf has put a chrome counter on the wooden sideboard that Hartmut built along the back wall, and he has added a big chrome-and-glass display cabinet—the kind of cabinet that holds the cheesecake and the banana-cream pie in American diners—and Strumpf uses the cabinet as a kind of menu. The day's dishes are on display there, announcing right off that there is no fancy food at Anton, that there is only plain Kreuzberg fare, like cold leek pie and frankfurter-and-mayonnaise salad. Half the people at Anton don't bother to eat at all, which may be just as well, because the food is leaden. They come to Anton because Strumpf's Anton, in Kreuzberg in 1988, is something like what Hartmut's Dziga Vertov film school must have been in 1968—an easy, authentic image of the Zeitgeist, a place that reflects and protects the mood around it. Strumpf does not use the word "authentic," although his friends at Heilehaus, the "social-medical natural-therapy center" on Waldemarstrasse, use "organic" when they talk about Anton. Strumpf prefers "letting things happen" or "saying O.K." It is hard to determine what Gabi says, because, regardless of Rosa Luxemburg and the women's groups and the radical-lesbian coalitions, the rule in Autonomen Kreuzberg in 1988 seems to be that the women do the work and the men do the talking. It is a function of that village ethic that Karl Schlögel discovered in the middle of his cosmopolitan Mitteleuropa city, the way Strumpf conferring with his friends in his old Freiburg dialect is a function of the same ethic.

Strumpf's real village is called Ulm. It is a hundred miles into the Black Forest from Freiburg, and Strumpf has not been back much since he moved to Kreuzberg, six years ago—long enough to have acquired the requisite leather and the spiky haircut and three-day stubble and the little silver earring in his left ear, and long enough to have taken up his parents' language. His father drives a truck in Freiburg. His mother works in a printing factory. They were like all the other parents in working-class West Germany, Strumpf says. They expected him to learn a trade and get a job. They sent him to Freiburg to apprentice as an auto mechanic, and he apprenticed for three years, and then one day, he says, "I decided to change my city"—which in Kreuzberg means that he decided to change his life. He was twenty when he left. He took his car and drove straight through West Germany and East Germany and into West Berlin—like a homing pigeon—to the door of a squat in Kreuzberg. He asked to sleep in the squat. He had no money and no job and no intention of going home and getting one—and especially no intention of showing up at the Ulm draft board for his year in the West German Army. Strumpf is an exceptionally peaceful person. He likes to say that some people want to destroy everything and some want to keep things peaceful, and that he is with the peaceful people. He does not believe in armies, although "if you do, that's O.K. too." He does not believe in jobs, either—not, at least, in the kind of jobs his parents wanted for him. His parents gave him three weeks in Kreuzberg. They thought he was "doing his Kreuzberg," like everybody else's children—but he never went home. He opened a coffee bar in the squat, and then for a while he had a small garage there, and *then*—it was when he decided that repairing cars was too cold and too dirty—he decided to sail around the world. He and a friend went to Bremen and started building a seventeen-meter schooner. When he and the friend "split," as Strumpf puts it, he kept on building. Two years ago, he and Gabi got together. They have a Kreuzberg arrangement. She lives in their old squat with Anton, and he lives in another converted squat with the dog and a couple of roommates —his partner from the squat garage and a friend named Andi from the social-medical natural-therapy center—and sleeps wherever he happens to end the day. "That's O.K.," he says. "That's O.K." sums up his philosophy.

Strumpf has what is often described as a "South German mentality." It means he thinks things over slowly and comes to conclusions slowly—and afterward is very settled inside, very sure, and never skeptical. Strumpf says that he "came to a conclusion about Anton." It involved the neighborhood and the Autonomen, and what the relation between Anton and the neighborhood and the Autonomen would be. Strumpf thinks of himself as a kind of

Autonomen alumnus. He used to be "organized" is how he puts it. His old squat was an Autonomen squat, and his friends at the natural-therapy center are what most other Berliners would call a "good" Autonomen group, but Strumpf does not know whether, properly speaking, you can call a group of friends a group, or whether you can even call *him* part of that group when he is the owner of a prosperous restaurant with people working daily shifts, and spends his own day buying cheese at the supermarket and bread at the bakery and checking supplies from the wholesaler and paying bills and, all in all, being a successful businessman. The question makes him reflective.

"With Maxwell, I asked my friends what *they* wanted," he says when he tries to explain how Maxwell turned into Anton—why, for example, he kept the Bitomskys' plain white plates but took away their napkins. "It was important for me to have friends speaking frankly. I had to know what to do about the tables, what was the right color for the neighborhood. And I had to know this: What was the right behavior for the boss of a restaurant in Kreuzberg? I didn't know how to be a boss. I didn't know how to tell anybody what to do, or how to give orders without shouting. I had to be straightened out. I had to admit that because of working, I had become less of an Autonomer and more of a liberal person—that something had changed in my mind since I came to Kreuzberg. At first, I thought it wasn't so important to work. Then I thought it was O.K. to work, but only in a collective. Now I think it's not so important—a collective. It's more important to look at work in terms of what's going on in the whole society around you. I'm not so interested now in daily political discussion, in all this talking about the revolution. For instance, all the people who work here are my friends. They're like me, they don't want a lot of money or cars or holidays. But I accept that if I'm here I have to be the boss, I have to control. Because I know now that people don't work without control. At first, I had a guy in the kitchen—he was a waiter in Charlottenburg, but he quit for a month and came here to train the girls for me and get the kitchen going—but once he left there was no chief in the kitchen and none of the girls would work and finally I had to say, 'Look, you have to vote and elect a chief of girls, and she gives the orders,' and that's what's happened. So here I am, a boss in Kreuzberg. And I know that if, because of this, I change my mind—if I decide, 'Let's put off the revolution until tomorrow'—I have to say so. But I also know that if I go to a meeting and the people say, 'What are you doing here, being a boss? You have to make Anton a cooperative'—well, that's O.K., too. What's important is this: What I think has to be the same as what I do. That's all that's important."

Strumpf is a lot like Hartmut Bitomsky, despite his being South German and twenty-six and dressed in leather and Hartmut's being North German and forty-six and dressed in jeans. Strumpf is small and fair and Hartmut tall and dark, but they share something almost physical, a deliberate calm, an almost willed mildness in their eyes. They come from different worlds—the apprentice shop and the university had divided Berliners long before the Wall—and the revolutions they talk about are certainly different, but in the little contact they had they got along. Strumpf was looking for a bar when he found Maxwell. He was thinking of a place for food and jazz concerts, but then he saw Maxwell, boarded up, and a few days later he began to ask around. He heard all about the discussions in the scene—how some Autonomen said that Maxwell was O.K. and others said it wasn't O.K. because of all the Schicki-Micki people looking out of the windows at the scene as if they were in a fancy glass lodge in a treetop in Africa, looking at animals. He had not known much about those discussions before, being one of the "peaceful people." When there is fighting in Kreuzberg, when the scene turns violent, Strumpf goes home and makes a cup of coffee. "That's just for me," he says. "I don't know what the others do." One thing he does not do is keep his restaurant open on May Day, the way Hartmut Bitomsky did. He closes the shutters and goes home. He is not a skeptic, but he is a realist—more of a realist, anyway, than Hartmut—and this perhaps is the real difference in the Kreuzberg generations. He is not even especially interested in restaurants. He says that Anton is something to do now, for a few years. When he is tired of Anton, he will move on to something else.

Strumpf is sensitive to what he calls "the mind control" in Kreuzberg, but he says that after the *Kübelaktion*—after all the discussions, and all the notices in the windows of Autonomen bars saying the *Kübelaktion* was good or the *Kübelaktion* was bad—the people who did it "had to accept the discussions in a self-reflecting way," and that, from Strumpf's perspective, is a kind of democracy. There is not much doubt that he knows who planned the *Kübelaktion*. People in the scene know these things, they know by instinct. They know the signals and the signs—they are alert to the signs—in ways that Hartmut, for all his semiology, did not. "Semiology" is not a word in Strumpf's vocabulary, but he probably would be amused to learn that there are people writing books about the semiology of Kreuzberg, and he certainly would be amused to learn that Hartmut Bitomsky considers himself a semiologist. What Strumpf thinks about are codes. "We are a few hundred people without politics but with a code" is how he describes his world.

Strumpf says that he "studied" Maxwell. He read the *Kübelaktion* clips in a scrapbook at the Autonomen bookstore M99, just off the Oranienstrasse, and decided that the problems at Maxwell were problems of code—that they had to do with whether you handed a beggar scraps in the kitchen or fed him in the dining room, like any other customer. He thinks that Hartmut Bitomsky broke the Kreuzberg code, but he thinks that Hardt-Waltherr Hämer probably broke it first when he tried to make the neighborhood clean and attractive. He says that "clean" and "attractive" are contradictions in a place where people are homeless or squatting. Officially, the squats have stopped, but the fact is that every few months people in Kreuzberg start squatting, and "squat spies" in the scene report them, and Wilhelm Kewenig sends the police to arrest them. Strumpf thinks that people without homes should squat. Two of his Kreuzberg friends—Kurdish refugees— are squatting now.

It is hard to imagine Strumpf talking about a minimalist aesthetic. Aesthetics have nothing to do with what he regards as an artful life, and anyway, Strumpf would say that talking about aesthetics is something bourgeois people do. He admires Hartmut but not for his taste or his movies. He has never seen one of Hartmut's movies. He admires Hartmut for being able to take two dilapidated secondhand shops and turn them into one big room all by himself. When he talks about Hartmut's good work, he means the plastering and the painting and the way the fixtures at Maxwell were secured and the fact that the kitchen Hartmut built was practical. When he talks about Hartmut's style, he means that Hartmut was friendly and straightforward in their dealings, and never resentful. He says that the people behind the *Kübelaktion* were "small" and that "by throwing shit at Maxwell they were throwing shit in all their neighbors' faces." They should have gone to Hartmut, he says, and made him part of the discussion, because "Maxwell was a little part of a whole story going on in Kreuzberg." His version of the story is simple. "Bitomsky was nice," Strumpf says, "but he didn't change the kind of eating at Maxwell, so he had to close."

PETER SCHMIDT

(JUNE 1990)

Peter Schmidt always wanted to leave East Germany. He did not so much want to go to West Germany as he wanted to get away from East Germany and from his angry father and his anxious mother and from all the policemen and plant managers and Party proselytizers whose job it was to undermine a dreamy teenage boy with a box of Jefferson Airplane tapes under the bed and a third-hand motorcycle chained to the banister. He wanted to be free, although he didn't really know what "freedom" meant besides freedom to stop school and never have to apprentice in a people's factory or play war games in the rain for the draft army of the German Democratic Republic. Peter was a *Schlüsselkind*—a latchkey child. He thought of himself as a "child of rock," but he was really more like one of those lonely, wistful boys sent into the world each morning with a key on a string around their necks and orders to stay in school until the janitor locked up and then to play in the parking lot and otherwise pass the time until a parent came home from work, or a neighbor arrived to make the cocoa, or the weather forced them to use their keys and wait indoors, in a small, cramped flat in a "new town" that was cut off from the city, and from the life of the city, by a four-lane ring road no one was allowed to cross. Peter did not have much of an education. He left school at sixteen to apprentice. He worked in a big Rostock garage, overhauling armored cars for the Warsaw Pact, and his ambition was to lie around all day and listen to his sixties tapes, from America, while his mother fussed over him and washed his jeans and maybe braised a juicy Polish ham—his mother was from Gdansk, and ham and potatoes were her specialty—or to get on his motorcycle and head west into the never-never land beyond the Schlutup-Selmsdorf checkpoint.

He would wait for his morning train at the South Rostock S-Bahn station and watch the Copenhagen express speed by on its special "transit" tracks, next to the subway tracks, and see the young Danes in their compartments, drinking, laughing, kissing, waving to *him,* and he would think about borders. Once, when he was visiting his grandmother—she lives in a village called Baumberg, on the Baltic coast, forty miles from the border—he picked up a Swedish hitchhiker with long hair and a Walkman and drove him on his motorcycle to the checkpoint and watched him walk across, whistling to the sound of Elton John, and saw for himself, he says, "where my world ended and his did not." That was when Peter decided to leave East Germany. It was April 10, 1981. The whole family knows the day. It marks their troubles, more than the day he actually tried to leave and was arrested, or the day he was sentenced and was sent to prison in a boxcar, or the day he was "bought" by West Germany for fifty thousand Deutsche marks, or the day he left for Hamburg, or even the day, this spring, he made his first trip home. "April 10, 1981," his mother, Hannelore, will say. "The day Peter met the Swedish hitchhiker." "April 10, 1981," his brother, Rainer, will say. "The day Peter was sad because the Swedish hitchhiker could go to Lübeck and he could not."

What Peter wanted in the West was not money or democracy, or even record stores with aisles devoted entirely to the Stones and the Grateful Dead and the other sounds that had arrived in the German Democratic Republic twenty years past their moment. He wanted something East Germany had lost, and he could not have described it except as a longing that was really a longing for himself, for an energy, an adequacy, a confidence that would connect him with the world. East Germany, trying to teach him *what* he was—trying to produce a worker for a workers' state, someone not too smart, not too skeptical, someone cooperative—had neglected to teach him anything about *who* he was or how to get to be himself. He longed for himself the way the boys he eventually got to know in Hamburg longed for girls or jobs or BMWs. It produced in him a deep passivity. He told his Hamburg friends that West Germany was too ambitious, too aggressive—he missed what he called the "closer, dirtier life" at home. At first, they thought he was exotic. They did not know what else to make of him. They thought he was laid back and supercool—that suffering had "detached" him, that it had given him a special claim on truth, which was unavailable to the radical sons and daughters of the Hamburg bourgeoisie, whose most defiant gestures had to do with drinking beer with the skinheads at their squats on the St. Pauli Hafenstrasse. But in the end they got impatient with Peter. They decided he was lazy, indolent, maybe a little strange. They did not know what he was waiting *for,* or why he expected to be taken care of— why he did not get up and go out and participate, like his roommate, Rudolf Klaassen, who was getting a doctorate in history and played guitar with a heavy-metal band and, whenever he was broke, went out and found himself a job. Rudolf was a proper Hamburg radical. It didn't matter to him if he made his money teaching typists how to use computers or hauling sacks at the post office or hawking the *Morgenpost* at traffic lights on the Reeperbahn or changing the labels on expired cans of mushrooms and tomatoes at a Hamburg wholesaler's warehouse. He could handle the system, whereas Peter Schmidt refused to take a job in the system. Peter refused to study in the system, or find a girl in the system, or even do the dishes in the system if he was not instructed to do the dishes. He could follow instructions, but it turned out that he could not easily be free. The freedom he dreamed of was always across some border, on the other side, away from prison or distress or the dinner dishes. It had as little to do with West Germany, with its strident competence, as it had to do with East Germany, with its strident apathy. Peter says that maybe the problem of being East German, the pity of being East German, is that you are always at your best, and your clearest, standing at a wall or a border or a prison door, reflecting on the other side.

∞

Germans talk about themselves. They talk about their pursuit of "Germanness" and their brooding interest in what being German means. They talk about *Innerlichkeit.* They say they want to find the space in their heads, the appropriate "innerness," where the German soul is located—where Germany is located—and in the end that space is so compelling that they tend to see it everywhere, to regard the world around them as a natural correlative of themselves. Whether they arrive as armies or as teenage refugees, like Peter, they carry with them a kind of blind entitlement. In their enthusiasm for themselves, they turn everything desirable into "Germany" and everything not Germany into a problem. They do not use the word *Lebensraum* anymore—they know that Hitler used it—but they think about *Lebensraum*. They talk about that space in their heads, with *its* borders, the way Helmut Kohl talked a couple of months ago about reviewing the status of the German-Polish border—as if the frustrations of a deepening, expanding, incorporating identity were their appropriate condition, the condition of being German. They talk about it the way Frenchmen talk about drinking wine as a condition of being French, and Englishmen talk about brawling at soccer matches as a condition of being English. Peter says he is "against nationalisms," but he talks about Germanness, too. He says that he never felt "so German" as he did in prison—which may be why he was so lost, and disappointed, outside. Being down and out at twenty-five in the city of Hamburg was not the kind of freedom he had come to believe in when he looked across the bay toward Lübeck—or, indeed, out the window of his prison cell. He had thought that "Peter Schmidt" left East Germany with the Swedish hitchhiker and was waiting for him across the border, emblematic and complete, like one of the Baltic pines on the hill behind his grandmother's farmhouse. He had thought that "Peter Schmidt" was there, waiting to be claimed.

∞

There are sixteen million East Germans and sixty-two million West Germans—which means that by the end of the year, when the two Germanys unite, there will be seventy-eight million new "German" citizens. There will be no more Bundis (West Germans are known in the G.D.R. as Bundis, because they come from the Bundesrepublik) crossing for the weekend in their Mercedeses, wearing Italian leather and designer jeans and wielding video cameras and waving fresh fruit and hard currency, like wampum, at the natives, trying to buy a piece of backward, "unspoiled" landscape for themselves. There will be no more Ossis (for *Ost*) like Peter, coming west on motorbikes or in their noxious, sputtering pink and blue Trabants, demanding housing allowances and health allowances and hardship allowances and, finally, the jobs and flats that Bundis claim were meant for them. There will be seventy-eight million "Germans" in the country that was properly theirs for less than seventy-five years. They will settle down with each other, and try to ignore their antipathy, wondering if the bargain they struck for each other is something good, something restorative, or a mail-order marriage of contentious strangers who have traveled too far and said too much—and spent too much—to separate.

It does not much matter in the end if the Ostmark and the Deutsche mark are exchanged at parity, which is what the East Germans demanded and got, or at a rate of two to one, which is what the West Germans (who are for all practical purposes buying East Germany) tried to propose. It does not much matter if the country unites according to Article 146 of the Basic Law—the law that has been West Germany's "provisional" constitution for forty years—and convokes constituent assemblies in Bonn or in Berlin and drafts a new German constitution, or according to Article 23, which establishes the right of the five old German states incorporated now as "East Germany" to vote themselves into existence again and then to "leave" East Germany and "adhere to Germany" (the way the Saarland did when it "left" France in 1957) and declare the Basic Law the official German constitution. It does not much matter if half the new democrats in East Germany were informers for the Stasi—the secret police in the G.D.R. was called the Staatssicherheitsdienst—or if the politicians in Bonn or Berlin or in a united Germany decide to destroy their files or expose them. What does matter is that the seventy-eight million Germans take a look at each other, fifty-seven years after Weimar, and try to decide what they mean by being German, and by being Germany. It is not entirely clear to many of them that they belong together, or even that they want to belong together.

When the Wall came down, in November of 1989—it was November 9, and while the date was familiar not many people in either Germany seemed to remember why it was familiar, or what had happened on Kristallnacht, fifty-one years earlier—it was, arguably, to keep East Germans in East Germany by offering them the freedom to go. No one talked then, at least in public, about uniting Germany. East Germans said that there was no question of uniting. They were going to find a "third way" and build a free

new country that would be better and more humane—"softer"—
than the Bundesrepublik, and it is interesting that even now, no
one in East Germany can say for sure who talked first about unification, or when, or which side of the Wall he came from. All they
can say is that sometime last fall demonstrators in Leipzig stopped
chanting "We are the people!" and started chanting "We are one
people!," and after that the only real question was how much
money it was going to cost West Germany to persuade Gorbachev.
But after twenty-eight years of a wall, Germans did not know each
other anymore. They did not know—whatever their claims to
"Germanness"—if they would get along. They had different priorities. They did not mean the same things by the words they used to
describe themselves. (The East German Christian Democrats are
Protestants, for example, and they were shocked to discover that
the West German Christian Democrats, many of them Catholic,
expected them to oppose abortion or, being "conservatives," to
save state money by shutting down their day-care centers.) Two
hundred thousand people moved west in the first two months after
the Wall came down, and another two hundred thousand have
moved this year, which would seem to suggest that some East Germans would rather *be* West Germans right away (and forget about
getting along with West Germans) than wait at home to join West
Germany as poor relations with their hands out and their embarrassing failure to account for.

In the end, it was mainly the West Germans who wanted them
to stay in the G.D.R. The politicians were slow to admit it, even
when workers in West Germany started trashing East German cars
and blocking checkpoints and occupying the school gyms where
some of the refugees were housed. Oskar Lafontaine, who is the
Social Democrats' candidate for chancellor, got up at a meeting in
December and talked about the social cost of the immigration, but
he was the first important West German politician who talked so
bluntly. He said that there was no "German" reason to be enthusiastic about taking hundreds of thousands of East Germans into
the Bundesrepublik, about offering them jobs and housing and all
the costly blessings of West Germany's bountiful welfare state. He
had lived his life in the West, and he felt as close to people in, say,
Austria as he did to East Germans. He had grown up knowing

Austrians, but he had never known many East Germans. The fact is that after the Wall went up not many West Germans had an interest in visiting East Germany. The trip was too difficult. The wait at the checkpoints was too long. The surveillance was too harrowing.

Willy Brandt, who was the West German chancellor from 1969 to 1974, had an interest in East Germany. Brandt and his ambassador in East Berlin, Günter Gaus, made a commitment to Ostpolitik. They wanted to keep lifelines open, though those lines were mainly for the East Germans, and had to do with a faith that somewhere, maybe in the old workers' cafés on the dim-lit streets of East Berlin, there were still socialists dreaming of a better world—that if those old socialists were acknowledged, and not abandoned, some of their dreams would survive, and even temper, the ideology of "economic miracle" in the Bundesrepublik. Ostpolitik did not do much for ordinary West Germans. It made a lot of businessmen rich and gave West Germany seven or eight billion Deutsche marks a year in East German markets, but the most that West Germany actually saw of East Germany was the relatives who got to visit once a year and the pensioners who were permitted, and even encouraged, to emigrate when they retired so that West Germany would have to pay their social security. For years, the only important West German presence in the G.D.R. was the garbage that the City of West Berlin (with nowhere else to put it) paid a fortune in hard currency to dump there. Some of the East Germans knew West Germany from the programs they picked up at night from West German television, but the West Germans didn't "know" East Germany. The myth in the West about the G.D.R. was always that it was in fact another "Germany"—the industrial power of Comecon, the vanguard of the East bloc. No one in the West except the businessmen who went to East Germany really knew the extent to which Communism had turned Germans into Russians. No one seemed to guess the depth of the disaffection, or the incompetence at the heart of Prussia. West Germans should have known. No country in Europe was more analyzed and observed and worried over than East Germany. The Allies, still formally in occupation, spied on East Germany for the West Germans, and the West Germans spied on East Germany for the Allies, and prisoners were "bought West," and spies were exchanged, and pensioners came with their lifetimes in a van, and businessmen went every year to the Leipzig Trade Fair and saw the pollution and the poverty and the corruption—and everyone still maintained the fiction that East Germans were the goose-step vanguard of the Communist world, drilled to obedience and production. No one anticipated how damaged East Germany still was. No one anticipated Peter Schmidt.

∞

Peter does not need much to get along. His brother, Rainer, who is married to a West German and lives in Hamburg now, says that Peter goes to the flea market every year and buys a pair of jeans, for one mark, "and with that he is happy." His jeans this year are black, faded to an enviable worn, smudgy color but intact, and every morning he puts them on, along with an old pink T-shirt and a purple sweatshirt and a pair of tan Jum Jog running shoes and, if it is cold, the old black motorcycle jacket he was wearing on January 29, 1984, the night he was arrested trying to cross the border to Lübeck. His mother bought him the motorcycle jacket, and his brother gave him the pink T-shirt after it shrank at the laundromat, and the purple sweatshirt is a hand-me-down from his roommate, Rudolf. Peter doesn't remember where he got the shoes. He thinks that somebody visiting from Berlin may have left them. He does not like to think about "things," he says, or worry about things, or even own things. He says that West Germans are "things people," that they live with what Ulrike Meinhof once called *Konsumterrorismus*—"the terrorism of things"—and know their neighbors not as neighbors but by the cars they drive and the size of their television sets. Peter likes watching television, but he would never want to own a television set. Rudolf had a television once. Peter would sit in the living room and watch it all day long while Rudolf was at school or playing with his band or working at one of his extra jobs, but then the picture started going, and Peter told Rudolf about it and waited for Rudolf to get it fixed, and every once in a while brought it up—"It'll be nice when the television is fixed," Peter would say—and never really understood why Rudolf got mad one night and picked up the television set and carried it down four flights of stairs and put it out with the garbage.

Rudolf says that it never occurred to Peter to fix the television set himself. "Peter expects everything and nothing at the same time" is the way Rudolf explains it. He calls it the East German disease. Peter's dark-brown hair will get long and flop into his eyes, and his mustache will droop into his mug of coffee, and Peter will wait until somebody—his brother's wife, maybe, or one of Rudolf's girlfriends—sees him and sighs and shakes her head and offers to cut his hair for him. If there is food in the house, he eats it. Otherwise, he forgets. He gets listless and scrawny, and eventually a friend comes to the flat and sees how terrible he looks—he was thin to begin with—and takes him out for a big meal, and even orders for him, because, as Peter says, "I don't think much about food." His brother says that Peter is "humble and shy, and his needs are small," and his mother, in Rostock, says, "Poor Peter, he can't take care of himself." But Rudolf Klaassen says that he's negative and arrogant and self-indulgent—that he has "a pain-in-the-ass East German purity." Rudolf does not see why his girlfriends should have to cut his roommate's hair just because his roommate is a refugee from the G.D.R. He thinks that Peter should get his own girlfriend, but he says that Peter is "shy *and* proud"—Peter thinks he's too good, and has suffered too profoundly, for a girl to understand.

∞

The Schmidts are an old Mecklenburg family. They talk to each other in Mecklenburg Plattdeutsch and hang Mecklenburg flags—red-yellow-and-blue striped flags—above their farmhouse doors and defer to Peter's elderly cousin Otto, the pig master at the Baumberg livestock cooperative, because of his cranky and successful resistance to uttering a word in High German. Otto used to say that one day all the Schmidts' Mecklenburg farms would be one big farm, and he was prescient. When the Russians came, in 1945, Schmidts had been farming the Baltic coast between Wismar and Rostock for two hundred years, and some of them had got rich on pigs and turnips and sugar beets, and had added land, to the south, and all the Russians had to do to secure the Schmidts for Communism was call the family together, declare their farms a cooperative, and make the village of Baumberg, where they had their barns and their houses, its headquarters.

There were six Schmidt brothers in Baumberg. They came drifting back from the front, or from prisoner-of-war camps, to learn that their sugar-beet beds were being put in grass for grazing, and their barns were being converted into feedlots and their family grange into a Party center for ideological education, and that all but fifty acres of the Schmidt land was now "the property of the people." They came back to find that the oaks they had planted for Hitler in 1934, when the Vaterland Chauvinistischer Verein was in the village recruiting, were thriving, but the plaques that marked them were in the mud on the bottom of the pond behind Peter's grandmother's house—which was just as well, because their children had already learned at school that the Baumberg Schmidts were never Nazis. The Baumberg Schmidts were always brave Communists, or would have been brave Communists if anyone had asked them. They were "Hitler's victims," not his followers. Hitler was an imperialist from "over there," in the Western Sector.

Of course, most of the villagers remembered very clearly how they had planted their Hitler oaks, and how enthusiastic they were—how everybody had a glass of sweet homemade cherry wine to toast the Führer, and how Cousin Otto, who was a boy then, attempted a stanza of "Deutschland Über Alles" in Mecklenburg Platt, and how that night the Baumberg Schmidts went to work on a family tree that took up twenty-eight pages of the village ledger, with six pages of addenda, to prove to the new "racial bureau" at the Wismar Rathaus that the Schmidts were an entirely unsullied Aryan clan. No one thought then that Schmidts would ever be leaving Baumberg. But after the war Otto's brother Erich came home from a prisoner-of-war camp in America, collected his young wife, and left the village for Baden-Würtemberg, and a few years later a cousin left, and by the time the Wall went up six more Schmidts had left Baumberg. Peter's father, Stefan, did not go west, but he left the farm for school in Rostock, where the only Schmidts were a family of apostate anthroposophists. Peter's great-uncle Horst went to America and got rich, everybody in the family says. His great-aunt Antraud, who had never found a husband (despite her dowry of fifty pigs and her trousseau chests full of linen and her turn-of-the-century feather beds), decided that she would never find one now, at forty-five, on a Communist livestock cooperative, and left for Bonn to answer the telephone at the Ministry of Agriculture.

Most of the Schmidts stayed. They started milking the cows and herding the pigs and plowing the beet fields and cleaning the stalls, and doing all the other steamy barnyard jobs that in the family's heyday had been left for Polish workers. They put their beautiful leather books in boxes in the attic and closed their upright pianos and stopped quoting Schiller and Goethe and started quoting Fritz Reuter, who wrote Mecklenburg genre novels, and telling nonsense stories in Mecklenburg Platt—stories that began with questions like "Do geese in America walk barefoot?" and ended with answers like "My shirt is full of boils." They went to church Sundays, the way they always had—they had a famous church, at the top of the village hill, which was as beckoning and severe as the sea beyond it—and after church the children would tumble down the hill to the stony beach and roll up their skirts or their trousers and wade into the lapping tide and hunt for shells. At night, on dares, the children would brave the small stone crypt that was dug into the hillside centuries ago, when there were priests instead of pastors in the church, and everybody worshiped statues, and dead children met their Maker with their own images carved, sleeping, into the marble lids of their coffins.

The Schmidts kept Pastor Busch busy, and Pastor Femfert, and, finally, Pastor Müller, who lives in the parsonage now and has one of Baumberg's three telephones. Every day, after the last milking, they climbed the church road with their rakes and hoes and their wheelbarrows filled with Osterglocke and potted lilies, and tended the graves in the churchyard, where eleven Schmidts had their family plots—proper Mecklenburg plots, with ivy hedges and plain square stones and neat clumps of country flowers. They did not think of church as a defiance, unless it was a defiance of Catholics. They seemed to settle into their Communist life. The Nazis had come and put their children in Hitler Youth and told them to prepare to die, that Germany was taking over the world. And then the Communists had come and put their children in Free German Youth and told them no, they had been on the wrong side—the

Communists were taking over the world. So it may be that the Schmidts took a long view of their own enthusiasms. They joined the Party and went to the weekly meetings at the Party center (it was at the foot of the village hill, just where the path to the church started) and eventually voted to merge their cooperative with the cooperatives in two villages up the coast, and ended up in a Kombinat with two thousand pigs, eight hundred cows, and a hundred and sixty people, including two Stasi spies and a Party manager who took a cut of the profits. They worked hard, and they did not complain publicly when one of the Schmidt girls was arrested in Schwerin—she was married, and was teaching kindergarten in Schwerin—and sent to prison for eight years for taking Stalin's picture off the kindergarten wall and putting up pictures of churches. They were pleased when another Schmidt girl became a "heroine of the state" for surpassing her milk quota and won a Brueghel print of peasants working, and a steamer trip down the Volga with a hundred other heroines. They lived with a Russian base not far away in Wismar, and with army maneuvers on their pastureland and the sound of *Tiefflieger* buzzing their farmhouses and scaring the calves, and they produced ruddy, rawboned children who wore overalls and little woolen caps and could muck a pig stall or a chicken coop at four on a January morning and never feel the cold and would greet the fighter planes with thick, comical Mecklenburg accents.

Their children had never heard of Schiller. Their children had nothing in common with the delicate children in old Schmidt-family photographs, who were dressed in organdie and sailor suits, like burghers' children, and looked as if the closest they ever came to a beet or a turnip was in a bowl of soup. The Schmidts were fond of their pigs and their cows, like the Schmidt *Bauern* eight generations before, like Cousin Otto. They were amateurs of Western life—they studied the clothes and the food and the furniture they saw at night on Norddeutsche Rundfunk—but they knew better than to waste their time dreaming about that life. They turned off desire when they turned off their television sets, at nine, and went to bed. Most of them never saw the border, forty miles away, although they all knew stories about people trying to flee, and getting caught on the barbed wire that was the Wall in most of East

Germany, and being torn apart by dogs. The older Schmidts allowed that they had had a terrible century, and they wanted to get on with it, as calmly and quickly as they could. They didn't want to think about glory anymore. They didn't want to think about war. They didn't want to believe in anything but the Bible, the way their children didn't want to believe in anything but the music that made its way to Baumberg on tapes smuggled into East Germany from America.

Peter has a cousin around his age in Baumberg. His name is Arnulf, and he is a sweet, goofy cowherd who loves Bob Dylan. He plays Bob Dylan at the feedlot. He dances alone, up and down the barn, in an electric-blue acetate jogging suit, every evening after the calves are fed. He dances to "Positively Fourth Street" and "Like a Rolling Stone" and talks with awe about the day Bob Dylan came to East Berlin to sing and eighty thousand people heard him. He says he wants to give Bob Dylan a hug. It is his greatest ambition. He tells everybody that. When Russian trucks come through Baumberg collecting potatoes—the Russians send trucks to Mecklenburg every year, and they go from village to village, taking everyone's potatoes, until they have got their quota of five hundred thousand tons—he tells the drivers about loving Bob Dylan, and wanting to hug Bob Dylan, and then he tells them how Bob Dylan's real name is Zimmerman, and asks if they have heard of other Jewish entertainers who changed their names. He wants to get tapes of those entertainers. He is sure that if he knows their names—knows who they are and what they call themselves—he will discover some wonderful music. He says he is keeping a list of Jewish entertainers with new names. He has been through seven years of school and through the Party youth group and through an agricultural apprenticeship, but he has never met any Jews (there are only four or five hundred practicing Jews left in East Germany) or learned anything about Jews. Peter, at school in Rostock, once read a book about a Jewish doctor, "Professor Mamlock," who lost his job because of the Nazis and committed suicide, but Professor Mamlock never made it to Baumberg. No one in Baumberg ever taught Arnulf or his cousins that there was anything odd, anything out of the ordinary, between Jews and Germans, any bad feeling, anything that might make people uneasy if they heard about a German keeping lists of Jewish entertainers who had changed their names.

Sometimes when the family is working in the feedlot, one of the Schmidts will point to a tag on the ear of a baby calf and say, "Hitler tried that." And another Schmidt will nod and say that Hitler "tried and succeeded, but now Germany is 'mixed' again." He will say it matter-of-factly, smiling—making a little aside in the conversation—and it is hard to know whether or not he approves of Germany's being "mixed" again. Or he will say, "Who would have thought November ninth would happen?" and you know that he is not talking about 1938 and Kristallnacht. He is talking about 1989 and the Wall. The Baumberg Schmidts are worried that November 9 has left them behind. They are a little embarrassed by their farmers' life and their country speech, and even by their affection for the cows, now that they have been to Lübeck and seen that "there is everything you want there, beginning with bananas." They are embarrassed that one Schmidt tried to resist and was sent to prison and another tried to escape and was sent to prison while they were quietly looking after pigs and cows in a village barn and keeping the rules, which were that you never talked politics in a bar, because a Stasi might hear you, or complained about anyone on the farm, because a Stasi might report you, or talked to strangers, because the strangers might be Stasis themselves. For six years—from the day Peter was arrested to the day he stopped at Baumberg on his way home to see his mother—no one talked about Peter Schmidt. Every Sunday, Schmidts came to his grandmother's house, which is a big farmhouse on the road to the church, and sat in her parlor and had a cup of tea or maybe a glass of schnapps and told a few family stories, but they never asked about Peter or about helping Peter. They did not want to attract attention to themselves.

There is a place near Baumberg where Peter would like to have a house. You can see it from the graveyard—you follow the roll of pasture eastward, about a quarter of a mile in from the sea, until you come to a windswept rise with a giant oak tree framed against the sky and the ruins of a windmill beside it, and that is the spot where Peter would build a house if he believed in property. It is a beautiful spot. Every weekend since November, West Germans from Hamburg and Lübeck, and even from as far away as Kiel, drive into Mecklenburg and admire the green pastures and the old brick farmsteads, with their courtyards roofed against the wet Baltic winter, and the ancient trees and the beautiful sweep of beach, and there are always BMWs and Mercedeses parked near Peter's spot, and Bundis with video cameras taking pictures, talking about how lovely Mecklenburg is, and how unspoiled—a landscape from another century, like Schleswig-Holstein before it got so crowded, a perfect German weekend landscape. When Peter stopped in Baumberg in March, a group of West Germans was around, looking for a path over the pasture and up the rise to the old tree and the windmill, and Peter was happy that the path he used to take was overgrown in the six years he had been away, because the Bundis had been asking if anybody knew who "owned" the land, and if it was for sale. They wanted to develop the beach near Baumberg. They thought it would make a great resort, as good as Travemünde. They wanted to get in early on the action, and it was obvious that Peter's spot, with its view of the sea on one side and pretty pastures on the other, and with the Baumberg steeple rising on its hill just across a valley planted in barley, was precisely the sort of place that they would find appealing.

Bundis had already been to Baumberg. Bundis had tried to buy a cottage that Peter's father had built, across the orchard from his grandmother's farmhouse. Bundis had paced the perimeter of Arnulf's house—which is three hundred years old and has the longest covered courtyard in Baumberg—with the whole village watching. Bundis were at the border every weekend, hawking plastic watches and rancid perfume to the farmers. They were at every flea market in Mecklenburg, hawking Holstein beer. They put out "HARD CURRENCY ONLY" signs on their folding tables and spread whatever junk they had bought cheap that week in the Bundesrepublik—whatever no one in Hamburg or Frankfurt or Cologne wanted. They sold cracked bathroom glasses for fifty marks and fake-brass candlesticks for a hundred and fifty marks, and the ones who weren't selling candlesticks or trying to buy beaches and farmhouses—they were called the good-will Bundis—arrived with bags of kiwis and bananas (having read in *Die Welt* that East Germans were so poor they never got to eat kiwis and bananas) and descended on farmers in the streets of Schwerin and stevedores on the Rostock docks, and, when the farmers and stevedores got scared or angry or abusive, threw the kiwis and bananas at them and ran to their beautiful cars and locked the doors and drove back to the Bundesrepublik as fast as they could manage on the narrow, bumpy East German roads.

Peter doesn't like Bundis coming to East Germany. He is proprietary about East Germany, even though he ran away and has a West German passport and is now officially a Bundi himself. He spent the trip from Hamburg to Rostock spotting Bundis—counting their West German cars among the little Trabants. He knows that "Trabis" are terrible cars. He calls them *Leukoplast-bomber*—Band-Aid bombers—and likes to quote an article he read somewhere about how one Trabi puts as much carbon monoxide into the air as a hundred West German cars. But sometimes he says that Trabis are "more natural" than Western cars. To Peter, "natural" means anything poor or shabby or familiar. An old car. A building that hasn't been pointed or painted for forty years. The life he had at home.

∞

When Peter was planning his escape, he found an old bicycle in his grandmother's garden shed. He fixed it up, pumped the tires, and attached a box for his map, a couple of bottles of beer and water, and a tin of liverwurst. The map was an old map. It marked the trails over country hills and along dunes and between pastures—the overgrown trails that the investors from the Bundesrepublik are trying to find now when they stop their cars and aim their field glasses at a particularly pretty stretch of scenery. Peter traced those trails with a fine pencil until he had charted what he considered a safe route to the border—a route that would take him through Wismar and then keep him under cover of hills or trees or dunes, invisible from the paved road. He finished his route four months after he met the Swedish hitchhiker. It took him two and a half years longer to get up the courage to go. He says he never had much courage. When the East German draft called him—he was stripped and locked in a room with twenty or thirty other apprentices, guarded by a soldier with a machine gun—the Stasi in charge of "security assessments" wanted to know what kind of "attitude" toward the state he had, and Peter shrugged and said, "I don't care about the state." He says he had no courage to admit that he hated the state, or even to lie and pretend that he loved it. The Stasi got mad and asked another question—"Would Peter Schmidt rather live in Hamburg or Rostock?"—and Peter shrugged again and said he didn't care. "*Ist mir egal.*" He was naked and scared and shivering. They thought he was subversive. They kept him locked in the room for eight hours before they let him go.

That night, he started writing letters. He wrote to the Wehrkreiskommando to say that he would not bear arms. He had nothing against the state, but he refused to bear arms *for* the state. He had "no courage." Then he wrote to the Rostock city council to say that maybe it would be better if he "gave up now" on being a perfect East German citizen. He had not liked working in a garage. He thought he might like working in a theater, or maybe becoming a dancer, but he had got a stage technician's job at the Rostock People's Theater as soon as his apprenticeship was over and had found that while the artists were "interesting," the "people's" operettas and plays and dances they had to perform were not. Once, he had tried to be an agricultural apprentice. He applied to a good agricultural program in a town called Dorf Mecklenburg, near Wismar, but his place was "canceled"—he figures someone with better Party connections got it—and he was sent to a little farm school in a village where there was nothing to do, and he got bored and hitched a ride home to Rostock. By then, the only apprenticeships left were in mechanics. He didn't like machines. As far as he was concerned, machines were more interesting to drive than to repair.

Finally, he wrote to the minister of the interior, in East Berlin, asking for permission to go. He wrote out draft after draft, by hand, because it was illegal to talk to anybody about emigrating or to ask anybody for help with your application, or even to borrow anybody's typewriter. In those days, an East German who lent a typewriter that turned out to have been used for an application to leave the G.D.R. went to prison himself.

Peter did not know what to say, really, on his application. He did not want to give in to the euphemisms of "official German," but he did not see how he could talk about Swedish hitchhikers, or Danes laughing on a train, or the boredom of the garage and the endless Socialist youth meetings every apprentice had to go to. He did not know how to describe—in official German—the claustrophobia at home, with his parents and brother, and sometimes even his brother's friends, sharing a two-and-a-half-room flat in a "housing cooperative" that his mother had subscribed to six years before she thought of having children. From the point of view of the East German state, the worst crime against the state was agitation and the next was dissidence and the third was shrugging your shoulders, like Peter, and asking to go. Emigration was the shameful secret of the G.D.R. Three and a half million Germans had fled to the West before the Wall went up—they were, indeed, why the Wall went up—and in the twenty-three years before Peter tried to leave more than two hundred East Germans had been killed trying and more than two hundred thousand thrown in jail for it.

Peter says he never really expected an exit visa. The Baumberg Schmidts might have been model farmers, but Peter was a Rostock Schmidt, and the Rostock Schmidts were already a suspect family. They were "cosmopolitan." They had contacts. There were files on the Rostock Schmidts at Stasi headquarters, beginning with Peter's father, Stefan, who was a ship's engineer, and his third cousin Adolphus, who was an anthroposophist preacher, and ending with his brother, Rainer, who had already met his West German, and fallen in love, and wanted permission to marry. Stefan Schmidt had already lost one job because of contacts. He had sailed with an ocean ferry that made the run from Rostock to a port in Denmark, and once, when the motor broke—it was a West German motor— and a West German mechanic came to Denmark to fix it, he bought the mechanic a beer, and someone reported him as a "class enemy," and he was grounded. He was forbidden to sail again— or, indeed, to leave East Germany at all. He lost his "West" passport (though not his Party card) and his rank and his engineer's salary, and ended up teaching on a training ship that was anchored permanently in Wismar Harbor. He got bitter and angry and possessive. He started saying that his family was all he had. He never minded that the apartment was small, because his children were, literally, never out of sight or sound. He tried to impress them, to make them proud, as if he were still at sea and sending them post-cards with foreign stamps and bringing them foreign toys and coming home like a hero—from someplace much farther away than Wismar—in his white uniform with beautiful gold braid. He framed his medals from the East German Merchant Marine for them, and hung the plaque he got in 1970 for "wonderful achieve-ments in building socialism." He told them stories. He told them about the day the Americans came to the Hitler Youth school in Wörth an der Donau, in Bavaria, where he was "training for Hitler," and arrested the principal and opened the dormitory doors and told everybody to start walking—about how he walked four hundred miles across Germany, to Baumberg, and found the Russians there, recruiting the village boys to "train for Marx." He said that after the Russians came he never felt the farm was his, even though they called it the property of the people. It seemed to him then that the only place that wasn't the property of the people was the sea at his back door—which was why he went to Rostock and took the tests for the marine academy.

Stefan Schmidt never got over the disgrace and the disappoint-ment of being grounded. He lost his nerve. He got plaintive and in-gratiating and deferential. He was terrified of being noticed. He did not want any of the Schmidts calling attention to themselves. He could not bear the thought of losing more. When Rainer applied to leave, Stefan wrote a letter to his Kombinat saying that he did not approve of his son's marriage. When Rainer was expelled from school—he was in law school—because of the application, it was his mother who went to the Rathaus and complained. Peter tried to keep his own application quiet. He says that no one in the fam-ily would have known except for the plumbing—which was "nat-ural" East German plumbing. He flushed his drafts down the toilet, and the toilet clogged, and his father went into the bathroom and found seven "applications to emigrate" floating in the toilet bowl and carried them into Peter's "room"—it was an alcove off the hall—shaking, shouting that now everyone in his family had betrayed him, that he was going to lose the last job he was likely to have. That night he threw Peter out.

Peter wandered around Rostock and knocked on doors, but no one he knew except the old anthroposophist preacher was willing

to risk putting up a boy whose father had lost his sailing papers because of "West contacts" and whose brother had lost his place in
school because of a "West fiancée." A few days later, the Stasi
picked Peter up at the theater. They held him for two days of interrogation. There were three of them, and they took turns. The
first Stasi would scream at Peter—his accusations had something
to do with anti-Soviet-military graffiti on Rostock walls—and then
the second would walk in, calm and smiling, and say to Peter, "Be
reasonable, we have all the power," and, finally, the third would
arrive and offer to let him go over to the Bundesrepublik if he did
a job for them in Lübeck. Peter tried to explain that he didn't care.
He didn't want to work for any system—he didn't *care* about any
system. Eventually, they let him go. He signed a form swearing that
their conversations had never taken place, and the Stasi sent him
home. A few days later, he got on a bus for Baumberg. He took the
bicycle from his grandmother's shed, and rode the forty miles to
the border. He was at the beach, crouched low, waiting to sprint
through the shallow water, when he stepped on a wire and flares
went off and the bay was suddenly so bright that he says he could
see "the honky-tonk of Lübeck." The border policemen tried to
find him. They searched for an hour and never thought to look behind the bush where Peter had run to hide. He figured that before
long they would bring the dogs in, so he called, "*Hier! Ich bin
hier!*" He asked them to return the bicycle to his grandmother's
house.

∞

Stefan Schmidt is living back in Baumberg now, and he wants to
write a book. Whenever a Bundi comes through Baumberg, Stefan
grabs him and takes him home for a schnapps and asks if maybe
he knows a good reporter—someone from *Stern,* say, or *Der
Spiegel*—to collaborate on this book, which will make their fortune. He wants to call it "From the Fascist Fanatics to the Red
Turncoats." It is about his life and his troubles and his bad luck.
He wants to tell the world what happened to a patriot who tried
to do the right thing for his family. He wants to explain why he
called the Stasi when Peter was arrested, and volunteered to take
over his *Umerziehung*—his reeducation—if Peter was returned.

Peter says that the only sleepless night he had in three months of detention in Rostock awaiting trial was the night he heard from a guard that his father was asking to reeducate him.

Peter was adjusting nicely to prison life. He was in a cell with a sailor of forty who had applied for an exit visa, and was refused, and applied again, and was arrested for "insistence." Peter himself was arrested and charged according to Article 213 of the East German penal code, which had to do with the crime of *Republik-flucht*—with trying to cross the border—and he says that when his father called he was finally getting interested in East German politics, talking to the sailor about how you could cross a border that the East Germans claimed was a fiction of the imperialists and the West Germans claimed was a fiction of the Communists. His father never came to see him. His mother came. It was always his mother who helped him. It was his mother who met with the lawyer appointed for his defense, and decided that he was useless and probably an informer, and fired him. It was his mother who took the train to East Berlin and saw the famous lawyer Wolfgang Vogel, who handled the "people trade"—people for Deutsche marks—between the two Germanys, and got him to assign Peter's case to a proper lawyer, who was his "Rostock representative."

Stefan Schmidt renounced Peter. He said that he was not responsible for the terrible behavior of children like Peter and his brother—children who complained, children who had no respect for their father *or* their country. When Hannelore cried and begged for help with Peter, he said they both owed it to the family to stay away from Peter, to keep the jobs they had. When she kept on crying, he started to stay out drinking, and then he started seeing a woman he had met, and then he left the apartment altogether, and eventually Hannelore went to Peter's lawyer—his name was Hans-Joachim Vormelker—and asked if he handled divorces, too.

Stefan Schmidt kept his job on the training ship for five more years. On October 4 last year, five weeks before the Wall came down, he invited the other officers on the ship to his cabin to say goodbye to a seaman's apprentice who had got his visa and was leaving for West Germany. It was a "friendly and polite farewell party," Stefan said later. He could not explain why a man who had renounced his children and lost his wife in order to keep his job and his small standing would risk everything to offer his cabin for coffee and cake in honor of a sailor who was giving up on the German Democratic Republic. It may be that he couldn't resist the attention—that he wanted to be the one to stand at the door welcoming guests and pouring coffee and making the little speech that sent the sailor on his way. It may be that the sailor, who was only a few years older than Peter, had been respectful and kind, and had listened to Stefan's stories with more attention than his children ever managed to give them. It may be that he finally had to break the rules, or break himself. That day, the Party representative on the ship stood up at a meeting and said that Stefan Schmidt was "not socialist enough." Stefan demanded an apology. When he didn't get one, he walked out of the meeting—and out of his job. He did it on impulse. He threw away fifteen years of caution. He lost his rank and his small pension. Five weeks later, East Germany had its "revolution," and the Party representative was fired.

Stefan Schmidt has a certain standing in the village now. He has nothing to do all day but think about his book, and he thinks about it too much and gets sentimental and weepy, but he is now the expert on dissent—the man who sacrificed himself for freedom and who brought up sons who sacrificed themselves for freedom—and his troubles have given him a kind of local authority. His cousins will pour him a schnapps when he makes his nightly rounds of the Schmidt households, and listen to his stories and nod thoughtfully when he announces that he is a Green now, or a Social Democrat, or is going to vote for the Christian Democrats, because East Germany needs money, or for the Independent Women's Union, because East Germany needs feminism, or is going to join Neues Forum and help run Rostock. He writes letters to his wife, asking to come home, and letters to the Justice Committee at the Rostock docks, asking to get back his sailing papers, and he spends his evenings rearranging the pictures in an old family album. He used to be a good-looking man, but his yellow hair is beginning to fade and his pale-blue sailor's eyes are getting weak, and bleary from schnapps, and seem to be looking for something far away. He is often confused. He has started showing up in Hamburg with a suitcase, or in Rostock, at his old apartment. He walks right into the flat where Hannelore and her boyfriend—who is a pleasant, portly accountant from the neighborhood—are sleeping, and starts talking about the day in 1981 they took a picnic to the beach, or the reunion they had with Peter in Prague in 1987. No one but Peter has the heart to send him away.

The family have stopped calling him Papa. Now they call him "poor Papa." Every day, he slips a little deeper into the dream that the Stefan Schmidts are a happy family. He sits at the table in his mother's parlor—an oval mahogany table covered with the trousseau damask that his mother, at eighty-five, bleaches in a pot on a wood stove and irons with a flatiron—and has his breakfast of farm eggs and tinned liver paste on what is left of the family Meissen, and then he reads aloud from the Ostsee *Zeitung,* as if the whole family were there instead of one old woman who prefers the *Neue Deutsche Bauernzeitung,* and is deaf anyway. The Ostsee *Zeitung* is the local Communist paper. It used to be called "the official organ of the Party," but now it has changed its logo to "the independent of the North" and only occasionally distorts the news.

Stefan Schmidt reads it every day. He is interested in the case of a Rostock civil-rights lawyer named Wolfgang Schnur, who turned out to have been a Stasi informer, with a set of code names and a bonus of five hundred marks for every piece of information he supplied. Schnur was a leader of one of the new parties—Democratic Awakening—in an election coalition with the Christian Democrats, and he was famous in Rostock. He claimed to have represented tens of thousands of political prisoners, and when the news about him broke, and he dropped out of the elections and disappeared into a hospital, Stefan told everyone in the village how smart he was to have chosen an honest lawyer for Peter—a lawyer with a white vest, the Germans say. He has forgotten that his only dealings with Peter's lawyer were when Vormelker served him with divorce papers. He thinks he knows Vormelker now. He talks about his friend Herr Rechtsanwalt Vormelker, and their sons, and about how his friend Vormelker's son was an important dissident, like Peter, and had helped lead the occupation of the Stasi building a month after the Wall came down, and how Vormelker himself had negotiated with the Stasi for Neues Forum—how he had talked the Stasi into surrendering completely and leaving the building for the people. He talks about asking Vormelker to handle his "rehabilitation," because Vormelker is an old Rostock maritime lawyer and is already working with the Justice Committee on the docks, negotiating reparations for seamen who have lost their jobs.

Rostock is the biggest port in East Germany. The Rostock Deutsche Seereederei—the state shipping company—used to provide the Stasi with a file on every East German who had ever been to sea. There were three hundred thousand seamen's files in the Stasi's Rostock headquarters when Neues Forum seized the building—and Stefan Schmidt wants to see the one on him. A hundred other seamen who had lost their right to sail because of "West contacts" have already released their files to the Justice Committee and got their compensation—it amounted to three years' salary—but, with the shipping business in decline, and not likely to improve once Rostock has to compete with enormous ports like Hamburg and Bremen, they do not have much chance of getting back their jobs. One of those seamen had lost his travel papers for sending a postcard to a woman he had met in port in Thailand, and another for signing a birthday card to an Englishman he had met in port in Angola, and another for having a wife who wrote a letter to a West German who had come for the weekend in 1952, and another for getting a letter from an unknown relative in America who had tracked him down. There were three thousand Stasis in Rostock reading letters and denunciations, and Stefan Schmidt has always suspected that they intercepted two Christmas cards he sent to an English soldier who gave him a lift when he was walking home from Bavaria in 1945. The pastor who confirmed Peter and his brother is on a seamen's commission of the Justice Committee, and could look in the file for him, but the pastor has three hundred other cases to consider first, and he does not have time to run his church and learn to drive the new Volkswagen he just received from a sister church in West Germany *and* answer the long letters Stefan Schmidt sends whenever he goes through his dossier and thinks about his problems. The anthroposophist preacher might have looked, too, but he went to Wiesbaden this winter for a Rudolf Steiner conference, and the family says he was so excited to be in the West, talking to other anthroposophists, that he dropped dead in the middle of a panel discussion.

Oma—everybody calls Peter's grandmother Oma—sitting straight at her table, reading her *Bauernzeitung* and chain-smoking City cigarettes, watches Stefan write his letters and tells him not to expect a miracle from this new Germany. She remembers the inflation after the First World War and the inflation after the Second World War, and how both of them destroyed her savings, and she worries about what will happen now, "after the Russians." She never minded the Russians. She says she was scared before the Russians came. Everybody ran around crying "The Russians are coming!" and hiding what little food they had, but the Russians got out of a big truck and shook everybody's hand, and the worst thing they did in Baumberg was take four bicycles at gunpoint. Erich Schmidt, the cousin who collected his bride in 1945 and went to Baden-Württemberg, wants to come back and take his land, and Oma does not know what will happen to the family if the cooperative shuts down and Schmidts arrive from all over Germany to claim their "inheritance." She wants to die "in tranquillity," she says, with enough of her savings left for a nice coffin. It makes her uneasy that tomatoes are up to eighteen marks a kilo at the Wismar market and that a head of cauliflower, which used to be one and a half marks, costs eight and a half marks now. A liter of milk in Wismar is still sixty pfennig, but across the border in Schleswig-Holstein it costs nearly twice that, and Oma is worried that in a few months it is going to cost just as much at home. She remembers the prices in 1929, when things were so bad in Mecklenburg that she and her husband had to leave the farm and work in Hamburg. Her husband got a job there selling cars—Opel, Mercedes, Wanderer, Horch, Audi, Hanomag, Hansalloyd, all the old German cars—and Oma ran a *Pension* on the Alster, and they did not come home until Hamburg was bombed.

Stefan was born in Hamburg. Lately, he likes to say that he is "from Hamburg." When he shows up in Hamburg now, carrying his suitcase and talking about "coming home," Peter usually hides in his room and doesn't come out until he knows that his father has gone. Peter doesn't like to see his father in Hamburg. He says that he doesn't blame his father for what his father did. He understands his father. He understands that "the system was responsible," and that if his father cannot apologize to them all, it is because the system destroyed him. The system made him craven.

∞

When Peter went back to Baumberg this spring, the family gathered in Cousin Arnulf's house and listened, rapt, to the story of his flight. They oohed and aahed as Peter bicycled through the clear, frosty January night and followed a path by a stream to the beach and saw the lights of Lübeck. They gasped when the flares went off, and held their breath when Peter was trapped behind the bush, with the policemen walking right by him, talking about the dogs. But Peter knew that they were disappointed in him and even a little smug about him. People who went west got rich and came home in BMWs wearing Italian bomber jackets and American cowboy boots, and here was Peter Schmidt, who had had to hitch a ride to Baumberg with a reporter heading east, and was dressed in flea-market jeans and a faded T-shirt and didn't have a coat, or even a sweater, to keep him warm. Peter was poor. He had left in pride, as far as the Baumberg Schmidts were concerned, and he had nothing to show for it. When they asked him about the West, he said, "I want to get rid of the West. The West is collapsed. The West destroys relations." When they asked him about his Cousin Erich, coming home to claim a farm, he said that Cousin Erich was immoral, that private property had made Cousin Erich aggressive, that Erich Schmidt looking at a field and saying "That's mine" was no better than Helmut Kohl looking at East Germany and saying "That's mine," or Volkswagen or Allianz AG or Deutsche Bank or any of the other big Bundi companies saying "That's mine." When they asked him about himself, he shrugged and said he didn't care about himself, one way or the other. They had been poor for forty years, and made the best of Communism, and now they were looking forward to a little fun and a little money, and Peter Schmidt mocked their poverty with his indifference.

∞

The political prison in Cottbus is sixty-five miles southeast of Berlin, near the Polish border. It is a square brick complex with high, barred windows. It has barbed wire and glass shards on top of the walls, and when Peter was there it had police dogs running along the walls and guards with Kalashnikovs on watchtower platforms. The kaiser had built Cottbus, and the Nazis had "secured" it, and by the time the Communists inherited it there was nothing to do except add a delicatessen by the front door so that mothers like Hannelore, on their monthly visit, would be tempted to spend money on smoked hams and gift boxes of expensive chocolates. Peter says that life in prison was not much different from life anywhere else in the G.D.R., except that prison was "more interesting." Prison was fantasy and at the same time history, and he liked the people there. He didn't have much to do with the criminals. He says the criminals at Cottbus were set apart. They got special treatment and special favors—more visitors and more food and the easy prison jobs, like working in the laundry or dishing out dinner. The people Peter knew were the political prisoners. They had yellow stripes on their sleeves and their pants, and they were all there, he says, "with the idea of being innocent." They lived in big cells—there were twelve prisoners in Peter's cell—and they talked a lot about being East German.

In Rostock, Peter hadn't known anyone who talked about being East German. He hadn't known anyone who talked about being German at all. All the conversations he had heard in groups in Rostock—at the Free German Union and the Free German Youth and all the other groups that he had had to join—were about how to integrate boys like Peter into what was called "the socialist community." In prison, his friends were dissenters and free spirits and intellectuals. He shared his cell with a theology student and a set designer and a waiter who had read all of Kant and Hegel and a Rostock shipyard worker with an earring and a tattoo who dreamed of moving to Kreuzberg or Neukölln, in West Berlin, and living in a commune with the Autonomen and listening to music and watching the world go by in a haze of marijuana and fellow-feeling. Peter met five Rostockers during the eleven months he was in Cottbus, but Max, the one with the earring, was his favorite, being "neither left nor right but healthy," and they stuck together.

Peter decided to be healthy too. He gave up cigarettes, and then he gave up eating meat and read a book about macrobiotics and tried to think "macrobiotically" about balancing the terrible fried, starchy prison food. The only thing he missed in prison was his mother's coffee—ground fresh and brewed in a paper filter and served, steaming, in a china cup. He says now it was the fellowship, the sense of being together and of being superior, that made the experience so satisfying. It was the first real fellowship he had had. He had worried about talking before. He had worried about having a beer with another apprentice in a bar and telling him about wanting to leave the G.D.R., and its turning out to be the *wrong* apprentice. He had worried about being denounced and ending up in a place like Cottbus, so he had decided that the fewer friends he had to worry about, the less he had to lose. But prison was like the folk song that goes *"Die Gedanken sind frei"*—thoughts were free in prison, and conversation was free, and the political prisoners talked all the time. They walked in the prison courtyard and looked through an iron gate at the neon sign of the factory across the street that printed *Neues Deutschland,* the national Communist Party paper, and tried to figure out how Germans could cause and experience such distress at the same time, and Peter says that for the first time he felt "the heaviness of the German experience." He wanted to read history, because he knew by then that the only history East Germany had acknowledged was the history of whatever in the German past was pleasant or fruitful or progressive. He wanted to read philosophy, like the waiter, because the only philosophy East Germany had acknowledged was the philosophy of Marx and Lenin. But there was no real history of the war in the prison library, and no Kant or Hegel, either. There were cheap novels and agitprop, and the Bible, put away in a drawer. Peter did not consider himself a Christian—no one in his cell was a practicing Christian except the theology student—but the student had permission to open the drawer and take the Bible out of the library, so the cell decided to study the Bible, just to pass the time and maybe see if there was anything in it to explain this problem of being East German. Every night after supper they read the Bible. They agreed that prison was the right place to read the Bible, because the Bible was all about dealing with people, and dealing with people was what you did in prison.

Peter liked the Bible. He says it gave him the idea that Christianity and Communism had a lot in common—that "in their pure form they were very similar and very good, all about community, but in practice they were both brutal in dealing with heretics." It made him think about how everything was political, everything was about power. And it made him think about resistance. His particular resistance was to stop working. He went to the prison factory, mornings, and took his place on a production line with a few hundred other political prisoners whose job it was to stamp out plastic camera parts for the state camera company (the name was Pentagon), and then he did nothing. He spent eight hours a day doing nothing. His shift was responsible for ten thousand parts a day, and the prisoners who worked hard making parts got real coffee, and the prisoners who didn't got solitary confinement, and Peter says the real sacrifice was the coffee. His friends covered for him. The theology student said he was "just like Gandhi," and Max said he was frail and just like Christ, and the waiter said he understood about the coffee. They slipped him parts down the production line. They told the guards that he was sick and shouldn't be working at all. They made him a cause—a kind of mascot—because he was so much younger than they were, and had made what they considered an amazing, instinctive, *natural* protest. He made them see that human beings were *naturally* political. He was an apprentice with no contacts among activists or intellectuals in his own town, and yet he knew all about the "politics of passivity." Max told him he was proof that the people could produce a "people's consciousness."

Peter enjoyed his celebrity. He enjoyed it so much that he was even a little disappointed when the guards came for him one day and gave him back his jeans and motorcycle jacket and told him he was going to West Germany. On April 2, 1985, Peter crossed the border in a bus convoy of seventy political prisoners and, he thinks, a couple of criminals being passed off as political prisoners. The convoy left from Karl-Marx-Stadt and deposited the prisoners at a refugee center in Giessen, where social workers from the Ministry for Inner-German Relations congratulated them on being free and gave each of them a hundred and fifty marks and asked them where they thought they would like to live. When the social workers got to Peter, he said he didn't care where he lived. He told them that as far as he was concerned one city was as good as the next—cities were all the same. He had no illusions about the West. He knew that capitalism couldn't be worse than Communism, but he didn't expect to be happy in the West, or even very balanced. They asked him what he meant by "balanced." He said, "Well, you know, spiritually and macrobiotically balanced." Then they said he had to go *somewhere.* They told him to just choose somewhere. So he wrote down Hamburg, because it was on the water, like Rostock, and he thought maybe it would have some of the same mentality—some of the East German feeling, dirty and close. Fritz Kepel, his only friend from the garage, had left the G.D.R. with his family, and *they* had chosen Hamburg, so he thought he'd try it. "What do I like? I'm a typical East German," he told the social worker who was filling in his "urgent need" certificate for the Hamburg housing office. "I can say what I don't like but not what I do like."

A day later, he had a room in a transient hotel in Ohlsdorf, near the Hamburg cemetery. He had a little cassette player, tapes by Pink Floyd, Grace Slick, and the Grateful Dead, a filter coffeepot, and two hundred and fifty grams of Jacobs Fein und Mild Guatemala-blend coffee. He had everything he needed until someone came and told him what to do.

∞

Hannelore Schmidt is a physiotherapist at one of the Rostock hospitals. She was an athlete as a girl—she swam and sprinted and skated in important East German tournaments—and there was no question of her not getting the training she wanted or the job she wanted. Athletes had privilege in Rostock. The Party had made the body a sort of public policy, and the "new" German man and woman were the gymnasts, the skaters, the swimmers, like Hannelore, not the musicians or the intellectuals, or even the Communists. They took their inspiration from the strapping bronze nudes playing with their strapping bronze children in the fountain in the middle of the Universitätsplatz—handsome people with fierce, honest, vacant faces, pursuing volleyballs and dolphins. Hannelore, growing up in Rostock after the war, wanted to help everybody be as handsome and healthy as a piece of Communist public sculpture. She was never in the Party, but she felt that she owed the Communists something. They had taken her on when she was a girl of eight with a father dead at the front and a mother nearly dead from the trip from Gdansk to Rostock with five small children. In a city that was half rubble (40 percent of Rostock was bombed out by 1945), they had found her a school and a place to swim and skate in the afternoon. They had sponsored her sports and then her training, and they ran the bank that had lent her money to join the building cooperative. She had met Stefan Schmidt at a Party youth meeting and had discovered physiotherapy at a Party career fair. She wanted to set an example with what she had. Her specialty at the hospital was taking heart patients for long walks up and down the beach, her theory being that if therapy was good for you, therapy in nature with an athlete like Hannelore Schmidt was better. The patients liked Hannelore. She had narrow blue eyes and blond bangs and a foxy, pointed face, and she was sympathetic. She would laugh when the patients told their jokes and cry quietly when they told their stories. Some of them were sick from being Stasi and some were sick from being persecuted by Stasi, and Hannelore says that at first, if she thought about the Stasi at all, and acknowledged the terrible things the Party did, it was because of those patients.

One of the men in her first walking group had been in prison in Waldheim. He was a young man. His parents were Stasi, and they had turned him in for being "antisocial." He was sent to prison and put in chains and left in water up to his chin, and eventually his teeth fell out and his heart weakened, and they let him out, but then his neighbors, who were respectable professional people—teachers and doctors—complained that it was bad for their building to have a tenant with chain scars on his wrists and no teeth when he smiled, and he lost his apartment and had a heart attack and was sent to Hannelore to be cured by walking on the beach.

Hannelore says that after a while she began to divide the people she knew into three generations: the children of the war, like her; the children of the state, like her patients; and the children of rock, like Peter and his friends. One reason she indulged Peter—paid for his tapes and let him lie around the apartment listening to them—was that she would rather have him at home, helpless and a little scattered, than send him into a world where the Stasi could arrest him. She worried all the time about Peter. Peter was ten when Stefan Schmidt lost his papers and had to start all over again, on the training ship, at only five hundred Ostmarks a month, and he was sixteen when Rainer Schmidt fell in love with a West German girl and was expelled from school and left the country, and after that Hannelore was determined to protect him. She was not a sophisticated woman. She was full of superstition and folk medicine (she never boiled the water she drank, but she boiled the water she used to wash her face and her stockings) and stubborn sentiment, and it was her belief that a mother in Rostock could keep a child who wanted to go. She says that she nearly went mad when Peter was arrested. The Stasi knocked on her door that night, and one of them said that she had educated her children wrong, and she started screaming. "Do you know how much pain that costs me?" she kept screaming. She sat there in a white nightgown, groggy from a tranquillizer she had taken because she "sensed" that something terrible was happening and couldn't sleep, and screamed at the policemen. She told them how she had always supported the Communists. She had insisted that Peter wear his Free German Youth sweatshirt, and he had always refused—and she knew now that he was right and she was wrong. She got the sweatshirt and showed it to them. She followed them down the stairs and into the parking lot and told them she was going to wait all day every day at Stasi headquarters until she knew where they had put her son and what the charges against him were. And that was what she did.

∞

The people trade started with the Wall. Lutherans in Württemberg raised money to save the life of a dissident East German pastor, and then Protestants all over the Bundesrepublik started raising money, and in a few years the trade was so big that the government took over, and opened the office it so delicately named the Ministry for Inner-German Relations. By the time Peter was arrested, West Germany was spending nearly a hundred and fifty million marks a year buying East German prisoners. Some of them were dissidents. Some had simply applied to leave, like Peter, and been arrested, like Peter—if not for actually trying to leave, then for having applied in the first place—and their parents had found their way to Wolfgang Vogel, like Hannelore, and Vogel had sent them home to one of his representatives, like Hans-Joachim Vormelker, and had started negotiating with the West Germans for the going rate. Vormelker was arguing seventy or eighty political cases a year in those days, and he says that while none of his clients were acquitted, in the end nearly all of them were "bought West." The most he could do for them in the short term was to make sure that their trials were "correct," and that their sentences were correct, and that they were not forgotten in prison. Vormelker had no stomach for the people trade. He likes to say that lawyers like him and his old friend Wolfgang Vogel were "democratic fig leaves" for the G.D.R.—they gave the regime a certain obscene legitimacy in the outside world, along with the hard currency they generated. But he had grown up in Rostock, and he knew everybody there, and, especially, he knew how to deal with the people in power there—and, when Vogel took over the people trade for East Germany, Vormelker figured he had a better chance of surviving in Rostock doing what he did than a lot of the younger lawyers around.

Peter Schmidt was not an important prisoner. He was not really "political," like the librarian from Rostock University who got ten years for trading East-bloc books for "West literature." He was not inventive, like the chemistry student who got five years for printing postcards with a montage of prison bars and the librarian's face. Vormelker says that Peter was young and helpless, and that the state had nothing to lose in letting him go. It was a question of money. Peter says now that he was "bought cheap." Fifty thousand Deutsche marks is what he remembers, but his mother insists that it was more. In her mind he has become a freedom fighter. She never asked him why he had to go or what his politics were or if he was in the underground, or even if he knew anybody in the underground—not when they met in Prague, not even when the Wall came down and they met in Hamburg. She waited until Peter was home in Rostock, and they were in the parlor eating gooseberry-cherry tart and drinking coffee, and the television was showing West German soccer—and everything, as Hannelore said, was "normal." Then she asked him.

Peter told Hannelore about how he made his passive resistance, and Hannelore told Peter about *her* resistance. She told him about showing his sweatshirt to the Stasi, and about what she said to the policemen outside the Stasi building on the day of his trial—she waited on the street that day, and saw him being taken away in a car, and it was terrible, because he was in handcuffs, and didn't have a sweater, and the day was cool. She told him about the day she came to Cottbus, and the guard said that Prisoner Schmidt couldn't get a food package—Prisoner Schmidt wasn't working hard enough to qualify for a food package. Hannelore had spoken right up and said that Prisoner Schmidt didn't work hard at home, either. He didn't pick up his underwear and he didn't make his bed and he didn't help with the dishes, but still she fed him. The guard was so impressed, Hannelore said, that he took her straight to the prison store, and together they bought Peter a box of chocolates for thirty-five marks. Hannelore cried, telling Peter her stories. "Can you believe it? Germans behaving so badly!" she would say, and Peter would nod and stretch and tilt back in his chair and scratch his chest, underneath his pink T-shirt, and once he spilled his coffee on the embroidered tablecloth. She started to scold him then, but stopped herself. "*Macht nichts,*" she said. "Never mind."

She was happy to have him home. She wasn't going to scold him because of a coffee stain on the tablecloth, or because of the ring he left when he put his beer glass on her beautiful new cabinet—the one with shelves and drawers and drop leaves and a mirrored bar—or because he drank up all the mineral water. She didn't complain when he stayed in, watching television, on his first night home instead of going with her to the Universitätsplatz to listen to Willy Brandt and Ibrahim Böhme make speeches. (She said later he was right, because Willy Brandt rambled, and Böhme, who was the head of the new East German Social Democrats, resigned from the Volkskammer in a week—*Der Spiegel* wrote that he had been a Stasi—and supposedly tried to commit suicide.) She didn't even complain when he took the big bed, and let her sleep on a mattress on the living-room floor. She said that her youngest son should have a proper bed on his first night home in six years, and Peter agreed with her. He got up the next morning and drank all the apple juice and all the mineral water and said that "relations" were much better in East Germany. People in East Germany were more caring. They were suspicious and they spied on each other, but they were not elbowy and aggressive and ungenerous and cold, like the West Germans. He wanted to warn his mother about the West Germans. Whenever she talked about East Germans, and asked what could be worse than East Germans, he said, "The West is worse."

Hannelore was going to vote for the Christian Democrats. She had listened to Helmut Kohl and found him "thrilling," and Peter could not imagine how someone as natural as his mother—someone who always talked about how she would rather ride her bicycle down a country road or take a picnic to the beach than spend her time making money, like a Bundi—could say that Helmut Kohl was thrilling or vote for his cold, capitalist party. Hannelore knew that politicians lied. She would start talking politics and all of a sudden stop and shake her head and say, "All those lies! Forty years of lies," but in the end she wanted to believe what Helmut Kohl was promising now. She couldn't explain why she believed Helmut Kohl more than Willy Brandt, except, maybe, because Brandt was old, and rambling. She said that Kohl was decisive. Kohl never asked questions. He told the East Germans exactly what to do. He told them that Christian Democrats had the power in West Germany, and controlled the money, and that there was no way they were going to give that money to the competition—by which he meant not only the Social Democrats in East Germany but all the new East German parties, and even the people in Neues Forum, who had made the "revolution" to begin with. He was right in the East German spirit. He was threatening and cajoling, like a Party boss, and he gave simple orders—"Vote money!"—while the local politicians, and even the other carpetbaggers from the Bundesrepublik, who weren't running for anything themselves but were putting themselves in place, and their people in place, for the first "German" elections, kept talking about how difficult and exciting the moment was, full of choices to make and directions to consider. The East Germans were bewildered by choices. They were terrified of choosing wrong. They believed the people who told them (with some reason) that choice in East Germany right now was an illusion, that West Germany already owned them, that there was no such thing as a "third way" between capitalism and Communism, that only Deutsche marks would save them.

"We need the money," Hannelore Schmidt said. She tried to tell

Peter about how poor the hospitals in Rostock were, and how dilapidated the factories were, and how polluted the city was getting, just like Dresden and Leipzig, and how corrupt the government still was, full of old Stasis. She said that was why they had to take the money the Christian Democrats offered. It was a terrible situation. Everyone was nervous. There were twenty-four political parties, and nothing but elections for the next year. Posters were going up and coming down all the time, because people were fighting and splitting and starting new parties. Helmut Kohl was fighting with Lothar de Maizière about kindergartens, and Oskar Lafontaine was fighting with Markus Meckel about the exchange rate, and Bundis at the Thursday market were trying to sell you last week's dirty laundry. Nothing was the way people wanted. The only thing to do was vote for the Bundis and take their money and four years later vote them out of power—because politics was *Schmutz* anyway, politics was dirty. You had to try to forget the Bundis at the beach, the Bundis at the market. You had to forget how arrogant the Bundis were. Everyone knew that Bundis were arrogant. The important thing right now was Rostock. The important thing was to get rid of the Communists, and there was no way to ensure that they were gone for good if everyone was poor. The new parties—Neues Forum and Democracy Now and the other citizens' groups that had for all practical purposes run the cities in East Germany since November—had nothing to suggest but hope and sacrifice and a lot of work. They didn't have the money for a proper campaign, let alone the money to save East Germany. Their telephones didn't work, and their posters were dingy and disintegrated in the rain, and their mimeograph machines ran purple, whereas the parties with West German connections could pay for thick white poster paper, and telephone lines, and Xerox machines, and laser printers.

Economists had said it would cost the West Germans thirty billion Deutsche marks a year to subsidize "Germany," but it had not cost more than a few posters and a couple of plane fares to convince Hannelore Schmidt that Helmut Kohl was going to solve her problems, and make Rostock so safe and so agreeable that Peter Schmidt would consider coming home.

∞

There were only a few hundred refugees in Hamburg when Peter got there. Most prisoners who came through the people trade stayed south, in Bavaria, or went straight to West Berlin, like Max, being more comfortable with the Wall and the Turkish workers and the spacey, subsidized Berlin life than with "reality" in a city like Hamburg, or Frankfurt or Cologne. Until Rainer Schmidt moved to Hamburg—he had been studying in Frankfurt—the only person Peter knew there was his friend Fritz, from the garage. He had cousins in Hamburg—distant cousins of his grandmother. He looked them up when he arrived, and even went to dinner at their house in Volksdorf and met their children, but he says the children were only interested in "consuming and careers and jobs that were going to give them 'standing' "—more interested, at any rate, than they were in Peter—and he never saw any of them again. He was counting on Fritz, because Fritz had "the East German mentality." Fritz had suffered the same system and the same distress and the same poverty, and Peter thought it would give them a solidarity, a common ground, that West Germans, with their busy and ambitious lives, their separate paths, could never share. They spent a couple of months together. The city gave each of them a living allowance of six hundred marks a month and a housing allowance of two hundred, and they used it to go back to school for what Germans call a *technisches Abitur*—a kind of vocational degree. But it was clear to Peter that Fritz had lost his "taste for adversity." Fritz studied hard and talked about going on to college and having a career as an engineer, while Peter did what he ruefully calls "the East German thing"—he backed off from the competition, and refused to study, and quit before the semester ended, complaining that everyone else at school knew more than he did.

Fritz left that winter for the Free University in West Berlin. Peter saw him off and remarked that Fritz had the West German mentality now, but he took the old East German stereo Fritz left him, and the tapes, and the textbooks, and the flannel sheets. For a while he stayed with Rainer and his wife in a small sublet off the Reeperbahn. They were together a year. But then Rainer got a good job, and he and his wife moved into a pretty flat in a fashionable part of town and bought Laura Ashley pillows and Habitat wicker chairs, and stripped the floors to a pale pine, and hung a Matisse poster from the Beaubourg on the wall instead of the funny Mecklenburg ceramics Hannelore sent them, and started eating Swiss Birchermuesli and imported tropical-fruit yogurts for breakfast, and there was not much left in their life to make Peter feel comfortable.

Eventually, he met Rudolf Klaassen. Rudolf had a group of friends who got together in his apartment once a week to argue. They read historians like Eric Hobsbawm and argued about social bandits, and one of the friends invited Peter, thinking it would cheer him up to argue, and that night Peter offered to put his housing allowance and some of his living allowance toward a room in Rudolf's apartment. He liked the apartment. It was a big, sunny, shabby fourth-floor walkup near the Goldbekplatz, where a lot of students live. It was "natural." Peter bought some plants for his room, and then a cat, and then a friend for the cat. He bought some pine boards for a cupboard and some matchstick shades to cover the cupboard. He hung a paper angel on the wall, and a Mecklenburg "Art and Memory" poster from his mother, and a bulletin board made from three squares of straw floor matting for his collection of Greens slogans and his postcards from the guys in his old Cottbus cell block. He put away his motorcycle jacket and his running shoes and T-shirt. He put his tapes in alphabetical order, and arranged his books: Stefan Aust on the Baader-Meinhof; Michael Herr on Vietnam; Max Frisch's *Tagebücher*; "Ansprachen," by Christa Wolf; and a couple of popular histories of the Second World War. He liked finally being able to read history. He liked the arguments he had with Rudolf and his friends about social bandits. It reminded him of prison.

"He was a nice, open guy," Rudolf says when he talks about Peter. He had thought then that Peter was an authentic East German radical, the kind of person you rarely got to see in Hamburg, someone on the order of his friend Freimut, from the Vereinigte Linke—the United Left—who had been an important activist in the G.D.R. and had organized in East Berlin for the Party and had come out only when it got too dangerous to stay. Freimut was smuggled West in the fake gas tank of a big truck, and now he was organizing in West Germany, occupying houses. He was the kind of person Rudolf imagined Peter to be when he took him on. A revolutionary. "Peter had some perspective then," Rudolf says. "He had a couple of friends like Max, in Berlin—Max was so kind, a real prole—and he said some good things. He was against the achievement system here. He didn't want to achieve anything for the state or for business, but the problem was he didn't want to achieve anything for himself, either. He had problems with achievement. He thought that *all* achievement was for the system, so he didn't try. He had pulled himself out of the G.D.R. He made a decision to leave and go to prison, but now I think it was a very personal decision. It was a decision to leave society—first his society, then *all* society. Most of the people I know from the G.D.R. came over to study, to work, to organize, to do music. They *had* something—a group, a profession, a politics. So maybe Peter was much more typical of East Germans. Maybe the system really shaped him, because he was so incapable. He was unfit for community. He had made a snail shell of his life. He did it to defend himself against the state, but when he left the G.D.R. he couldn't get out of it, and I think he didn't want to get out of it. He thought he was an anarchist or a rebel or a revolutionary, but he was really a snail. All he had was his opposition."

After a few months, Peter and Rudolf really started arguing. They argued about the Palestine question and about the nationalism question and about the question of socialism. Peter said one night that the Israelis were just like Nazis, and then that the Communists were just like Nazis, and Rudolf blew up and said that it wasn't true—that Peter had to give up monocausal explanations, that "history" rejected monocausal explanations. He wanted to know if Peter had thought about Auschwitz, because if Peter had really thought about Auschwitz he would never be calling all bad behavior Nazi. He would understand that you had to accept the horrible *particularity* of the Holocaust if you were going to talk about being German at all. Rudolf had had this argument before, with his friends in the United Left. His friends were very pro-Palestinian, and Rudolf did not see why supporting the Palestinians had to mean making all the Israelis evil. He "understood" the Israelis. He had been to Israel, like a lot of West German students, and had worked on a kibbutz and hitchhiked around. He did not much like the government there—in fact, he spent a lot of his time demonstrating against it—but he liked his radical Israeli friends, and he did not want anyone to call them Nazis. He wondered what Peter would say if people started calling *him* a Nazi because he was German. He told Peter that whatever Peter might have thought about Auschwitz, it was clear he had never made a serious moral judgment about Auschwitz, and Peter replied that no one had really told him about Auschwitz—all he knew was that nationalism was bad. Rudolf said that that was "typically East German."

Rudolf considers himself the *real* German left. He has the friendly confidence of a well-brought-up bourgeois. His father is a teacher and his mother is the librarian at an economics archive, and his freedom, like his future, has always been something given, something guaranteed. He plays classical and flamenco guitar along with his heavy metal, and dreams of having a digital synthesizer, like the Synclavier that Sting uses—one he can attach to a Macintosh and use for composing. With all his odd jobs and his rich talent, he probably will. He has had a special kind of nurturing. When he and his friends put together their first rock group, Cyberdeath, and started playing the clubs and squats on the St. Pauli Hafenstrasse—"We were slower and more emotional, but we were *heavy,* I mean we looked for violence and blood to caricature" is the way he describes it—everybody smiled and said that Rudolf was doing his thing, Rudolf was "being young," Rudolf was gifted. When he came to the *Gymnasium* in the suburbs for his student teaching, with his long brown curls and his funny psychedelic sweater, the one with the wool that glowed in the physics lab when the lights were off, everybody smiled and said that Rudolf was a bird of paradise among the Hamburg shrubs. When he began his thesis, about the terrible treatment of dissident Communists during Weimar, everybody smiled and said that it was an appropriate thesis—that young people like Rudolf Klaassen *should* be angry. Rudolf, of course, is not angry. He has a sweetness that comes in part from a gentle nature and in part from believing that life will never really do him harm. It gives him a freedom to worry about the people who *are* harmed. The people like Peter.

At first, Rudolf talked Peter into one more try at school. He stayed home every night for an hour to help Peter with his math. But Peter, he says, had angst about math. Peter was afraid of tests. He was afraid of failing and also of trying not to fail. He would work on his math with Rudolf for ten minutes, and then he would have trouble concentrating. He would start to complain. He would get up and walk around and put on a tape—the Stones or the Jefferson Airplane or T. Rex—and Rudolf would leave the room, exasperated, because Peter had such "typical East German taste," and the music he played had nothing to do with the music that was really happening, with Queensrÿche doing "Operation: mindcrime" on twelve voice tracks, or with Sabotage, or with the black metal band called Living Colour. And then, instead of studying math, they would argue about music. Or they would argue about work, because Peter refused to work, and as far as Rudolf was concerned, the only excuse for refusing to work was making music. Or about love. Rudolf did not know how Peter could love his mother and never write a letter to her—how he could get a long letter from Rostock every week and never answer one and still say he loved his mother. He did not know how Peter could love his friends and never answer any phone calls. He did not know how Peter could stay in his room all day with the door shut and his cups of perfect coffee and never call a friend or answer the phone when a friend called him.

Peter got better and better at making coffee, but that was the only thing he did. He talked for a while last year about moving to West Berlin. He had read Max Frisch about "the inspiring sky of Berlin" and had seen Wim Wenders's movie *The Sky Over Berlin,* about the romance of Berlin—"about how everything passes, but to live the fantasy you have to give up your immortal life for mortal life, and Berlin is mortal"—and thought that maybe the contrast of East and West Berlin mirrored some of his own ambivalence. He went to Berlin for a weekend when the Wall came down, and a few days later his friend Max found him a place in Neukölln—a room in a house that was once a squat and was now a "legal squat"—but Peter kept putting off moving, and by the time he was ready to go, the West German draft had called him and assigned him to "alternative service" on the AIDS-and-cancer floors of a hospital near the Hamburg docks. It is, finally, a job he

likes—helping people with dinner trays and baths and thermome-
ters and bedpans. He calls it "a simple job, nothing ambitious." It
comes with six weeks' holiday, and some of the nice East German
feeling. He wouldn't mind staying on at the hospital, though he
would never study nursing—he wouldn't want to hassle the competition at nursing school. He talks sometimes about moving to
America. Rainer and his wife took a trip across America last summer, and told him about some mountains—in Wyoming, he
thinks, or maybe Montana—where there were no cities and no cars
and no elbowy, ambitious people talking about money and politics, and Peter thinks that maybe he could find a job in those mountains. A janitor's job. Nothing special. Rudolf doubts if he will ever
go. Rudolf told him a year ago to look for his own apartment.
Peter agreed, but it is hard to rent an apartment in Hamburg without a job, and Peter never started looking anyway. He says there is
no point in looking now—not with people crossing daily from the
G.D.R., and all of them needing apartments. There is too much
competition for apartments, Peter says, and Rudolf admits that
this is true. Every couple of months, Rudolf says politely, "Please
go." And Peter, just as politely, stays.

∞

Fifteen thousand of the five hundred and fifty thousand East Germans who moved to West Germany over the past year are living in
Hamburg. They started to come last summer, when Hungary and
then Czechoslovakia opened their western borders and for a few
months any East German with an East-bloc passport had a safe
route out. The exodus was so great, and so constant, that West
Germany tried to spread the burden, and the cost, by assigning
every state a share of the refugees to support. Hamburg got 3.1
percent. It was a makeshift figure. It had to do with population but
not with population density, or housing, or employment, or unemployment (two million people are unemployed right now in
West Germany), or professional demographics.

The first immigrants—the ones, say, who came through Czechoslovakia into Bavaria—were mainly families. Some of them had
been waiting to leave for years. They were young craftsmen and
skilled workers and technicians who had more energy and ambi-

tion than they could satisfy in the moribund Kombinats of the
G.D.R., where people worked four hours a day and stopped and
(unlike the Hungarians or the Poles, who put their best efforts into
moonlighting) seemed to have no appetite for what East Europeans call the "second economy." Nearly everyone liked the first
immigrants. People in Hamburg say now that they were actually
looking forward to having a few nice young East German families
like the ones they read about in *Der Spiegel*. They were disappointed when most of those families stayed in Bavaria, which is
pretty and prosperous, the way they were disappointed when the
artists and intellectuals they expected—the ones who had not been
sent away during the years that East Germany was "exporting"
dissent, and people like Wolf Biermann and Monika Maron came
to Hamburg—told them they had no intention of moving west just
at the moment East Germany was changing. Hamburg's 3.1 percent tended to have "grease in their hair and tattoos on their
arms," as one of the tabloids put it. They drove their Trabis across
the border, and abandoned them cheerfully, and told the waiting
reporters and cameramen that what they wanted out of Western
life was a Volkswagen Golf. So many of them said it so often that
the refrain became part of a television comedy routine: A West
German reporter asks a pretty East German girl if she wants freedom, and the girl says no, certainly not, what she wants is *"ein
Golf GTI, Marlboros, und ein Video-Recorder."*

Nikolaus Piper, who writes about East European economics for
Die Zeit, once said that the East Germans who came to Hamburg
"thought in consumer terms but not in economic terms," by which
he meant that in the West you had to earn money in order to spend
it, and that was something the East Germans didn't know. The fact
is that for months there was nothing to persuade the East Germans
to think in economic terms. They heard in Rostock that in Hamburg immigrants were getting nice new clothes and apartments
with television sets and freezers; that immigrants were getting unemployment checks for far more money than they earned at home;
that immigrants were getting government-backed loans for seven
thousand marks at almost no interest. So they came. A few were
professional people. (There are, for example, four Rostock doctors
at one Hamburg hospital, and a couple of other Rostock doctors

are on unemployment in the city, getting twice the money they made at home working.) But most of them were workers. They were farmworkers and industrial workers, but they were not the Brechtian proletariat that the Hamburg intelligentsia expected. They had—this shocked the Hamburgers—petit-bourgeois values. They spent their "urgent need" allowances on huge knickknack cabinets and horrible flowered couches, and had never heard of Neues Forum.

There are fifty to a hundred new immigrants every day in Hamburg. They did not stop coming when Hamburg filled its quota, and they did not stop coming when immigration was "officially" suspended, and by now not even the promise of parity by July keeps them home. They stay in trailer camps and school gyms and in army barracks in the countryside and in converted sex hotels on the Reeperbahn and in Yugoslav ferries and Norwegian oil-rig housing stations leased by the city and anchored along the Alster. They spend their time shopping. They are almost entirely uncritical. They will not go to symposia to tell the Bundis what it feels like to have "missed post-materialism" (intellectuals in West Germany call the nineteen-sixties post-materialism), or even what they are going to do to catch up with democracy. They get confused and say that they are too busy for politics—that they don't know right politics from wrong politics anyway, and are not much interested in learning.

A young radio journalist named Maren Wintersberg followed a group of East German immigrants during their first six months in Hamburg, and wrote a radio series about them, and decided in the end that the people she had got to know had been damaged by the "East symbiosis" of friendship and favors. They came to the West and didn't know they were alone. They were met by people who said, "Hello! We're your friends, and here's your new refrigerator," and didn't understand why a week later those friendly people had disappeared. In the G.D.R., a new refrigerator meant friendship, even if it was friendship based on getting and giving favors. A new refrigerator meant protection. It meant that someone was going to take you by the hand, that your worries were over, that you had a friend with connections.

Maren Wintersberg says that the hardest thing *her* East Germans had to learn was that no one in the West helps anyone else voluntarily. They arrived like pioneers, on an adventure, and they were not strong enough, or educated enough, to accept that simple fact of capitalist life, and now they are in danger of falling through the net of a welfare state that supplies their needs but doesn't implicate them. Their apathy, like Peter's, is a kind of fear. They laugh at the West Germans who go shopping in the G.D.R. as if they were in Portugal on holiday, and buy all sorts of terrible things they don't need because the things are cheap, and the West Germans laugh at them, in Hamburg, buying all sorts of terrible things they don't need because the things are expensive. Peter does not think much of the refugees. He has heard about how Germany recovered after the Second World War by devaluing money so that German products were competitive and everybody started buying, and he thinks that East Germany should do that now. He thinks that East Germans should stay at home, and stop thinking about reunifying and getting rich, and start thinking about their country. He doesn't see any of the people who have come over from Rostock. He doesn't want to see them. They have none of the problems he had. It is easy for them at the border, easy for them at home. They are free at home, and he does not know why anyone free to leave Rostock would not be happy to stay in Rostock forever, keeping that nice, close, dirty East German feeling.

∽

"I think a lot about it now," Peter says. "I spend a lot of time avoiding stress, but I think, Why me? I had no idea of going West. I knew nothing about the West. There was no Western television—the antenna in Rostock then wasn't strong enough. All I knew was the music. I couldn't talk to my parents. I'd ask them about the West, but West Germany was taboo, the border was taboo. They knew it was stupid, but they had no answers and they had this typical East German thing about repressing everything they couldn't answer. Everyone I knew was like that. I see East Germans out demonstrating now and I think, Where did all these people come from? Because when I was there no one did anything. They knew the G.D.R. was crap, but they wouldn't say so. They were passive. *I* was passive. I went to school and I got this strong class-enemy picture of West Germany—we were the socialist citizens of the G.D.R., and West Germany was this imperialist power concentrated against us; the Second World War was never a German war, it was a fascist attack against *us;* we were the anti-fascists, and the fascists were still in power in West Germany. And my attitude was, Let them talk but don't believe them. I didn't see why the others believed them. Most of us had parents who had fought in the war. Anyway, they told us we had to integrate into the socialist workers' world, we had to find our identity in the larger German workers' movement, and I said to myself, Wait a minute! I didn't make this. I didn't ask to be born here. Why couldn't I have been a Dane? Or a Swede? Or even a West German? Why am I alone? I didn't meet the people who were radical. My brother wanted to leave, but that was only to marry. *His* conflict with the G.D.R. began when they wouldn't let him go. The only real radical I knew was Fritz, and when he and his family left, it was like with the Swedish hitch-hiker—I was totally conscious that they were in a different world. I thought about the close quarters at home—four people in two and a half rooms—and the bullshit, the animosity, this personal dissatisfaction I had with the system, and I said to myself, No, I can't survive here. The enemy was now *East* Germany. I thought, The West? It can't be worse.

"I started making plans. I knew my application would sit around in East Berlin for five, six years. I had wanted to leave legally, but all I got for trying was threats from one Stasi and a job offer from another. I knew I'd have to leave illegally. I thought, I'll go to prison, but I'll do it anyway. I considered Hungary, but it was complicated for a kid to go by Hungary. My most fantastical plan was to steal a boat and cross the Baltic. There were stories of people who crossed the Baltic to Denmark, stories of people who drifted around in rowboats until they were finally picked up by Danish ferries. But I knew in the end that it would have to be the border at home. When I was planning my route, I made a trial run to the border. It was a terrible wet, stormy night. I took paths through the fields, and then—it was two miles from the border—I thought of the possibilities, like stepping on a mine and getting blown up, or even getting arrested, and I stressed out and smoked and smoked, and rode back to Baumberg and called my mother.

"Even when I did try, I didn't think I'd actually succeed. It was just that I knew I couldn't stay. I couldn't survive that brutal protection against the rest of the world. I couldn't stand borders. I couldn't stand not talking about borders. I tried once going into church circles—what interested me about the church was the *oppositional* aspect—but the topics I wanted to discuss, topics like borders, were not discussed in church circles. I think now that East Germans like me were formed by a system that meant they couldn't live a life in East Germany. They had the solidarity that came from that horrible social reality—from wanting to live under different circumstances. Here that solidarity is lost. People are more assured. It's easier for them to be individuals, but they're disconnected from each other. That's why I think that whoever is idealistic now—after the fall of the Wall, the fall of the Communists—should stay in East Germany. After five years, I can say *I* wouldn't have come over. It would have been enough if the Communists had changed.

"There have been so many changes—the empire, Weimar, fascism, division, Communism, and now this. East Germans have shaken off the system themselves, without the West. If Gorbachev had been around twenty years ago, they would have done it then, without the West. I try to put myself in my mother's place, voting for the West, and the sad thing is that maybe the chance won't come again for forty more years. I tried voting here. I voted for the Greens, but I don't think the Greens know what's happening any more than the rest of the West German left. The Greens know more about Australia than they do about East Germany. They did nothing for the East Germans. At first, they were all for asylum, like everybody else, but now, like everybody else, they say that all the East Germans are 'consumer idiots.' People don't realize that all foreigners 'consume' here. They don't ask where this consumerism comes from—from decades of withdrawal. They just say they are against the 'ecstasy' of the East Germans.

"Maybe it's hard to understand if you come from a full, satisfied country. They say we're one people, but I think Czechoslovakia and East Germany have more in common than East and West Germany—they both have nothing. I don't mind having nothing. I don't like the West. It's not worth striving for. I was never *going* West. I was determined to leave, but not to *go* West. I was determined to leave the East the shortest possible way."

BERLIN

(NOVEMBER 1991)

A few weeks ago, I ran into my daughter's friend Tilo, who is a cool, competent, and ambitious young man from Frankfurt with a degree in economics, five or six languages in his head, and a jet-age *Wandervogel* intimacy with the scene on several continents. Tilo has a good measure of impatience with the million and a half people in the East of what is now his capital. He used to like Berlin better when it had a wall, and the closest you got to Mitteleuropa was the poetry readings at the Schlesisches Tor subway station. Berlin was the place his friends went to beat the draft and collect subsidies, like allowance, and check out the Kreuzberg clubs and try on selves, like funny clothes from one of the Berlin "alternative" stores—the place where they were not accountable for their identity or their adventures. The Wall protected them. The press called Berlin an island, and the politicians called Berlin a fortress, but to Tilo and his friends Berlin was a party. It had nothing to do with serious grown-up life or with serious grown-up work or with serious grown-up commitments. It was where reality stopped. Reality was what their parents practiced in the Bundesrepublik, two or three hundred miles away, leading lives that were orderly, practical, and prosperous.

To the bourgeois boys and girls in West Berlin, Marx was a radical born in 1968, in time for the student protests, and had more to do with hating the war in Vietnam and getting the curriculum changed at the Free University than with the invisible, anonymous, unhappy people across the Wall in the German Democratic Republic. Poverty had more to do with Turks and *Schlüsselkinder* making house squats in abandoned Kreuzberg clothes factories than with those mysterious "other" Berliners who lived across the Spree from Kreuzberg, in the projects of Marzahn and Hellersdorf—in apartment blocks for a hundred and fifty thousand people. Ecology had more to do with yin and yang and macrobiotic rock clubs and saving rain forests in the Mato Grosso than with the pollution that is still so thick it literally clogs your lungs when you drive a couple of miles out of town past Potsdam. Tilo says he probably thought more about the Wall and the Cold War at his university, in Mannheim, than his Berlin friends ever thought about them—though some of those friends had a big commune on Köpenicker Strasse, and could see the Wall, and the buildings behind it, from their living-room window. His friends had no interest in crossing Checkpoint Charlie—it meant having to trade in twenty-five good West German marks for twenty-five worthless marks from the G.D.R., and it meant a hassle at the checkpoint, and it meant drinking warm beer and listening to terrible East Bloc rock while they sized up girls who turned out to have fake jeans and unshaved armpits—but Tilo crossed a couple of times. He figured that someone curious enough about the world to have hitch-hiked from Bombay to Shanghai and camped in the outback in Australia and followed the Big Wave to Costa Rica could take the time for Charlie, though it was more a duty than an adventure.

Tilo crossed, of course, when the Wall came down. Every student in West Germany seems to have crossed on November 9, 1989, because for a couple of weeks after that East Berlin was right in the West Berlin style, a piece of street theater, with Mstislav Rostropovich sitting on top of what was left of the Wall playing Bach on his cello while hustlers from twenty or thirty countries chipped away at the bottom, taking the best parts—the bright, graffiti parts—and gluing pins on them and selling them to the incredulous East Berliners as jewelry. It was an instructive couple of weeks for everyone. The young West Berlin writer Wiglaf Droste says that the first night was sentimental and cathartic but after that there was "no dignity at all." What shocked him most was the bananas. People in West Berlin, like people everywhere else in West Germany, had read about there being no fruit in the state grocery stores of East Germany, and they arrived at the Wall with big bunches of bananas—and Wiglaf still doesn't know if it was the arrogance of the West Berliners throwing bananas at the East Berliners that shocked him, or the abjectness of the East Berliners catching the bananas, or both. He agrees with Tilo that the only people who behaved correctly were the Turkish *Gastarbeiter* from West Berlin, who saw the situation for what it was and bought bananas and sold them in East Berlin at a profit. Tilo says now that if you had thought about it at all, you could have predicted the whole complicated and disquieting exchange that eventually produced one Berlin, and one Germany, from those first little exchanges of fruit at the Berlin Wall.

∞

There are many versions of what Berliners sometimes call "the process of unification" (if they are on the left, and think that "Germany" properly began with the fall of the Reich, in 1945) and sometimes "the process of reunification" (if they are on the right, and think that "Germany" was something merely interrupted by Hitler). The political version dates it, formally, from Helmut Kohl's announcement of a ten-point "unity plan" in November of 1989. The popular version dates it, sentimentally, from the day that summer when demonstrators here stopped chanting "We are the People," and started chanting "We are one people." But the fact is that Berliners were not one people then and may even be less one people now. They still refer to the city by its old halves, as East Berlin and West Berlin, or, more politely, east Berlin and west Berlin—it is their way of saying who they are and what they are and, maybe more important, how capable they are, or are not, and what other people can expect of them. For West Berliners it is a matter of vanity, entitlement, and status. For East Berliners it is more often a matter of apology—for the wrong clothes, the wrong jobs, the wrong taste, and even the wrong accents, because the German in East Berlin is so thick it amounts to a dialect. Sometimes it is a matter of resentment, too, and has to do with a kind of bitter purity where lack of money or competence or confidence or sophistication is concerned.

In Dresden or Leipzig—in the other big cities of the "Germany" that Germans who want to be politically correct call, neutrally and cautiously, the *fünf neue Bundesländer,* or five new states—the galling differences between East and West are less apparent, for the simple reason that the West is somewhere else. Wiglaf, who has been giving readings in the East, says that the people he meets outside Berlin are pretty relaxed now, and are even getting confident. Westerners who work in the East have to get along with the Easterners. It doesn't matter if they are in the East because of greed or commitment or because they are racking up duty points in the bureaucracy—they do better if they get along. But in Berlin, where the only official difference anymore between East and West has to do with turning right on a red light, there is no way to avoid the contrast, and maybe even to avoid identifying with the contrast.

The only neutral place in Berlin is the no-man's-land where the Wall once stood. It is a bicycle path now, occasionally invaded for drag races by the young East Berliners who crash around town on their Harley-Davidsons and call themselves Rubis, which they say is American for "rich urban bikers," but generally empty of "East" and "West" in everything except the sinister-looking curved gray lampposts of the East bowing across the path to the bright, upright lampposts of the West in a gesture that was never intended when the East German *Grenzkommando* installed them. But the land around the path is being contested, not so much as real estate but as symbolic space. A lot of Berliners believe the new Germany is going to take its purpose and its moral tone from the purpose and tone of the reconstruction of what in the gruesome glory days of the Third Reich used to be the center of the capital. There are people who want to open the Reichstag for the Bundestag, which is the West German parliament, and others who say no, because for them the Reichstag is associated with Hitler. But the truth is that Hitler hated the Reichstag and never spoke there before it burned. The great Social Democratic speeches of Weimar Germany were Reichstag speeches, and the building that chills the tourists now is not Hitler's, anyway, but Kaiser Wilhelm's, restored by Bonn in 1970.

Almost everything in the new Berlin is being contested, from the tenancy of the Reichstag to the choice of the eagle restored to Gottfried Schadow's Quadriga on top of the Brandenburg Gate—some people thought it would have been a lot more seemly to use the peaceful perched eagle that Schadow put there in 1793 rather than the martial eagle and iron cross that replaced it after the Prussian victory over Napoleon in 1814—and the enormous corporate complex that Daimler-Benz is planning for the Potsdamer Platz. Two years ago, the Potsdamer Platz was literally up against the wall. It was the East of the West, as far as you could go in West

Berlin, and the result was that no one did go—certainly not the people from Daimler-Benz. The famous Mercedes logo that turned above West Berlin turned, appropriately, above the pricey commerce of the Kurfürstendamm, like a rotating corporate steeple or, as the kids in Berlin called it, Mammon. But a few months before the Wall came down, Edzard Reuter, the head of Daimler-Benz, started negotiating for fifteen acres of rubble on what had once been the busiest square in the capital, and eventually bought it from the government of West Berlin—the Senat—for ninety-three million marks, which is about fifty-five million dollars, and anywhere from a third to a seventh of what real-estate people figured was its market value. The Senat, which had always had trouble keeping corporations in West Berlin after the Wall went up, called Reuter's interest in the Platz a sign of his great faith in the divided city, and in the future of the city, and made much of the fact that Ernst Reuter, the first mayor of West Berlin, was Edzard's father. By then, of course, anyone with friends in Bonn knew for a fact that West Germany was buying East Germany from the Russians—sixteen million East German citizens for thirty-four billion Deutsche marks was the first deal struck, with Gorbachev talking Kohl into an extra seven billion at the last minute—and that Daimler-Benz was getting in early, and getting a bargain on what would soon be some of the most valuable property in the country. A lot of people thought it looked bad for Germany, and maybe *was* bad, that a large chunk of the historic center of Berlin was going to be turned into a monument to capital instead of into a place where ordinary people lived and worked and went to cafés and did their marketing and kept their shops, and did whatever Berliners, who have never known Berlin as a "normal" city and are quite sentimental in their images of old Berlin, think ordinary people in a normal city do.

Right now, the Potsdamer Platz looks like a large back yard that no one has bothered to tend for fifty years. The Allies bombed it continuously from 1943 to 1945, and the rubble is overgrown with weeds and scrub and crabgrass, and the grass has got so long it bends in the wind, like beach grass. But it was once a hub, and the people who used to avoid it have started using it again, if they are on foot and in a hurry, because it makes such a good diagonal shortcut from the Tiergarten to East Berlin, and maybe because, being so bleak still, it makes an interesting kind of transition between the two Berlins—a liminal space where the soul of the city seems indeed suspended.

The Potsdamer Platz is so big, and so conspicuously bombed out, that it is an easy symbol, but in a way all Berlin is symbols. A few of those symbols are, literally, too shaming to acknowledge. Very few Berliners will tell you which of the overgrown lots in the middle of town, near the Potsdamer Platz, is the site of Hitler's bunker—or, rather, each Berliner you ask will assure you it's not the lot the last one said it was. (The bunker was in fact under the Chancellery, on Wilhelmstrasse.) For years in Germany, the Second World War was a bland page, if not a blank page, in the history books. In West Germany, it was the time when all the fathers and brothers went to a terrible place called the Russian front and fought Communists, and if the silence about Nazism drove some people mad—troubled children of the war, like Ulrike Meinhof— that silence was somehow considered indispensable to what Germans called "the recovery," and was only slowly challenged, and by the time it *was* challenged, "recovery" in Germany had become entirely an economic, and not a moral, word.

In East Germany, the silence never lifted. East Germans grew up to an official history that described Nazism as a capitalists' adventure, something that the "other side" invented, the other side being the people across the border in the Bundesrepublik. They inherited a topsy-turvy war in which East Germans were the liberators and West Germans—and, by extension, the West itself—were the fascists. To the extent that East Germans believed this about their country, the regime claimed what shallow legitimacy it had. To the extent that East Germans believed it about themselves, they lost their bearings in history and claimed, at most, a kind of unremembered collective memory that the state persuaded them was theirs. It is a habit they still have trouble shaking.

The West Germans are spending hundreds of billions of dollars a year on East Germany, counting on the fact that another economic miracle will mean "recovery" for a people whose habits of authority, intimidation, and self-deception were so ingrained, and so accepted, that when the Wall fell more than a million of them were paid informers for the Stasi. The East Germans, for their part, are adjusting memory to accommodate the change. Somebody has opened an amusement park on the old Marx-Engels-Platz—it is now the Karl-Liebknecht-Platz—in front of the Volkskammer, where the Communists had their parliament, and the Ferris wheel nicely blocks the entrance—and, in fact, blocks the Volkskammer itself—from people walking down Unter den Linden toward it. Somebody else has gone to the suburb of Wandlitz and turned the walled forest where Erich Honecker and his Politburo had villas into a "stress clinic" for the state of Brandenburg. The Kalashnikovs are gone from the gun emplacements in the forest wall, and the security gates are open now. If you drive north from East Berlin and follow the six-lane highway that is pointedly heading nowhere, you will eventually get to Wandlitz, and if you ask for Honecker's house, as Tilo and I did one afternoon, the locals will point vaguely to the left or the right and say, "You can't miss it." But in reality the compound is as secret now as it was when the Party bosses hid there and called it home, and the only reference to the old regime is a handmade wooden plaque, inside the main gate, that the clinic put there and that says, "We are here for healing, not privilege." The only people who talk about the old prime minister are the patients, who live in the Politburo villas and wander around the grounds, with their volleyballs and badminton racquets, in a pleasant Valium daze, and will point the way down a forest path to Honecker's drab brown house—as if Honecker were another spacey patient, but one who happened to precede them.

The theory, of course, is that East Berlin will somehow return to "normal" if the remnants of the old regime are put to "normal" use, and the fact is that the shortage of buildings in East Berlin seems to demand it. There is a big glass convention center—the Lichtenberger Congress Center—in the "reception hall" at Stasi headquarters, and across the courtyard, where political prisoners were brought for interrogation, is an office with a sign on the door saying "Victims of Stalinism." The Russian Cultural Center, on Friedrichstrasse, makes its money showing Terence Hill Westerns and selling Cokes and Ninja Turtles, and the Communist ministries in the enormous building that Göring built for his Luftwaffe have been redecorated for the Treuhandanstalt, the federal holding company that is trying to sell off East Germany's state industries. But all this is really camouflage, because in the end the problem is not Berlin or how many Berlin streets change their names but the fact that in making Berlin the capital of a new Germany, Germans have collapsed their two very different and elaborate memories of "Germany" in the city where those memories were purchased—and now no one seems to know which memory is real, or what "being German" is supposed to mean, or what Germany should look like or act like or build like when it builds its capital, if it tries to dismiss the last forty or fifty or sixty years.

∞

Legally, Berlin was always the capital. Bonn was a provisional arrangement, because the West German constitution was a provisional constitution, a piece of enabling legislation at the discretion of what until last year were the occupying armies of France, Britain, and the United States, and had been drafted so that West Germany could go about its business as a country without precisely being one. The constitution named Bonn to represent this provisional country called West Germany until it could join the other provisional country called East Germany and become "Germany" again, with—it was understood—Berlin again the seat of government. That, at least, is what the West said. East Germany did not. The Russians let East Germany declare itself a real country in 1949—although, with half a million Soviet troops installed in its five *Länder,* East Germany accepted another form of occupation—and it followed that, for the East, West Germany was a real country, too. The rhetoric of partition was complicated and exacting—East German Communists were careful never to refer to West Berlin as "West Berlin" but always as Westberlin, as if it were a new city and had nothing to do with the real Berlin or with who owned it or whose capital it was—but what it came down to was that East Germany's interest lay in recognizing West Germany whether or not West Germany wanted to be recognized.

West Germany certainly never recognized East Germany, though for forty years the two did a great deal of business. The West Germans sent "mission chiefs" to East Berlin but never "ambassadors," and the Allies, who had to send ambassadors if they wanted embassies in East Berlin, and diplomatic status, called those embassies "embassies *to* the German Democratic Republic," and never "embassies *in* the German Democratic Republic." This, of course, had nothing to do with the realities of political or economic life in the East or the West, and it didn't keep either of the Germanys from sending missions to the United Nations, or from joining NATO or the Warsaw Pact, or, for that matter, the Common Market or Comecon. In the end, the rhetoric of German unity was mainly the stuff of West German campaign speeches, because the idea of keeping the size and shape and status of "Germany" open was a convenient Cold War notion and a convenient political notion. The irony is that it lasted long after anyone on either side believed in a united—or reunited—Germany.

The politicians in the West got used to Bonn. They grumbled at first, but eventually most of them decided that the boring town Konrad Adenauer had chosen for the capital—mainly because he had a house near Bonn, and liked to water his roses in the afternoon, and, being Catholic and usually outnumbered by Protestants in West Germany, he appreciated the fact that in Bonn the Catholics outnumbered the Protestants—had its uses. The deadly rectitude of the place was not the least of those uses; no one else wanted to be in Bonn, certainly not the reporters who had to cover it, and for a long time this left the politicians and the tenured *Beamten* of the bureaucracy remarkably unscrutinized.

There were (and still are) forty-five thousand people in Bonn involved one way or another in running Germany, and for them the city was a captain's paradise. Deputies and ministers and important bureaucrats who kept their wives and families at home in Düsseldorf or Stuttgart—it is a mark of status in Bonn to commute—bought pretty villas in the suburbs and installed their girlfriends and hired cooks and decorators and learned to enjoy the arrangement, proving that the highest form of decadence in Germany is a secret *bürgerlich* life. They put their money in property, and paid prices that they could never recover if the capital moved—which is one reason so many of them voted against moving it.

Two years ago, it was hard for any politician in West *or* East Germany to imagine that Bonn would not go on, provisionally, forever. Erich Honecker said that the Wall would be here in a hundred years, and Helmut Kohl, who dreamed publicly and profitably about reclaiming Berlin for "democracy," razed more than a hundred beautiful old Bonn houses to expand the capital he had. When the Wall came down, and in the public mind—for reasons no one has really explained completely—the eventuality of a democratic East Germany became the inevitability of *one* Germany, a lot of people had forgotten that Bonn was not, legally, anybody's capital. No one anticipated the argument between the Bonn partisans and the Berlin partisans which started then—any more than anyone anticipated that three hundred thousand East Germans would move west into the Bundesrepublik in a matter of a few weeks, and make the promise of a quick unification the only way to keep the rest of them home.

The fact that Berlin was the de facto capital of the new Germany was in most ways beside the point of the argument; constitutions, and certainly provisional constitutions, change. The argument was about politics, and about money, but mainly it was about the ambition and the direction of the country. It had to do with whether Germany was going to be an "East-looking" country or a "West-looking" country. It was a way of talking about nationalism, and about what the connection was between German nationalism and the old capital of German nationalism, and about how long a salubrious German "Europeanism" would survive if Bonn was abandoned for a city whose history and "instinct" pointed Germany eastward. It was a way of wondering whether a new Germany would be frightening again or collegial at last, and it was complicated by the fact that nobody really knew where the East ended and the West began in the German consciousness—in 1871, Berlin was actually the middle of "Germany," four hundred miles from its eastern border—or whether in Germany "East" was a matter of politics or the church or *jus sanguinis* or temperament or propaganda or culture or "destiny." All anyone knew was that Bonn stood clearly for "West"—for Europe, for the European Community, for partnership, for a kinder, gentler German, for the peaceful eagle that always votes with the other birds instead of swooping down and taking the spoils for himself. Bonn people pointed out that Berlin had been their capital for a very short time—from

1871, when Bismarck collected the various kingdoms, duchies, principalities, and Hanseatic states of "Germany" and put them under Prussian rule, to 1945, when the Reich fell—and that "not the best things in German history happened then." My friend Spiros Simitis, who teaches constitutional law at the University of Frankfurt and was a Bonn advocate, told me before I came here to remember, in the excitement of Berlin, what a critical symbolic value Bonn has had as Germany's capital, because it represented "what has been good in Germany since 1945."

∞

Everyone knows the story about François Mauriac's telling a reporter that he loved Germany so much he was glad there were two of them. It was an obvious postwar tenet that a divided Germany would be a safer (for everybody else) Germany. But it was also believed—by liberals in West Germany like Professor Simitis—that West Germany would be safer if power were literally spread across the country. The Bundesrepublik was structured as a decentralized federal state. The Chancellery, the ministries, and the two houses of parliament were built in Bonn, but the West German Constitutional Court sat in Karlsruhe, the Bundesbank was in Frankfurt, the Bundeskriminalamt, which is Germany's F.B.I., was in Wiesbaden (along with the Hessen office of the Data Protection Agencies conceived by Professor Simitis to protect West Germans from the information the *Länder* collect about them), and, in fact, the Social Security office, which is the biggest bureaucracy in the country, was in West Berlin. Trains ran and planes flew and roads were built to accommodate the considerable distances between the offices of the men (and the few women) who governed and administered the country. It was not unusual for a German politician to start the day in, say, Hamburg, stop at the Bundestag in Bonn, fly to a meeting in Saarbrücken, and end the afternoon in Stuttgart—and never leave the bureaucracy of the Federal Republic. Centralism meant one thing in West Germany—Germany's disastrous experience of concentrated power—and people adjusted their lives to avoid it. Liberals feared that putting authority in one place in Germany would eventually mean putting the wrong authority in one place. They felt that the democracy here was still too fragile to be exposed even to a physical concentration of offices and functions, and said that Germans could not afford the pleasure and status of a real capital, like London or Paris. Bonn was "necessary."

In 1949, of course, centralism meant nationalism—not Churchill or de Gaulle but Hitler. The gangs of skinheads and neo-Nazis and new German "Klansmen" who started attacking immigrants and firebombing refugee shelters this fall are not necessarily Berliners. Many of them come from cities in West Germany. But the worst of the violence took place on the first anniversary of unification (which, to avoid arguments about "unification" and "reunification," was celebrated as "Unity Day"), and after six hundred attacks, and six or seven deaths, it was obvious that the rhetoric of Blood and Soil and keeping Germany "German" and free from contamination by foreigners had been revived and, liberals feared, endorsed by unification, which included the ascendancy of Berlin, with all its confusing symbolism. It is hard to separate the excitement of unification—of being "Germany" again—from the illusion of exoneration, and this is the warning that liberal Germans are trying to give.

There was a lot of protest from liberals last summer when Helmut Kohl showed up at Hohenzollern family ceremonies at Sanssouci, the old imperial palace, for Frederick the Great's "homecoming." The Hohenzollerns had moved Frederick to West Germany a few years after the war—to a tomb in Burg Hechingen, near Stuttgart—and once the Communists were gone they had got permission to bring him back and bury him according to the instructions in his will, under the palace terrace. No one here seriously worries about the Hohenzollerns' taking over Germany—most Germans were surprised there were any Hohenzollerns left in Germany—but the fact that Kohl turned their ceremony into a state occasion worried many Germans, and even reminded some of them of Hitler and Hindenburg standing over Frederick's tomb in the Garrison Church in Potsdam in March of 1933, at the birth of the Third Reich. Kohl himself had lobbied harder than anybody else except, possibly, the mayor of Berlin to move the capital here—something that did not sit well with the planners and preservationists who had fought to save those hundred or so Bonn houses and had lost to Kohl's argument about needing land for a proper capital there. Kohl decided early in the Bonn-Berlin debate that Berlin was not only Germany's historic capital and its constitutional capital but its "natural" capital, and while the Bonn people argued about the burdens of cost and dislocation and relocation—the country is going to have to spend something between one and a half and two trillion Deutsche marks to absorb its five new states, and moving the capital will add billions more to the public cost—Kohl was bound to win, for the simple reason that Berlin was pretty much all East Germany had to offer, economically and psychologically, to the new Germany, and that without the government here to draw investment eastward, East Germany would very likely become a kind of German Mezzogiorno, and everybody would leave.

There are six hundred and sixty-two deputies in the Bundestag, and when they voted for a capital last June three hundred and thirty-seven of them voted for Berlin, including most of the new East German deputies. Fifteen out of sixteen deputies from the Party of Democratic Socialism, which is the new name for East Germany's old Communist Party, and which has no members outside the five new states, voted for Berlin, and their votes gave the Berlin people their majority. The Berlin people celebrated, and the price of Berlin real estate, East and West, doubled overnight—it had already doubled and in some neighborhoods tripled the day after the Wall came down—but the Bonn people said that Germany had left Europe, that Germany was rebuilding its Wall on the east bank of the Rhine, and the irony was that in their last gasp of power in the new Germany the Communists had had the last word. The real irony, of course, was that there were Communists in the Bundestag at all. The Communists had turned over two billion Deutsche marks' worth of Party property and stock to the Treuhandanstalt, and by election time they were exempt from the federal election laws, which do not seat any party in the Bundestag unless that party gets over 5 percent of the national vote. The Communists got to the Bundestag with less than 2.5 percent.

∞

Wolf Jobst Siedler, the Berlin historian and publisher, likes to say that the problem in Berlin right now is all the Berliners who are *not* here—the Jews, the intellectuals, the aristocrats, the *Bürgertum,* the farmers, the plumbers. He says there are no "Berliners" anymore besides the children of a handful of old West Berlin families, like his own, who couldn't bear to leave the city, and the children of the old East Berlin workers who couldn't afford to. Siedler is the great-great-great-grandson of Gottfried Schadow, the sculptor who put the horses on the Brandenburg Gate. His family has been in Berlin for three hundred years, and in the same Grunewald house for the last hundred of those years, and as far as he is concerned Berlin has been a kind of family destiny. There are three and a half million people living in Berlin today, but the West imported its Berliners with promises of tax breaks and subsidies and extra salaries, and the East, of course, kept its Berliners with a wall, and even so, from Wolf Jobst Siedler's point of view, "Berlin is empty." Three million Berliners went West after the war, and never came back. West Berlin repopulated itself, so to speak, with the young who came for the scene, the old who came for the fat pensions, the bureaucrats who came for the salaries, and the artists and intellectuals who were cycled through Berlin with pomp and perks, and could be said to have come for the glory. East Berlin, quite simply, lost its smartest people.

Berlin was a vibrantly cosmopolitan city before Hitler. The only German city with anything like its variety—its ethnic mix and its intellectual spice and its liberal appetites—was Frankfurt. The famous *Berliner Mentalität*—the Berlin mentality—was fast, funny, sly, skeptical, worldly, and enlightened, and the people who created that mentality were long gone by the time the Communists came. A hundred and seventy thousand Jews lived in Berlin before the Nazi putsch. Berlin's Jewish bourgeoisie was like fin de siècle Vienna's Jewish bourgeoisie—assimilated, educated people who built beautiful houses in Grunewald and Schöneberg and Dahlem and worshiped culture and entertained, and often produced, the artists and intellectuals with the Berlin mentality. They left Germany or they died in the camps. Most of the very few who managed to survive emigrated, and, by their own accounts, the Jews who did come back to Berlin—there were six thousand Jews in West Berlin when the Wall came down, and since then six thousand more have arrived from the Soviet Union—were mainly ordinary working people without connections in the West, and were too shattered to begin their lives again someplace else, or to expect anything from Berlin beyond the small comfort of a familiar street or a neighborhood where they would not get lost and have to ask directions.

Siedler is a conservative, and he likes to shock his liberal friends—friends like me—by talking about elites, but he is right about Berlin's elites: they tempered the Prussian rigidity and the chaotic Slavic politics of Weimar Berlin and, for a while, made this the most interesting and progressive city in Germany—made it in every way a capital. He calls the problem now "a problem of personnel." West Berlin was able to buy its managers and its investors and its intellectuals, but for years after the war anybody who wanted to have a "serious" life and make an important career did it in the Bundesrepublik, and if people stopped in Berlin on the way to that serious life, it was usually a chapter in their bildungsroman—a fling or an adventure or a rite of passage—and not the end of the story. West Berlin may have been the biggest industrial city of, if not precisely *in,* West Germany, but the power and most of the ambition in West Germany were always somewhere else. There was no important television network here when the Wall came down. There was no important paper or magazine. The only important West German industry with headquarters in Berlin was Schering Pharmaceutical—Siemens had moved to Munich, Borsig to Düsseldorf, MBB and Telefunken to Stuttgart. The Berlin factories that did piecework on parts or materials cycled through Berlin for the tax breaks rarely saw a finished product. The major investment here was in real estate, and, by extension, the major industry was construction. The important politicians—Willy Brandt, say, or Richard von Weizsäcker—were West Germans trying out for power in Bonn. The important radicals—the Greens and the Marxists—were experimenting with ideas that went West if they were successful or attracted attention, or else got left in the "scene" here, like scented candles and Baader-Meinhof buttons, for the teenage tourists.

West Berlin was fed by the West German recovery, but it had very little to do with that recovery. Its only product was a kind of official "culture." By the time the Wall came down, the culture budget here was six hundred and twenty million marks—which amounts to three hundred and sixty-five million dollars a year, and is more than the government spends on culture in the United States. Bureaucrats who worked in Berlin got 17 percent "Berlin pay" added onto their West German salary. The arts were subsidized, the institutes were subsidized, the think tanks were subsidized. When West Germans came to Berlin to visit, they went to the theater and listened to concerts and looked at daring and expensive new buildings that as often as not had been commissioned from architects at home—and West Berlin thrived in a full circle of exchanges, importing its famous scene and then the audience for its scene. In a way, it was a kind of hyper-West—the postmodernists would say a meta-West—with all the ambitious, ambiguous achievements of the Bundesrepublik replicated on a hundred and eighty-five bombed-out square miles inside a wall.

Not many East Berliners saw it, or had permission to see it, unless they were the dissidents bought out by the West, or the compliant intellectuals rewarded by travel in the West, or the old workers encouraged to leave when the time came to collect their pensions, because West Germany, by not recognizing East Germany, was obliged to consider them "German" citizens, and to offer them all the West German benefits and social services. The West Berlin that most East Berliners knew was the city they saw on West German television—a sitcom-and-soap-opera city of beautiful girls and rich boys enjoying endless rock and wild sex and expensive shopping. The Communists tried to jam West German television for about ten years after the Wall went up, and then gave up trying. "West Berlin" was free entertainment, and for a long time it was too spectacularly different from reality in the G.D.R. to be taken as anything but fantasy. Still, it is probably true that on November 9, 1989, East Berliners knew more about the KaDeWe, the department store across the Wall on the Kurfürstendamm, than they did about the Christian Democratic Union or the Social Democratic Party or the Free Democratic Party or any of the other West German parties that had been winning and losing elections on the issue of what the policy toward *them* should be.

∞

There was very little public dissent in East Germany. The fact that for years, dissidents who had not already fled West were either put on a bus, driven to a checkpoint, and deposited in the West (if they were too well known to disappear into an East German prison) or arrested and eventually "sold West" left East Germany with a remarkably passive population—disorganized, dispirited, doing nothing very well except waiting for bad news. With its war dead, and its professionals long gone, and its dissidents systematically exported, East Germany had reverted. It was a peasant state in industrial clothes, more like Russia than Prussia. Nothing worked in East Germany. Its factories made terrible things that no one wanted. Its farms produced, per acre, a third of what the West German farms produced. Its buildings started falling apart before the tenants had unpacked. Its schools taught a mixture of political propaganda and obsolete science. Its avant-garde—like the Berliner Ensemble, in East Berlin—was stuck in a kind of frozen modernism, and produced death masks of art and theater.

The people in East Germany who survived with some sense of their civilization intact were usually the people who could carry it in their heads—Lutheran pastors with a commitment to witness and testify; musicians with a commitment to centuries of German music; scientists who had mastered a language that was too difficult for the Party to discredit or distort. Most East Germans were edgy, acquiescent, and bewildered people. Their education was distorted. Their "history" was an invention. They had no way to evaluate what being German had meant, or could mean, no parallel truth about themselves with which to exorcise or investigate, or even balance, the official truths—none of the stubborn, sustaining identity of the Czechs or the Poles or the Hungarians. They were to a large extent without community—except, maybe, the ambiguous community of the informed-against and their informers. It is not surprising that over a million of them *were* informers, or that the Stasi's domestic files covered four million people—one of every four East Germans—nor is it surprising that there was nothing in East Germany like Solidarity, or the Hungarians' revolution of 1956, or the Prague Spring of 1968.

Jens Reich is the East Berlin molecular biologist who—with a pastor named Wolfgang Ullmann and a painter named Bärbel Bohley—led the citizens' movement that for practical purposes ran East Germany for the first four months after the Wall fell, while the country got ready for elections. Reich is an introspective and, by his own admission, troubled person, and talks reluctantly to strangers, but when he does he says that "the tragedy of East Germany" haunts him; he cannot come to terms with his own part, and the part that intellectuals like him played, in that tragedy. People trying to explain something of the last forty years in East Germany often talk about the reluctance of East Germans to accept the leadership of intellectuals—they mean, of course, dissident intellectuals—but Dr. Reich talks about the reluctance of those intellectuals to lead.

There were no Václav Havels or Andrei Sakharovs in East Germany. Men and women who were "on their way," as Reich puts it, were ruined or exiled without any real protest, or they were ruined if not by working for the regime then by a kind of complicity with the regime. They purchased privilege or peace or simply safety with their compliance, and everybody knew it, and they were thus discredited. People associated them with everything else that was "official" in East Germany ("We were like everybody else who purported to know what was good for Germany," Reich says), and the lesson those people learned was that intellectuals were cowards. The protests of 1968 in West Berlin were repeated in East Berlin as demonstrations against Americans in Vietnam, not against the terrorism of the state at home. And, even so, the young people who dominated those demonstrations, the ones the state considered dangerous or charismatic or subversive, were rock musicians and folksingers, not students. Some of them were given a couple of hours to pack, and then were deposited in West Berlin. They left behind a generation of artists and intellectuals who complained among themselves but enjoyed enormous privilege—good cars, travel in the West, country houses, books and records bought with hard-currency accounts that were unavailable to ordinary East German citizens.

There is a lot of bitterness in East Germany right now, and a lot of cynicism in West Germany, about the privilege and compromise of East German intellectuals who stayed. Christa Wolf, who, at sixty-two, is arguably the best writer in East Germany, was a Party member. Last year, she published a book, *Was Bleibt?* ("What Remains?"), about a day in 1979 when she was being watched by Stasi, and while the book is an honest and honorable document, young East Germans wonder why she never took a risk and published it then, when it might have helped or taught or inspired *them,* instead of waiting until it was safe for *her.* Reich says that this sort of passivity, this retreat of intellectuals from public life, will mark the intelligentsia in East Berlin for decades. "It's not a miracle that no one wants us now," he says whenever he talks about the impatience of the West Germans with East German pieties about fighting Communism. "I reproach myself. I reproach my friends. We tolerated the nonsense for so long. We ceased to be credible. We kept silent because of careers, because of children. But how do you say to your children, after a lifetime of waiting, 'I was waiting for better times'?"

Reich thinks that the real dissent began when children started telling their parents they were going to leave East Germany—"because when your children refuse your life it's time to do something." For years, he and his wife and a lot of other liberal parents had met in what he calls "white circles." They met privately and were "anxious not to be overheard," and they talked mainly about their children—how to counter some of the ideological pressure on their children at school, how to keep the minds of their children open, how to discredit the idea of "enemies" with which their children were being indoctrinated. They had contact with church groups, with peace groups—after Chernobyl, Reich and some of his friends at the Academy of Sciences got involved with Physicians Against Nuclear War—and tried to let the people around them know what was happening in the Soviet Union. But they did not really organize an opposition until the summer of 1989, when Hungary opened its border with the West and thousands of young East Germans did start leaving, and Reich says that now they will never know what would have happened if they *had* organized, or at what point the regime would have lost its will or its power to terrorize them.

It may be that the guilt East Germans feel now, as the "last dissenters" in the East Bloc, accounts for some of the aggressive apathy you often feel in East Berlin. They seem to like not so much their distress as surrendering to their distress. It is a national habit. The students in West Berlin, who pride themselves on their cool, say that the East Berlin students they are meeting now are very emotional, just like their parents, and make them uncomfortable, talking all the time about "true values" and whether or not they have them. The East Berliners pride themselves on their preoccupation. They defer to the West Germans who arrive to run their schools—and their politics and their offices and their factories—and complain quite cheerfully that they are incapable, incompetent, undeserving, that they have no good reason to resist the "colonialists" they resent (the metaphor here for German East-West arrangements is colonialism, and in most ways it is accurate), that they deserve the colonialists, that they have nothing to show for themselves as East Germans on their own. They concede to West Germans a kind of entitlement.

Dr. Reich, who sat in the first free East German Volkskammer and was supposed to run for the Bundestag, decided against it a month or two before the election. He says that by then East Germany was "full of tycoons dancing around" and they made it clear that East Germans who did not belong, in every sense, to one of the big West German parties would be token Ossis in Bonn, memento mori of a grass-roots movement that had lasted only as long as a free and independent East Germany lasted—which was less than a year. That was how most Germans—even East Germans—seemed to want it. When East Germans went to the polls in March of 1990 and voted freely for the first time, they voted "West German" in that they voted Christian Democrat and Social Democrat and Free Democrat. They voted for West German parties that had fielded candidates in the East and been able to pay millions of marks to get them elected. In fact, they managed to reproduce in East Germany—and with some accuracy—the political composition of the Bundesrepublik, and the only surprise then was that anyone in East Germany voted Communist. Nearly 10 percent of the East Germans did. By the time they voted again it was as "Germans," and it was nine months later. People from the citizens' movement of 1989—they called their party Bündnis '90—shared a list with the East German Greens, and, even so, won only eight seats in a parliament of six hundred and sixty-two. Reich says that the vote was "hormonal." It was as if West Germany were an impulse East Germans had—something involuntary, something they could not help reproducing. And East Germany's "political class"—its potential political class—"was not in a resisting mood." There was probably no way to have resisted. East Germans longed for the West, but they had no competence in judging and evaluating the West. The politicians with the fresh four-color posters and the fax machines and the telephones and the money for a "Western" campaign were the politicians people voted for, and any enthusiasm East Germans may have had for a free and independent East Germany disappeared under the shiny West German sell. Dr. Reich put it this way: "After an outburst of political energy, a great resignation took over."

The grass-roots amateur politicians here—like Dr. Reich; like Pastor Ullmann, who got elected to the Bundestag; like Frau Bohley, who sat on the Berlin city council—never really had the money or the experience or the platform to build anything like a majority party. They were idealistic, or foolish (or both), and they thought that East Germans would want to keep "East Germany" for at least a few years longer. They thought that now that East Germany was free, East Germans would want to settle their own future, and settle their scores among themselves, and arrive at some agreement about who they were morally *and* politically and what kind of society they wanted, and, with that agreement, some confidence as a people. They thought East Germans wouldn't want to lose, summarily, what little "good" they had managed to achieve. They talked about kindergartens and day care and women getting twenty free days at home a year if they had sick children, and they wanted to know what East German women were going to do about abortion—abortion was legal in East Germany, and the state paid—once they belonged to a country where conservative Catholics from Bavaria wrote the abortion laws. They wanted to temper the punishing costs, in jobs and lives, of a quick conversion to a free market.

The people from Bündnis '90 did the best they could, but they were amateurs, and they ran amateur campaigns, and they brought up complicated issues that they had no competence to address, let alone resolve, and that few people wanted to hear, and even fewer people had the understanding to acknowledge. The argument on the other side was simple, and it was paid for, and in the end it was irresistible. It was that East Germany would be rich if East

Germans left their future to the West Germans, and that East Germany would be poor if East Germans tried to represent themselves. And the irony was that the same East Germans who complained about being owned by West Germans and, in fact, overrun by West Germans were the ones who believed that they had no choice except to do what the Communists had taught them to do—let the people who "knew better" make the decisions. They did not seem to understand that whatever East Germany chose, it was in West Germany's great interest to support them. It did not take long for Bündnis '90 to start looking like a student movement run by grown-ups.

Today, the groups in Bündnis '90 share the top floors of an old building on the corner of Friedrichstrasse and Behrenstrasse. They borrow each other's typewriters and photocopy machines and telephones, and hang up posters about Gray Panther evenings and Palestinian plays and "Work for Peace" meetings and "dialogue" between the Soviet Union and the United States—as if Germany were still ground zero in a cold war. It is disturbing to go there, because the ground floor of the building is a beautiful new West German bookstore, with wood paneling and rare editions and English hunting prints that sell for four and five hundred dollars. To the West Germans at the bookstore, the Bündnis '90 people are not the people who took to the streets in 1989 and helped make East Germany free. They are (with a shrug and a tolerant smile) "the people upstairs," and in this new Germany they seem as innocent and anachronistic as their posters. The causes that are left to fight for are the ones they inherited—and are so benign that even the Communists permitted them—but no one bothers to help them figure out what their real causes could be. The polls say that 10 percent of the people in East Germany are "in sympathy" with them. But the majority thinks that they did their job in '89, and that now they should be sensible and go home and leave politics to the professionals. Tilo tells me that the worst thing you can call somebody in the new Germany is an amateur.

∾

The priorities in East Berlin are obvious. You learn them walking down the street and looking at buildings, at which buildings have the fresh paint and the sleek West German furniture and the telephones that work and the secretaries who speak English instead of Russian to a foreigner—and the building that had them first is the Treuhandanstalt, where more than three thousand people are occupied in what is known as "privatizing" East Germany. Treuhand has been done up in international corporate style. The enormous hall with the massive columns and the stone walls that Göring built for intimidation is fitted out with chrome-and-leather couches, lit with designer tensor lamps, and decorated with mysterious white cubes that are either sculpture or bases for sculpture that somebody forgot to order. No one at Treuhand seems to know, but the people who work there are instructed to be agreeable to anyone who looks American or Japanese, so they leave the decision to you.

In fact, no one from Japan has bought property from Treuhand, and only ten Americans have, though Treuhand has about six thousand of its ten thousand companies left to sell, and is running what could be called a perpetual white sale. Treuhand calls it "the sale of the century." The Japanese take a long view of their investments, but not, apparently, long enough to take on any of East Germany's dilapidated plants or old Party managers or badly trained workers, or to put their money into businesses that West Germans were (unofficially) offered first and, for various good reasons, rejected. The Treuhand was not actually a West German invention. It was the Communists' idea—an attempt to save themselves by bringing foreign capital into the country. Hans Modrow, who was the last Communist prime minister in the G.D.R., thought up Treuhand. He named sixty East German bureaucrats to the staff, and eventually the West German minister for economic affairs sent five or six of his bureaucrats to help them, but the East Germans were no more adept at liquidating or selling factories—which was what they were told to do—than they were at managing factories. They were Party people, and what they did best was put other Party people into easy jobs.

Volker Hillebrandt, who comes from West Germany and handles Berlin property for Treuhand now, says that the system in East Germany was a "simple protecting system": workers had nothing to do when they got to work, but they could not be fired, so in the end everyone had an interest in holding up the house of cards. The first director of Treuhand was an East German who lasted three and a half months. The man who replaced him was a West German who gave up after a couple of weeks. The third Treuhand director—he was a steel executive from Düsseldorf named Detlev Rohwedder—did what he said any sane industrialist coming to Treuhand would do. He added hundreds of West Germans to the original five, and kept adding West Germans until virtually everyone with authority at Treuhand came from the Bundesrepublik, and then he transferred all of East Germany's industries, along with twenty thousand farms, forests, shops, services, and pieces of real estate, to nine Treuhand holding companies, organized by industrial sector and, taken together, the biggest company in the country.

Rohwedder was a smart man but, from the East German perspective, a ruthless man. His mandate was to sell East Germany, not necessarily to save East Germans. He closed down hundreds of factories; the ones he sold were as often as not sold for the land they sat on, and the people who bought them either closed them too, claiming bankruptcy, or fired as many workers as they could and started over. Rohwedder was shot at the beginning of April this year. (He was at home in Düsseldorf, and someone—the police say a terrorist from the Red Army Faction—fired into his window from a garden and killed him.) But by April nearly a million people were out of work in the five new states, and more than two million people were working "short time," which is an old East German euphemism for showing up for a few hours every week, collecting your pay, and thereby keeping the real unemployment figures hidden, and Rohwedder was so unpopular among East Germans that when he died, hundreds of them put on buttons saying "It wasn't me!" The story went around that the only company in East Germany with a profit was the company that made the buttons. The next story was that the company was West German.

The problem for Treuhand is that Germany doesn't really need the East German factories. They duplicate the products and processes in West Germany, and do it poorly, and West German businessmen claim that by increasing their own production by 10 or 15 percent (and in some industries 5 percent) they could supply the five new states and do it for less money, and at more profit, than by modernizing East German plants and maintaining East German workers. It isn't surprising that businessmen are self-righteous about investing in the East. They expect Treuhand to accommodate them as long as they are paying, and they resent having to cover for the government's wisdom that it is cheaper to let *them* pay people to produce badly than for the government to pay those people not to produce at all. Right now, Treuhand has to choose between their demands and the demands of workers with nowhere else to go, and the best it can do is try to balance the costs, including the social costs. It is a question of intentions and priorities. Germany needs to keep millions of East Germans from moving West, and the only way to do that is to make life attractive for them at home—which obviously includes their having jobs at home—but Germany also needs to finance that attractive German life with investment, and no sensible investor wants a company with a padded work roll or bad management or terrible products.

The problem is complicated by the fact that a lot of people who buy property through Treuhand are not even sensible investors. They are what Rohwedder once called "Wild Westerners"—land speculators and developers and a few criminals—and they run a gamut from the young man who bought a construction company in Cottbus, cleared out the company account, and disappeared, to the West Berlin developers who bought a lightbulb factory called Narva in East Berlin (over the bids of two real lightbulb manufacturers) on promises of an investment of five hundred and seventy million marks, and it turned out that only seventy million of those marks were going to be used for making lightbulbs and the rest were for developing the property. The sale was just canceled.

Treuhand has no trouble selling property in Berlin when there are no factories on it—or claims or entailments. Hillebrandt says that land here is more expensive now than land in Hamburg or Munich; there is a village called Falkensee, just east of Berlin, where the price of a square foot went from under one Deutsche mark to forty Deutsche marks in a few weeks. Hillebrandt's job gets much harder when the property he has to sell is anywhere farther from Berlin than about thirty miles—which means when it is anywhere else in East Germany. Officially, people are not supposed to be speculating on Treuhand land; they are supposed to be investing in Germany's future. If one investor makes an offer that involves laying off a hundred workers, and another investor wants to lay off two hundred workers, Treuhand is supposed to weigh the hundred lost jobs when it makes a decision. There are fines and penalties and all sorts of other deterrents to keep people from buying a factory and firing everybody in it and then tearing the factory down and selling the land, at a profit, to someone else, but there are nearly as many ways to get around this. The developers who tried to buy the lightbulb factory—Klingbeil is the name of their group—had an agreement that left them free to fire any worker if they "compensated" that worker to the amount of twenty thousand marks, which is less than twelve thousand dollars. After 1992, they were free to fire workers with no compensation at all. There were about twelve hundred people working at Narva when Klingbeil signed for the factory. Klingbeil, by contract, was to keep a thousand. Once *they* were gone—for severance pay amounting to twelve million dollars—the developers would have cleared a million square feet of land in the center of Berlin which is already worth hundreds of millions of dollars.

Treuhand has sold a hundred and sixty-five of its nine hundred Berlin companies so far, and says it expects to "sell Berlin" entirely in the next two years. The new director, Birgit Breuel—she was a finance minister in Lower Saxony, and Kohl chose her on the advice that a professional bureaucrat would go down better in East Germany than another professional capitalist—has tried to establish "neutral" guidelines to the effect that if a company is losing ten million marks a month, and no one wants it, the old management has three months to begin to turn it around, and after that Treuhand shuts it down. But East Berliners think that Treuhand should be "protecting" its holdings, socially (from their point of view) and politically (from its own). Some people in East Berlin want Treuhand to turn their factories into cooperatives, or to agree to more worker or management buyouts, but that also means lending the money for the buyouts, or finding somebody else to lend it, and Hillebrandt says that when West Germans talk about lending money to East German management he knows for sure that somewhere along the line a not very savory deal has been made. People who look like East Germans—people with synthetic suits and used cars and xeroxed calling cards—have a hard time getting through the door at Treuhand. People who look rich can get appointments and attention and a glossy portfolio to take home, and sometimes even the offer of a company underwritten by the German government.

A couple of months ago, two reporters from Cologne television presented themselves at Treuhand with nothing to show for themselves but fake calling cards marked "Euro Consult," a rented Mercedes with a telephone, and a story about representing a Japanese-American group that wanted to buy film and tape factories in Wolfen and Dessau. The man they saw at Treuhand—he was the director of the "chemicals sector"—was so delighted at the prospect of rich foreign buyers for a couple of factories no West Germans wanted that he never asked the reporters for references or financial statements or seemed the least put off when they said that their "clients" were thinking of producing pesticides and planned to burn their waste, unfiltered, in the neighborhood, or even that they were hoping to lay off a hundred workers in one factory right away and fire fifteen thousand in the other factory in the next three years. The reporters came home with a deal: they got the factories for twenty-five million marks less than their own appraisal; Treuhand was going to help out by building a highway for them; and the German government was paying them nearly sixty-five thousand marks for every hundred thousand marks they invested.

The fact is that the best properties in East Germany went fast, and always to other Germans. Volkswagen got the Trabant plants to convert. Faber got the oil refineries in Schwedt an der Oder. BASF got its choice of the chemical plants near Dresden. When foreigners were courted at all, it was usually to raise the bids on companies that West Germans eventually bought—like the East German airline Interflug, which was taken over in the end by Piper. Now the foreigners are being courted—there is a new Treuhand "sales office" in New York—for the leavings. It has always been hard to buy into Germany if Germany doesn't want you. People in the European Community complain about it all the time. They say that the Common Market is a pretty concept designed for Germans investing in *their* countries, but that at home in Germany there are books full of regulations and pockets full of I.O.U.s that every banker and bureaucrat knows when and how to remember. A good German bureaucrat can head off the most determined businessman, and he can do it with maddening hospitality and correctness. Only two hundred Treuhand companies have gone to foreigners, and many of those foreigners were Swiss and Austrians, who had an obvious advantage. Most foreigners who want to buy into East Germany try to buy land directly, or through German middlemen or German partners, because when Treuhand sells quickly to a foreigner it usually means that the company is hopeless even by the old East German standards—like the company in Dresden that was trucking crushed stone four hundred miles north to the Baltic and had never figured out why it was losing money. Treuhand tried to sell *that* company to some Georgia businessmen who carried Bibles and looked like rubes but did know that you don't truck crushed stone to the Baltic if you want to make a profit.

∽

The status of East Berlin land has been complicated by the many claims on it. Germans whose land was seized by the Communists can claim it if it was not taken during the four years of the Russian occupation. Jews whose land was seized by the Nazis can claim it anytime if records exist—they often do not—proving it was theirs. The only businesses to make a profit, or break even, in the five new states over the past year were cleaning businesses—West Germans hired maids from them—and construction businesses, and contractors say that half of East Berlin would be under construction if the developers could afford the risk of starting work on a piece of property they thought was free and then having to stop and wait out an investigation because somebody filed a claim. There are a hundred and twenty thousand claims pending in Berlin (and more than a million in all of East Germany). Treuhand is working on formulas that involve giving the money it gets for contested property to people who arrive with valid claims after a sale is made and work is started—but not giving back the property itself. Right now, a company that buys from Treuhand has to stop restoring or constructing—or, more likely, decides to stop—if someone else claims the property, and in Berlin the black market in title searches and fake deeds is nearly as big, and as dirty, as the market in working papers. Friedrich Weber, a West Berlin architect whose company designs the Klingbeil projects—he is currently turning the Leipzig train station, which is the biggest and one of the handsomest stations in Europe, into a restaurant and shopping mall—says that one particularly repulsive specialty of the new property and title searchers has to do with identifying Jews who died, tracking down the land or the house or the shop they owned, and selling the information.

The registry office for East Berlin is in the Rotes Rathaus—the old town hall, a few blocks east of Unter den Linden—and Weber says it's almost impossible to trace the original titles there. The registry books are blackened and crumbling, and over the years thousands of pages were removed by Nazis and Communists who wanted somebody else's property for themselves. Weber had to stop work on a development in East Berlin because someone filed a claim saying that a piece of land in the middle of the development had belonged to his family, and he wanted it back. The man turned out to be another West Berlin developer. Still, Weber says he prefers building in East Berlin because there are always West Berliners in the bureaucracy who can handle problems; he says that in towns like Leipzig the people he sees are good, young, motivated people, but they have no experience in dealing with architects or developers, let alone shady strangers who appear suddenly with fake deeds and fake claims and batteries of expensive West German lawyers. Weber's developers are the biggest in Berlin, and he has projects all over the East, but he says that because of problems of provenance, only one of those projects is actually under construction.

Weber is from Dresden, and when he talks about what he really wants to do he talks about building something *there*—a nice apartment house or a symphony hall—on a piece of land on the Elbe that his father, who was also an architect, dreamed of owning fifty years ago, and that Weber grew up dreaming about too, and was finally able to buy in August. People who work for developers in Germany rarely get to build symphony halls, or even apartment houses. They build office buildings and hotels and shopping centers and business centers, because developers make more money in commercial property, and because an architect's job is a lot easier when he is designing offices and malls than when he is trying to make families feel at home in a housing project. There is so much confusion in East Berlin about who owns the apartment houses that are already there that Western developers are putting almost all their money into commercial space, hoping to get it out fast, before the market is glutted. There is already a shortage of two hundred and fifty thousand apartments in Berlin. Two hundred thousand refugees arrived in Germany this year, and most of them came through Berlin, and many of them stayed here. The shortage will get worse when the capital begins to move.

In East Berlin, most of the public housing is so bad anyway that it is reasonable to say *everyone* needs a new apartment, or work on the apartment he has. The few good apartments are being rented or sold to Wessis—Bundis are known as Wessis now that Germany is united—for the simple reason that Wessis can pay, and neighborhoods like the one around Kollwitzplatz, in Prenzlauer Berg, where the Communists restored a couple of pretty nineteenth-century streets, are filling up with young West Berliners and now have art galleries and good bookstores and the requisite punk cafés featuring black leather and vegetarian sandwiches. Kids from Kreuzberg started squatting in Prenzlauer Berg right after the Wall came down—the word was that the scene was "purer" and more "authentic" there—though the Kollwitzplatz, at least, was never the *gemütlich* workers' quarter the Communists claimed but an old bourgeois neighborhood noted for the age and coolness of its wine cellars, and a lot of interesting East Berliners lived there in whatever apartments the Stasi hadn't already commandeered. The way it worked in neighborhoods like that was for the local housing institutes—which managed the apartments and chose the tenants—to rent a place to Party people or Stasi people for a couple of dollars a month, and for those people to sublet at a profit. When the Wall came down, *their* tenants sublet, at an even bigger profit, to the West Germans. Now everybody wants the apartments back. A student I know named Dorothea, who lives in West Berlin, house-sits for a couple of friends on the Kollwitzplatz when they go away on vacation—because these days when somebody with a good apartment in East Berlin leaves town, somebody else is apt to put the furniture on the sidewalk and take the apartment himself.

Rents are supposed to be stable in East and West Berlin, and raised only by fixed percentages over specified periods, but the Berlin Senat is in the process of decontrolling rents, East and West, as salaries are adjusted (right now salaries in East Berlin—or, more accurately, the salaries of East Berliners in East Berlin—are only about 60 percent of West Berlin salaries), and last month the official rents in apartments in the East quadrupled. When the Senat finishes adjusting, apartments in the East will cost about ten times what East Berliners are paying for them now. Shops will cost even more. This means that people in the East *and* the West who might normally move—to another apartment, to the suburbs, to another town—are sitting on the apartments they rent or own or control, knowing that in a little while they can make money on them. Dorothea's landlord in West Berlin is paying his way through school in Saarbrücken on the rent she and her roommates give him. She would like to move. She thinks it would be nice to live in one of the town houses off Kollwitzplatz, but the neighborhood has got too chic for students—when Berlin was celebrating Unity Day last year, the fashionable people in Prenzlauer Berg threw an anti-unity party on Kollwitzplatz that all the other fashionable Berliners wanted to go to, and ten thousand did go to—and she says that in another couple of years it will be all "stockbrokers and fashion models."

The real workers' neighborhoods have a different "West" clientele. The dropouts squat there. The radical students squat. The Autonomen squat. The skinheads squat. The street gangs squat. The only Berlin gangs that are not squatting somewhere in East Berlin are the Turkish gangs, because East Berlin is too dangerous for them. Not many East Berliners had ever seen a Turk before the Wall came down, but they must have heard that West Berliners didn't like Turks, because they made it a mark of sophistication to dislike them, too. The polls that Wessis are always taking in East Berlin rank Turks as the people East Berliners "hate most" (though, judging by the conditions in which their own Vietnamese migrant workers are forced to live, and the confusion and loneliness of those workers, it is safe to say that they are being disingenuous). The Turkish kids here, being smart, have kept their squats in Neukölln and Kreuzberg, where they are in fact helpful and agreeable neighbors.

There are a lot of empty buildings in East Berlin. Some of the early projects—the hideous tile apartment blocks along the Karl-Marx-Allee, which runs east from Alexanderplatz—are empty because the housing institutes that control them are waiting for windfall rents when the capital arrives. In some of the smaller buildings only three or four of twenty or thirty flats have tenants. East Berliners talk a lot about the market, but they do not have much to say about the social contract. People in East Berlin get rich being "capitalists," like Wessis. They speculate on their neighbors' apartments. They sell fake insurance and phony stocks. Hustlers roam the corridors of the Charité—the biggest East Berlin hospital—demanding money from patients for the ambulance rides that brought them there, and the patients pay, because difficult patients under the old regime used to wake up from operations and discover that the surgeon had removed their kidney and put it in a transplant bank for the families of the Politburo. The East Berliners are scared of the Wessis now, and scared of each other. They are scared of losing their jobs, scared of not being able to pay for the flats they have, scared of not being able to give a "West" life to their children. It isn't just a problem for the poor. By the end of the year, three-quarters of the scientists at the Academy of Sciences in East Berlin will be out of work. Most of the teachers at Humboldt University are already out of work. They were fired for incompetence—the argument was that they were not as qualified as West Berlin teachers, and that their students would suffer—and by the end of a year's reprieve all the good teachers had gone and only the terrible ones had stayed. West Berlin students, who always considered themselves more spiritual than other West German students, complain that now the talk at school is all about money. They say that students come to their classes from East Berlin and sit in the front row in "environmentally correct" hand-knit sweaters and interrupt everybody with their terrible accents, and after they parade their innerness by talking about serious things, they want to know how to get ahead, how to get rich on what they learn, how to beat the other guy, even if the subject is Renaissance poetry or analytic philosophy. Mainly, they want to know how to make a deal on their grandmother's apartment. Real estate is the only currency they have.

∞

Before the Wall fell, East Berlin was a restricted city, like Moscow. You couldn't move there without permission, and if you got it you had a certain status in the G.D.R. Your invitation to Berlin carried the imprimatur of the Party, or the Stasi, or the important research institutes or government offices, and if your job was good, it didn't matter so much if you lived in a project or didn't have a telephone or if your flat was moldy. It was no surprise to East Berliners that 30 percent of the people in Marzahn, the worst of the projects— Germans call them "sleeping cities"—voted Communist last year, or that the deputy mayor of Berlin, a research pharmacist named Christina Bergmann, who ran as a Social Democrat, talked proudly about her flat in one of the other sleeping cities, Hellersdorf. About four hundred and fifty thousand people live in the projects of Marzahn, Hellersdorf, and Hohenschönhausen, and the average age is twenty-three. Marzahn was built in 1976 and is already a slum by any Western standard—there are said to be more gangs there, and more crime, than anywhere else in the city. It is hard for a stranger to see much of a difference between Marzahn and Hellersdorf, which is only eight years old, but Berliners see it. Hellersdorf people still associate the place with a kind of privilege, and they hang flower boxes from their windowsills and their balcony railings, and when they have the cash they fill their tiny apartments with West German stereos and television sets and complicated module furniture. Hellersdorf was a slum designed as a showplace, but the streets are alleys, and some have never been paved, and it is still impossible for most people to get a telephone.

One of the problems for planners in Berlin—and one reason so few builders want to get involved in East Berlin housing—is what to do with projects like Marzahn and Hellersdorf, with their staggering concentration of people. It would be cheaper to tear down the sleeping cities and start all over than to renovate and restore them, but no one knows where to put half a million Berliners in the meantime, and even if there *were* someplace to put them, the politics of relocation in Berlin would be daunting. Planners at the

Stadtforum—the commission set up to advise on the unification of the two Berlins and the planning of the capital—want to restore the housing that exists now, to keep people where they live and where they have friends and neighbors and playmates for their children, but it is one thing to restore a solid building that has survived the Allied bombings and forty-six years of neglect and another to take on projects that are only a few years old and were built so cheaply and so badly to begin with that they are already falling down. A lot of private housing in East Berlin is being restored now—houses that were owned or inherited or claimed as family property when the government changed, or apartment buildings that were claimed by old owners or sold by Treuhand. People with real privilege in the East—Stasi officers, Party functionaries, compliant artists and intellectuals and performers— often had permission to keep their family house, or to buy into a housing cooperative that the state managed. But there were never that many houses in Berlin for them, given the fact that 45 percent of "old" Berlin was lost in the bombings, and that anything solid built since then was built in West Berlin.

∞

In 1927, a radical German architect named Ludwig Hilberseimer came up with a plan to create a "new" Berlin by leveling the entire center of the city and starting over. The plan was famous in modernist circles—like Le Corbusier's *plan voisin* for central Paris— and infamous almost everywhere else people talked about architecture, because the early modernists like Hilberseimer and Le Corbusier believed that you could literally "build" social change by taking over the social environment and shaping it to control what you thought values and behavior should be. The critics (talking about Le Corbusier) called these plans a "Trojan horse of Bolshevism," but in fact they attracted ideologues on the left *and* the right, wherever the state wanted to control people in cities and how they lived and where they lived, because the random and chaotic spread of cities—the mix in cities—has always produced contacts, and politics, that are more anarchic than obedient. The plans led to Brasília, and to the Socialist new towns of France and Sweden. They led to the fascist fantasy of society as a *Gesamtkunstwerk,* and to Albert Speer's "Germania." They led to a couple of generations of postwar planners who meant quite well in believing they could draft human satisfaction on blueprints and sewage maps and demography charts, and to a couple of generations of developers who needed a respectable utilitarian pitch to cover for their exploitations. Hilberseimer never got to raze Berlin. The war did it for him, and the Wall kept it that way, and the irony is that now Berlin *needs* planning. There is not much of what the planners call an infrastructure in the East—meaning an infrastructure adequate by Western standards. The city has to lay trunk lines in East Berlin and install hundreds of thousands of telephones (right now, nobody in West Berlin, including the mayor and the president of Germany, can get a call through to East Berlin), and the demand for lines is so daunting that the Bundestag may have to exempt Berlin from the public-service laws and sell the telephone system to private companies. The city has to build roads to accommodate the traffic from hundreds of thousands of new cars. The city has to link the two Berlins with coherent public transportation and see that children can get to school and grown-ups can get to work and patients can get to the hospital. The city has to join the electric lines and the gas lines and the sewage pipes, and now that the East belongs to the West the city also has to figure out where to put the Berlin waste, because in the old days West Berlin paid East Berlin to take its waste, and East Berlin dumped it in Brandenburg. The city has to take this new Berlin and connect it to the land around it, because right now West Berlin stops where the Wall stood, and East Berlin, having been a restricted city, stops at the city limits and turns abruptly into pastures.

Berlin needs all this now—before Berliners can settle down to their united city, before the rhythms of ordinary life and trade can begin to become apparent. The decision to move the government here has put a stop to whatever was "natural" in the new Berlin. Even the Berlin advocates—the people who said that Bonn was a hothouse, and that the politicians in Bonn were making laws about life in Germany with no real experience of life in Germany—admit that moving the government to Berlin has ended an exceptionally open moment, though they also admit that there would be much less money for that moment if the government had decided to stay home.

People began "planning" Berlin long before the capital vote in

June. Last January, the Deutsches Architektur-Museum in Frankfurt and the *Frankfurter Allgemeine Zeitung* asked seventeen architects (only a few of them German) to imagine the new Berlin, and in March a show of their blueprints and maquettes opened, called "Berlin Morgen." The results did not solve the plumbing problem here, or come to grips with the problem of whether Berlin should have a central train station, with spoke lines moving people out of the city, or a ring of stations, with branch lines moving people into the city. One architects' collective, called Coop Himmelblau, from Vienna wanted the middle of Berlin to look like children's building blocks. Zaha Hadid, who comes from Baghdad, wanted to paint Berlin red and brown. Giorgio Grassi, the Italian architect, wanted to turn Berlin into an op-art experience by making patterns of windows all over the city, and Jean Nouvel, the French architect, wanted to link Berlin semiologically, so to speak, by writing things like "Protect Me From What" and "Grass Roots Agit" on the buildings. While the developers were making their deals with Treuhand and the architects were fantasizing, the Stadtforum tried to negotiate among the citizens' groups and government groups and interest groups and business groups, and come up with some ideas about what Berlin might actually look like, and how it would grow, and in what direction, and where in fact the center of town would be, not to mention where Germany's government would be.

The Stadtforum was put together by Volker Hassemer, who is the minister for urban development and environment in Berlin. Hassemer used to be the minister for culture. He made his name promoting Berlin (and buying talent for Berlin) as a cultural center. He was a fierce Berlin advocate in the capital campaign. His plan was to center the government on the Museumsinsel, in the Spree—the island where Unter den Linden meets the old Marx-Engels-Platz, and where some of the great public buildings of neoclassical nineteenth-century Berlin, like the National Gallery and the Pergamon Museum, still stand—and, while it is unlikely that Helmut Kohl will move into the Pergamon, Hassemer got to be known in Bonn as someone who understood Kohl's Berlin ambitions. In April, he called on some local planners and architects who had been meeting informally to talk about Berlin, and eventually he put together a group of sixty experts and advocates and politicians to meet a couple of times a month and report back to him with recommendations. The group meets now in an old insurance building in West Berlin, and has a *Werkbank* of young town planners and programmers doing research and putting together statistics, but there is not much the experts and advocates and politicians agree on. The traffic people want to turn the Leipzigerstrasse into a six-lane highway, and the planners—many of them are disciples of Helga Fassbinder, the planner who advised on the restoration of Rotterdam, and who sits on the Stadtforum board and tries to convert the traffic people to "a Dutch solidarity with nature"—want to make neighborhoods where people live and work, and the real-estate people want to raise the air rights in the center of town from four to nine stories (the Allies fixed them at seventy meters, because of air traffic), and the businessmen want to put parking lots under the Potsdamer Platz, and the politicians, who talk about putting "the heart of Germany in the heart of Berlin," want the best land for their offices. There is so much data already on the new Berlin that the only person with any idea of *how* much is a young woman paying her way through a doctorate in comparative religion at the Free University by working the Stadtforum computer, and there is so much fashionable theory loose about "the idea of Berlin" that Hassemer invited Jacques Derrida and Wim Wenders to contribute to the discussion.

Hassemer wants a glamorous Berlin—one of his ideas for solving the Berlin housing problem was to take the eighteen thousand bureaucrats at the Social Security office and send them to Bonn when the capital moves here. But, for a politician, he seems to appreciate Berlin's complicated character. A couple of years ago, he stopped the mayor, Eberhard Diepgen, from rebuilding the palace—it was the Prinz Albrecht Palace—where the Gestapo had had its headquarters, and kept the site in rubble for an exhibit called "Topography of the Terror," and people on the left acknowledged that "Hassemer has learned about fighting for the revelation." He is certainly as credible in Berlin's defense as Diepgen or any of the other Christian Democrats who run the city in a very *berlinerisch* coalition with the Social Democrats. Berlin politicians do not have much of a reputation for brilliance or charisma. Hassemer was one of the good ones—the ones who used to be sent here from the Bundesrepublik, to put in time for their parties—and he was also one of the few who stayed. He was not brilliant, but he was an oddity in a city where the resident politicians were provincial if not corrupt and the mayors came and went according to the city's real-estate and construction scandals. Hassemer's enthusiasm for the city, and maybe his arrogance about the city, kept him clean.

There were a lot of protests here when the Potsdamer Platz was sold—people who opposed the sale say "donated"—to Daimler-Benz. (Actually, Daimler got the Platz from Potsdamerstrasse to Eichhornstrasse, and Sony Europa, the department-store chain Hertie, and the electronics company Asea-Brown-Boveri divided the rest.) Hassemer tried to appease the protesters by persuading Daimler and the other investors to let their architect, Richard Rogers, design a project for the Potsdamer Platz that would make them happy *and* make the Berliners happy, but the Stadtforum was planning a competition for the Platz, and had set conditions involving the ratio of private to public transportation and of commercial to residential space, and Daimler had declared Rogers's plan to be "outside" the competition and thus the rules of the competition. In effect, it was already outside them, because Daimler paid for it. Hassemer says now that the plan was never meant to be binding—that it was intended to open discussion about the neighborhood, to stimulate "the idea of Berlin." But the Stadtforum people were furious, and it didn't matter to them that, whatever its problems, the Rogers plan was beautiful, or that it turned two-thirds of the Platz into public park, or that Rogers himself called it "A People's Place." When all the designs were in, they chose a model for the Potsdamer Platz by a couple of Munich architects named Heinz Hilmer and Christoph Sattler that reminded some Berliners of the "Trojan horse of Bolshevism" and others of something Speer might have submitted. In fact, it was mainly ugly. Daimler and the other investors in the Potsdamer Platz called it "provincial" and "mediocre" and "a disgrace," and threatened to take their money out of the project unless the plan they paid for was used. Edzard Reuter said that Berlin was, after all, not Posemuckel—Posemuckel is the German Podunk—but "the German metropolis in Europe."

∞

The old West Berlin radical architect Hardt-Waltherr Hämer is one of six architects on the Stadtforum's "creative review" board. Right now, Hämer is in charge of a city project for what he calls the "step-by-step renewing" of thirty thousand more Kreuzberg apartments, as well as, in the East, fifty thousand Tiergarten apartments and a hundred thousand apartments in "the real Prenzlauer Berg," which is desperately poor—so it isn't surprising that he was one of the architects who disapproved of the Daimler-Benz sale. He thought that giving the most interesting part of the city to a company that makes so much of its money producing arms was a disastrous "signal about Berlin" to begin with, and became an even worse signal when the job of "translating" between the city and its investors was done on the investors' checkbook. He says that money for projects like his Prenzlauer Berg project, which are intended to confirm "the value of usage over time," and to give people a chance to work on their own homes and their own neighborhoods at a moment when jobs in Berlin are scarce—and maybe even keep them from chasing rainbows in West Germany—has been held up because Bonn is really only interested in projects with "traditional investors," by which he means not neighbors with time to work but corporations like Daimler-Benz with power to confer. Hämer knows that the power of West German capital to remake Berlin will help East Berliners—especially given the distress in East Berlin, and the longing of East Berliners for change. But he also knows that it will not do much to help those East Berliners think about their lives and their part of the city in a processual way, in the "step-by-step" way he and his friend Helga Fassbinder admire, and that a rampant exploitation of East Berlin, whether you call it "colonialism" or "conquest" or "the Wild West in the East" (he prefers to call it "two continental plates colliding"), will have a substantial if not a sinister effect on the mentality of everybody here.

The truth is that neither the subsidized island city that was West Berlin nor the subsidized Communist city that was East Berlin has had any real experience of venture capital or a buccaneer market. Neither side really understands what is happening to the city now, or how different it is from other Western cities, or why, with Treuhand as the biggest landlord in East Berlin, and the city itself the second biggest, investors are not much interested in consulting or cooperating with the people who live there. Treuhand's charter is to privatize, and nothing else. It is not legally accountable to anything but its board and its balance sheets, and it does not have any of the checks and balances of productive West German companies—which have union contracts and workers sitting on the board and are part of a carefully calibrated arrangement between labor and management to meet West Germany's growth schedules and economic directives.

Christina Bergmann, the deputy mayor, is the Berlin minister for work and women—which means that she is the minister who usually has to take on Treuhand in an emergency. She was never in politics until the Wall fell. She is fifty-two, and says it was hard for anyone her age in East Berlin to trust a politician, and for a woman it was probably harder, because being a woman in East Germany was like "having somebody hold a big thumb on your head any time you tried to rise." But she wanted to do something. She joined the S.P.D. "because of Ostpolitik and Willy Brandt," and got on the Social Democratic list and, to her great surprise, did well in the elections here. Diepgen needed an East Berliner *and* a Social Democrat for his deputy, and he gave Frau Bergmann the job. She is one of three women—all of them Social Democrats—in the Senat, and one of her standing complaints at Treuhand is that women are always fired first when Treuhand lets workers go or sells a company to someone who lets them go. She is not a party to Treuhand's negotiations; Treuhand is a federal company, and local politicians have no authority there. When Frau Bergmann gets information about a deal in the works she goes to Treuhand and demands the plans and the contracts, and "negotiates" in the only way she can—by threatening public action against it.

Hämer says that the corruption at Treuhand is immeasurable—"out of every control"—and Frau Bergmann has had some experience of that. When Klingbeil wanted to buy the lightbulb factory, she tried to get the developers to guarantee the jobs, and lost. Then she tried to get them to keep on a few hundred extra workers for "reeducation," with the government paying their salaries, and lost. Then she tried to get them to promise to keep making lightbulbs, and lost again. East German politicians, and especially novices like Frau Bergmann, don't have the contacts in the West, or the favors to call in, that would give them leverage in this sort of negotiation. Berlin cynics would say that this is why she got her job to begin with, but in the end she won.

Only about forty thousand workers are training for new jobs in East Berlin. About thirty thousand more are supposed to be going into "environmental" community programs, and will presumably be trained to restore houses and plant trees and clean up pollution, with Berlin organizing the programs and Bonn paying for them out of federal taxes. Everybody in West Germany was taxed an extra 7 percent this year to help pay for unification, and paid a special surcharge of twenty-five pfennigs on every liter of gasoline and heating oil. The VAT—which is a sales and service tax—went up from 12 to 14 percent. Politicians on the left want some of that money used for public-works projects, something on the order of the W.P.A. projects in America during the Depression—they talk about creating four hundred and fifty thousand jobs in East Germany that way—but the conservatives who run the country say that works projects are "against the ethic of a free market," no matter how much East Germany, which is dangerously polluted, needs them or wants them. In Berlin, being against the ethic of a free market used to mean being a Communist; now it means being worried.

∞

One of the nicest buildings in East Berlin is a turn-of-the-century house on the corner of Behrenstrasse and Glinkastrasse, just down the street from the Komische Oper. It has arched windows framed by delicate fluted columns, a stone eagle peering out of its rounded cornice, and a coat of thick, cream paint that sets it off from the gray stone buildings around it. The Stasi, which used the building to spy on the missions and embassies in the neighborhood, restored it in 1988. (The policeman who guards it now says that that was the last thing the Stasi did in East Germany.) Today, twenty East and West Berliners work there for a man named Joachim Gauck, a Lutheran pastor of remarkable fortitude who helped disband the Stasi in the months before Germany was united, and has the unenviable job of putting its files in order so that the four million East Germans and two million West Germans in those files will be able to read what their friends and neighbors said about them to the secret police.

The Stasi files are arguably the most dangerous and damaging documents in East Germany. Michael Zabel, a West Berliner with a law degree who used to work for the Berlin Data Protection Agency and now works for Pastor Gauck, running the office that will actually release those files to the people in them, says that so many East Germans informed so much on other East Germans that he counts them in miles: fifty miles of Stasi files in Berlin alone, and another seventy-five miles in the Stasi's fifteen district headquarters. The government figures that it will take three thousand people just to guard the files once they are open to the Stasi's victims, in January next year. Two thousand people are already guarding them now.

In the winter of 1989, just after the Wall fell, East Germans occupied Stasi offices all over East Germany, and when the Stasi fled they took what they could carry—usually the files involving *them* or the files on important new East German politicians, which could be sold or used as blackmail. The information they had was a kind of hard currency. It bought Deutsche marks. It bought protection. Everybody wanted it. The press wanted it—magazines like *Der Spiegel* and *Stern* bought so many files from Stasi that every week for a year somebody "pure" from East Germany was exposed at the newsstands as a Stasi agent or informer. Bonn wanted it—and got *its* files from the East German interior minister, Peter-Michael Diestel. So many people wanted to make use of the Stasi files, and were stealing or selling or destroying Stasi files, or trading Stasi files for protection, that one horrified painter from the Neues Forum actually disappeared with the Erfurt files, occasionally sending word that he was keeping them safe until the Stasi's victims were free to read them.

He had a point, because there were months in the fall of 1989 and the winter of 1990 when people in East German towns could walk right into a Stasi headquarters that was being occupied, and find a friend, and walk out with the files they wanted. Little by little, the files were closed, and most of the stealing stopped, though the files in Berlin—they are stored in the Stasi headquarters here, in blue and orange folders—were broken into last year, and the guards say that probably the only safe files are the files in Cottbus, which are in a bunker in the middle of a forest. One of the problems for Gauck's commission is that Erich Mielke, the Stasi boss, didn't like computers. He was an old man—eighty-two when the Wall fell—and he liked to say that he was too old for computers. When East Berliners took over his headquarters, the only computerized files they found were the master codes and the Stasi's personnel files of officers, agents, and informers, and those files were on BASF disks and programs that Mielke seems to have bought from West Germany with a busload of political prisoners. The six million "victims" files that those officers, agents, and informers had produced were all over East Germany in their folders.

Joachim Lass was one of the East Berliners who occupied the Stasi headquarters. He is a gentle, middle-aged man from Hellersdorf, and when the Wall fell he had a reasonable job at the East German Labor Ministry, but his office was infiltrated by Stasi, and on the first day of the occupation he left work and walked into the Stasi headquarters, on Normannenstrasse, "out of curiosity," and saw the interrogation rooms and the cells and the cries of "Help!" scratched into the walls, and that day he joined the Berlin burgher committee and volunteered for the occupation. He says now that the problems with the Stasi files began that day, when it was clear that nobody in the building, not even the Stasi guarding the files, knew anything about the fancy West German software with the master codes and the personnel files. The burgher committee didn't know anything, and the Citizens' Round Table—people from the government and the parties and from Neues Forum and the other citizens' groups, who were pretty much running East Berlin then—didn't know anything. They started negotiating with the Stasi, and eventually—it took three months, because at first the Stasi refused to talk about the disks unless someone in charge promised immunity from prosecution—they made a deal by which the Stasi got to destroy its personnel files in exchange for opening the files with the master codes.

It was not a deal that went down well in East Germany. Most East Germans would have agreed with Lass, who wanted to see all the files saved, whether or not anyone got to read them, and who quit the occupation after he found out what had happened. The East Germans were left with their folders, and with the codes for sorting them, but there was no agreement on how to use them, or on who should see them, and after unification Bonn closed the files until the Bundestag could draft a law on the conditions of access. There was no way to stop the leaks, though, or the damage they did, or the breakdowns and suicides they caused. Two men in Gauck's office leaked the story about Lothar de Maizière having been a salaried Stasi informer. De Maizière was the Christian Democratic prime minister of East Germany from April of 1990 until unification in December, and at the time of the leak he was running for a seat in the Bundestag, and was certain to win it. The men who leaked the file were fired, but no one at Gauck's commission denied the story, and after the campaign it was rumored that de Maizière had bought protection in Bonn early on, by leaking information himself.

Some Germans wanted the fate of the Stasi files left to the five new states. They thought that the files were East Germany's business, and that only East Germans could know what they meant and whom they would hurt, and, as victims *and* informers, had to come to terms with each other alone. The other argument was formal. People who wanted the files under federal law said that the Stasi, having been a state police, was the responsibility of the state as it existed now—that is, the united German state, run from Bonn and three-quarters "Western." They thought there should be formal and uniform laws of access, and said that, anyway, West Germans were the only people in the country who knew anything about administering law, about legal procedure and due process— which, unhappily, was true.

Hansjürgen Garstka, a West German jurist who runs the Data Protection Agency in Berlin, tells me that after a year of experience with East Germans he has just begun to realize how difficult it is for them to understand the law as protection. He says they were controlled in every detail of their lives for so long that now they think of "law" as a kind of control too, something necessarily against them. "They are full of heart, but they have no feeling for *Rechtsstaatlichkeit,*" Garstka says, "and in their hands the law breaks down." East Berliners are still calling up their friends at the Stasi archives and demanding to know whether someone informed on them in, say, 1975, and who that person was, and where to find him, and when West Berliners tell them that they shouldn't just call like that—that they should wait for a law to pass so *everyone* can call—the East Berliners think the West Berliners are talking like policemen.

At first, a lot of people didn't think East Germany could survive opening the Stasi files. They thought that what little community Germans in the East had would disappear if they knew the worst about one another, and how casual most of their betrayals had been. One of my Berlin friends says, "Imagine this. You sit down, you read what your daughter said about you, you read what *I* said about you. You want to get a knife and kill us. But what have we really said? And by what unspeakable means did the Stasi come by this information? How can you know the truth?" My friend was one of the people who wanted to burn the files, or lock them in vaults for some other, stronger generation, or even ignore them, the way the Poles have ignored the crimes of their secret police. He was frightened, because so many people who had been betrayed wanted vengeance.

No one who has worked on the Stasi files, or knows anything about the Stasi files, has had an easy time deciding what the law should be, or how to determine access. Spiros Simitis, who was the West German adviser to Pastor Gauck's commission, and was skeptical at first, decided finally that people had to have access, because they were so determined to have it. He says that nothing good will come out of this, except that maybe Germans will see how disgusting the entire system was—how everybody ended up lying. The agents lied. The informers lied. They made up stories to get more money, or to cancel the lies about *them,* and everyone was dirtied, everyone was damaged. Civil libertarians like Professor Simitis are more uneasy now about government access, because the government will be able to use the Stasi files on the ground of "national security"—a concept that governments tend to define loosely when it suits their interest. Professor Simitis thinks that information gathered by "illegal and unacceptable means" is, logically, illegal and unacceptable information. He is uneasy because

German secret services—and, by extension, a lot of other secret services—will be using the files, along with public prosecutors and the police, who will be able to subpoena information for criminal investigations. Stasi members can be prosecuted now only for what the Germans call "ordinary crimes," like torture and murder and—there is some argument on this—spying. When prosecutors looked for actionable ordinary crimes involving Erich Mielke, the ones they came up with had nothing to do with the terror Mielke inflicted on East Germany for so many years but with his pocketing Stasi money, and murdering a couple of policemen in 1931.

∾

The Berlin philosopher Ernst Tugendhat grew up in Mies van der Rohe's famous Tugendhat House, in Brno. He fled the Anschluss, lived in Venezuela, studied in America, and in 1949 arrived in West Germany, and he says that the best thing about being in Germany for the past forty years is that "we had to say 'I am a citizen of the Bundesrepublik.' We couldn't say 'I am a German.' " He is leaving now, with sadness and some relief, and one reason for the relief has to do with his not wanting to be a witness to what he calls the "annexation" of the G.D.R. He does not find Germans very admirable right now. He says that Detlev Rohwedder used to tell visitors to Treuhand, "I have so-and-so-many colleagues, and so-and-so-many Ossis," and that Erich Böhme, who came from *Der Spiegel* to take over the old Communist paper *Berliner Zeitung*, tells *his* visitors, "I have Wessis and Ossis who sit at the same desk and do the same work, and the Ossis get half the pay." Tugendhat's own colleagues at the Free University were so worried about having too many Ossis in their classes that they introduced what amounts to "an East German numerus clausus." What saddens Professor Tugendhat is that for forty years West German intellectuals were engaged in Germany's problems—they spoke up, wrote things, got excited, signed petitions, organized protests, and did what they could to encourage what they took to be a democratic "European" consciousness—but now that "this enormous thing" has happened, all that most of them seem to do is stand back and watch, dumbfounded, unable to contribute. Tugendhat says he can count the few who did contribute. Spiros Simitis spoke up. Jürgen

Habermas spoke up—he wanted the two Germanys to write a constitution together, and see what history they shared, or wanted to share, and *then* decide if they wanted to unite. Günter Grass spoke up—he said he was against the unification, because "Auschwitz speaks against even a right of self-determination," let alone against "a strong, united Germany." But he had been to Calcutta and perhaps encountered karma, because when he came home he dropped out and left Berlin for Schleswig-Holstein, where his nearest neighbors are cows. Many of the other important West German intellectuals never spoke up at all, except to speculate on the confusion. Tugendhat says that maybe it was impossible for them to say much. The East demanded unity, and there was no way to avoid or deny the terrible differences between East and West. Tugendhat remembers when one of the best philosophers from Humboldt University came to lecture at the Free University, and ten minutes into his lecture all the Western philosophers were sleeping. What troubles Tugendhat is that the *imagination* to do something to ease those encounters or stop the humiliation is gone.

In the beginning, it was fashionable for West Berliners to have what the kids here call a *vorzeige* Ossi—a demonstration-model East German—to hang around with and show off. Now the West Berliners complain because the East Berliners are passive and don't make the effort to get to know *them;* the East Berliners complain because the West Berliners make them feel like poor tourists in a foreign country, unless those Wessis are the "bad" brash Wessis and are with an Ossi on business. There is so much bad faith and bitterness and suspicion between East and West Berliners that sometimes the only thing they have in common is what Wiglaf Droste calls their "barking, bad-manners Berlin chauvinism." He says that before the Wall came down he thought, We've got enough fascists here, we don't need more. Now the situation is so disturbing that the only time he feels "a nice, peaceful atmosphere" in Berlin is when he takes a walk from Schlesiches Tor to Schöneberg at four in the morning. He says that the famous scene has gone, because the people who made it are either leftover radicals, who still talk about preserving the right of the proletariat to "choose" to live without plumbing, or leftover punks, who sound like the old S.A., and demonstrate for Saddam Hussein, shouting

"The Jews are responsible." And, according to Wiglaf, the scene in East Berlin is not much better, because people *there* are either too naïve—long beards and "Man is good" and God instead of politics—or too angry to think clearly and be professional and try to get on with their lives. There are hot lines now in East Berlin called *Wut-Telefon*—rage telephones—where people call up and scream about hating Wessis, hating the government they elected, hating the things that never work, including the telephone that goes dead in the middle of their call. There are "rage newspapers," like the tabloid called *Super! Zeitung,* which sells five hundred thousand copies a day in the five new states and features stories like one about a "boastful Wessi" who was beaten to death with a beer bottle in the town of Bernau; it ran with the headline "ALL BERNAU IS HAPPY."

The truth is that East and West Berlin may not have much to say to each other for a couple of generations. Tilo says that one of his West Berlin friends, who runs a performance group in East Berlin, told him it was easier to work in France or Italy than with his own East German group, because "the actors who are open don't have skills, and the ones who have them are closed, and sit in their apartments, working, and never go out into the world." Wolf Jobst Siedler says it is even worse with *his* colleagues in East Berlin, because they are fifty or sixty years old and literally speak another language when it comes to the world—they don't know how to read a local paper like the *Tageszeitung,* let alone a real European paper—and this makes conversation impossible. West Berliners talk a lot about language when they talk about East Berliners. Brigitte Hammer, who works at a museum here, said the other day that collaborating with the curators in East Berlin was impossible, "because you speak the same language and mean something very different—and the difference starts with the word 'art.' " Frau Hammer tells a story about trying to put together an exhibit of Berlin art, East and West. East Berlin was supposed to send seventy-five paintings and West Berlin was supposed to send seventy-five paintings. The difference was that the West Berlin jury held a competition, got two hundred and eighty submissions, and *then* chose the paintings, whereas the East Berlin jury made a list of sixty painters from the state artists' association and presented the list, and that was that.

My friend Dorothea plays the flute, and sometimes she plays with a young East Berlin pianist near the Frankfurter Allee. The first time she went to his place, to practice, she thought it was his mother's or his grandmother's apartment, because it was full of terrible Romantic paintings and fake-Biedermeier furniture, and there was a brown tablecloth on the table. But he was proud of his flat. He was very concerned about having a nice place to show his Wessi flutist, and Dorothea says that for her the hardest thing about their friendship was accepting that "nice" meant something very different to him than it did to her—or probably would have to any West Berlin student—and that even music meant something different, since he will play only Bach, and Dorothea and her West Berlin friends are interested in trying the new French composers who write for synthesizers. She often wonders what it's like to be an East German who has worked as hard as her friend has to make something of himself in a terrible system, and finds suddenly that everything in his life, from his taste in music to his taste in table-cloths, has to be "adjusted" to another system. Many people here wonder. Hansjürgen Garstka, who is forty-four, asked me, "What can I possibly say to an East Berlin scientist who, after years of try-ing, finally gets permission to travel, and buys an old piece of West-ern equipment for his lab, and spends a year rebuilding it, and is proud of it—and then scientists from the West arrive and say, 'This East German science is ridiculous,' and his lab is closed." The trou-ble is that he can't really say anything.

∞

The night Germany united, the actor Hanns Zischler had a read-ing at his apartment, in Charlottenburg, a few blocks from the Paris Bar. He invited some West Berlin friends, and his West Berlin friends brought East Berlin friends, and at midnight—"at the first stroke of 'Germany,'" Zischler says—everyone had finished din-ner and was sitting in the living room in a circle, and he was read-ing aloud from Goethe's "Das Märchen." The moment was so unreal, he says, and so extraordinary, that he knew it couldn't be grasped in any "orderly German way," and he was "clutching at Goethe" to try to explain it. The East Germans thought they had come for a party. It was their first "West party," and when they had to sit down and listen to literature they were bored, and a little bewildered, but in the end, Zischler says, "they accepted what you might call the subtext—which was that this immense, incomprehensible event, this sudden metamorphosis of Germany, was not something any of us, East Berliners or West Berliners, could master." Zischler often has readings in his flat—they are part of the Berlin scene, and people like to be invited. This time, he didn't know what to read. He had thought of choosing something political, but finally he chose Goethe's fairy tale—because it seemed to him that the presence of so many East Berliners in a Charlottenburg living room was as fantastical, in its way, as the lilies and will-o'-the-wisps and talking cauliflowers that consort in Goethe's story. He and his friends heard the whistle of the night train, heading east to the Zoo Station, and knew that for the first time in more than forty years it wouldn't be stopping at a checkpoint, or taking on policemen. No one knew what to say, so they kept listening to Goethe.

STASI

(MAY 1992)

Wolf Biermann is a folksinger. When he was a young man, in East Berlin, he was called the Bob Dylan of the German Democratic Republic. He would come to the Alexanderplatz with his guitar and sing sad, intimate protest songs that were really poems —about being German and wanting simple, impossible things like truth and peace, and not knowing how to find them—and thousands of East Berliners would come to hear him. They thought that hearing Biermann sing in the Alexanderplatz was just like hearing Dylan sing in Berkeley during the Vietnam War—except, of course, that in their case the police came too, and stopped the concerts, and sometimes arrested a couple of hundred kids and put them in jail for a few cold nights of self-criticism and reflection. Usually they arrested Biermann, too. They did not know what to make of this *Liedermacher* who claimed to be a socialist, like them —a better socialist than they were—and then insisted that the past was *theirs,* the Wall was theirs (when everyone knew that Nazism and the Cold War were something West Germans had invented), and even that their socialism was corrupted and cruel, and not at all like the "true" socialism of poets and folksingers and ecological housewives and peace-movement Protestant pastors.

Biermann was too famous to lock up for very long—to send to Waldheim or Cottbus until West Germany "bought" him out with hard currency and computer systems and limousines for the Politburo. Besides, Wolf Biermann made a convenient dissident, a symbol of East German tolerance, though the police preferred it when he sang for his friends, alone, in places that were less conspicuous than the center of the East German capital—in neighborhoods like Prenzlauer Berg, where a lot of the houses were still gutted from the war and nobody went except the kids who wanted to write or paint or start a rock band, and who were beginning to arrive from all over East Germany and squat in the abandoned houses until the government found them, and they became "tenants" and had to pay.

The police gave up on Biermann in the end. He asked permission to sing in West Germany—the West German Metal Workers Union had invited him to give some concerts—and they let him go, and somewhere between Cologne and Bochum he heard on a car radio that his East German citizenship had been "canceled," and he could not come home. He ended up back in Hamburg, where he was born, singing sad songs and writing sad poems about the corruptions of exile, and wondering why, for a *Liedermacher,* there seemed to be so few friendly, "socialist" alternatives to fighting devotedly for socialism in East Germany or fighting devotedly against it.

That was in November of 1976. By the time the Wall came down, Wolf Biermann was as much a stranger in East Germany as he claimed to be in West Germany. The young Prenzlauer Berg poets were writing Dada—which some of them believed was a French post-structuralist invention. The young *Liedermacher* were into punk rock and heavy metal. In Prenzlauer Berg, Wolf Biermann seemed as folkloric as his songs—an aging Hamburg hippie with a droopy mustache and a guitar-strap slouch who in moments of national nostalgia occasionally broke the charts, and was, in fact, suspected in the East of being a millionaire. The new *spiritus rector* of the Prenzlauer Berg scene was a poet named Alexander Anderson. He was not a very good poet, but as much as anyone else he was responsible for what in East Germany passed for bohemia. The French have a word for Anderson: he was *débrouillard,* which means he was foxy and knew his way around and was able to work the system in his own interests. He was famous in his small world as an organizer and entrepreneur. He had introduced the writers he knew to the rock groups he knew, and the rock groups to the painters, and he was famous for the parties he threw at his girlfriend's place—parties where the painters hung their pictures and the writers read their poems and the rock groups played their songs, and everybody had a good time and said that protest was indeed alive and well in East Germany. He had put together little homemade books of their drawings and verse and seen to it that the books were passed around Prenzlauer Berg. He had promoted the Prenzlauer Berg scene long before there was a scene—which meant that West Berliners looking for samizdat in East Berlin came to Prenzlauer Berg, and carried out the books and the paintings they saw there, and made the "West contacts" with galleries and publishers that brought in money and word processors and tubes of paint and, most important, the West Berlin attention that was an East Berlin artist's best protection. He was a constant and mysterious source of equipment and news and tapes and books by people no one in Prenzlauer Berg had ever heard of.

Anderson was sent West in 1986, but by the time he left he had got the poets in Prenzlauer Berg out of their squats and reciting Schwitters's sound poems and having debates about Jacques Derrida and Jean-François Lyotard and Jean Baudrillard, and convinced they were an avant-garde—not only post-structuralist but post-deconstructionist and post-materialist and postmodern and post-political and whatever other "post"s Anderson claimed were happening across the Wall. Being the children of police-state schools, they were often unburdened by poetics or aesthetics or craft. The Prenzlauer Berg style was to go home after one of Sascha Anderson's evenings and write a couple of hundred poems by morning and call it Dada, or City Lights, or simply cool. Sascha was cool. He cultivated a three-day beard, like Yasir Arafat and the men in American underwear ads, and wore an overcoat to his toes and little round granny glasses, and he kept his blond hair short and spiky. He never talked about the repression in East Germany. He seemed to be saying that the ultimate politics was no politics, and the ultimate protest was detachment, and possibly that the ultimate art was puerile or incomprehensible, or both, but no one really knew, because he never talked about what he thought. He never talked about himself at all. No one knew anything about Sascha Anderson. No one knew why the Stasi hadn't come for him earlier, though people assumed it was the Stasi who finally expelled him. His friends at home were happy to have Sascha Anderson in West Berlin, working to promote them. He was a one-man East-West cultural impresario, creating little sensations of celebrity and exchange—nothing, they said, like Wolf Biermann, who sat in Hamburg getting rich on sadness and sentiment. It was said that there was bad feeling between Biermann and Anderson, and that it was a matter of literature, because Biermann was an old-fashioned writer—a sixties sort of writer—and wrote what he felt in a thick, direct, embarrassing sort of way, while Anderson and his friends were allusive and modern and wrote things nobody could decipher. Or it was said that it was a matter of attitude, because Biermann had lost his cool and protested, while Anderson had waited and "done his thing" and let politics happen. Or that it was a matter of politics, because Biermann, whose father was a Jew, objected to German "pacifism" during the Gulf War—he said that being against war was like being *for* motherhood, and he didn't know what it meant, really—while Anderson, of course, never said anything about war. But in the end it turned out to be a matter of reputation.

Last spring, Biermann won the Georg Büchner Prize, which is the country's important literary prize and is given yearly to "writers and poets who write in German . . . and have had an important influence in shaping contemporary German culture." He accepted it formally in October, at a ceremony at the Rathaus in Darmstadt, where Büchner was born, and gave an angry speech about the "dark times" in Germany, and about what a real socialist like Büchner would have made of the socialists of the German Democratic Republic, who had kept their power because a hundred thousand Stasi kept everyone else spying on friends, and people were so compliant that they never produced a workers' movement like Solidarity or a rights movement like Chapter 77. He said there was not much courage in the G.D.R. There were a few courageous people—he named some of them—but in the end even the "opposition" turned out to be full of Stasi spies and informers, and he named some of *them*. The last informer on his list was Sascha Anderson. He did not say, "Sascha Anderson." He said, "The untalented bullshitter Sascha-Asshole, a Stasi spy, who is still playing the son of the Muse hoping that his files will never appear"—because everybody knew who Sascha was, everybody called him Sascha. Sascha had seen to his reputation. He was *débrouillard*. He was a paid informer. He was thirty-eight, and he had been spying on his friends, in East Germany and then in West Germany, since he was seventeen.

∾

There are people in Germany who believe that the Prenzlauer Berg scene was a Stasi invention, and that it was all about the German language—about controlling the political possibilities and "subversive" uses of German by taking a generation of would-be Biermanns and getting them out of the house to meetings and readings and underground presses, where they could be watched and encouraged to betray themselves, and then diverting them from politics and protest with obscure texts and sophisticated aesthetic models they had neither the education nor the experience nor, often, the wit to understand. Those people say to remember that Biermann's German—crude, concrete, and relatively "harmless" in West Germany—was considered wildly subversive in East Germany, whereas the "cloudy, metaphoric stuff" that Anderson was promoting was considered harmless in East Germany but was certainly sensational and subversive by West German standards. Of course, it is impossible to know if the Prenzlauer Berg style was a cynically programmed style, or a mirror image of the obfuscations of official agitprop, or a commentary on it, or a flight from it, or simply posturing adolescent verse. An old Prenzlauer Berg novelist named Adolf Endler replied to the Büchner speech by accusing Biermann of talking "Wehrmacht Deutsch" (the implication, according to Biermann, was that anyone who talked straight and told the truth was a fascist and should be put in army boots, along, perhaps, with Luther, Brecht, and Büchner), and, indeed, a German journalist I know says that after the speech she heard people at fashionable Hamburg dinner parties describing Biermann as "our best writer after Martin Luther." It may be that Germans today see "German" as carrying such moral imperatives because Germans have abused the language so often in the past, and in the interest of causes far more chilling than free verse. The Swiss novelist Jürg Laederach, who spends a lot of his time in Germany, once said that what makes Germany so merciless—viewed from across the Rhine in German-speaking Basel—is that Germans can use "acts of language" to exterminate.

Günter Grass, who was at Darmstadt with Biermann, accused Biermann of using "Stasi language" in his speech, and called him "Wolf Grand Inquisitor." Ulrich Greiner, the cultural editor of *Die Zeit,* accused him of putting the attack before the evidence, because he talked about "assholes," and another journalist said he was using the language of a "sixties radical in Earth shoes." Freimut Duve, the Social Democratic deputy, said in the *Frank-*

furter Rundschau that he didn't have manners and should certainly return his Büchner money, which amounted to thirty-six thousand dollars. And Laederach himself said that making political attacks on your poetry competition, so to speak, was "against the principles of political discourse." What they were saying was that Germans using "acts of language" to attack other Germans made everybody nervous.

Of course, the real attack was Anderson's. He may have written lines like "for i am your/sister your lap & the two/facelike mask without profile all/seizing a pot full of chaos full of holes/of the single-sciences" in Prenzlauer Berg, but the lines he wrote to his control, a couple of miles away at the Stasi complex on Normannenstrasse, were factual, plainspoken, direct, and damaging. The friends he betrayed—the ones who have started reading through Anderson's reports on *them*—say that they still admire at least his discipline, that as an informer Sascha was scrupulous. Sascha's reports were never cloudy, like his poems, or speculative or exaggerated or emotional, like the reports of a lot of other Prenzlauer Berg informers. They were models of accuracy, and even objectivity—the sort of work that gets passed around to first-year students in journalism schools. Maybe he should have been a journalist, because what gets written about Anderson in the newspaper now is rarely the "facts" about Anderson but an exploration of what the proper German feelings about Anderson should be. It is about what makes "good Germans" and what makes "bad Germans" and about whether good Germans turn into bad Germans if they accept an Anderson or tolerate or excuse an Anderson, or if they expose or reject or punish an Anderson.

The German government has an academy in Rome called Villa Massimo, and before the Büchner speech Anderson was invited to stay there for a couple of months. After the speech, some of the writers at the villa complained, and eventually—reluctantly—Anderson agreed to stay home. The *Süddeutsche Zeitung* reported it this way: "The Berlin poet Sascha Anderson, who is suspected of being a Stasi spy, has voluntarily renounced a grant at the Villa Massimo in Rome." Biermann thought it should have been reported *this* way: "Protests by all the grant holders at the Villa Massimo have forced the dabbler Alexander Anderson, who was unmasked as a long-term spy, to abandon his plans to go to Rome

at the expense of the German taxpayer." Anderson might have put
it a third way, if he were reporting to Normannenstrasse. He might
have written, "The Villa Massimo withdrew an invitation to the
Berlin poet Sascha Anderson, who was accused in October of informing for the Stasi, after the accusations were confirmed in January"—because that is what in fact happened.

∞

There was never a revolution in East Germany. People talk about
"the revolution," and the painter Bärbel Bohley is sometimes referred to as the "mother of the revolution," but the Wall came
down in East Germany because East Germany was literally coming apart—and it had very little to do with the Prenzlauer Berg
poets, or with the thousands of political prisoners, or even with the
crowds that marched in Leipzig and Dresden and Berlin chanting,
"We are the people!" East Germany fell because the state was
bankrupt, industry was bankrupt, agriculture was bankrupt, and
there was no money, and thus there was no way short of a mas-
sacre to stop East Germans from leaving. There was no way because East Germany had got to be too expensive and too
embarrassing for Mikhail Gorbachev's new *perestroika* East, and
in the end Gorbachev was happy to let it go.

Wolf Biermann said, in Darmstadt, that for him "We are the
people!" had less to do with the demonstrators of 1989 than with
the angry mob in *Danton's Death*—Büchner's 1835 play about the
Terror in France. The reference was instructive, because in Germany *Das Volk* have usually been invoked when lawlessness becomes "the law"—which is pretty much what happened in the east
of Germany during the sixty years most East Germans have been
alive. The revolution in East Germany was not the peaceful revolution of the Czechs, or the monetary revolution of the Hungarians, or the labor revolution of the Poles. In some ways, it was just
Germans following orders to be free. Hansjörg Geiger, a West
German jurist who runs the commission charged with providing
Germans with access to the reports filed on them by informers like
Sascha Anderson, says that sometimes he wishes the G.D.R. had
lasted one more year, and the economy had *totally* collapsed, so
that East Germans would be disabused of this myth of a revolution. Most East Germans *were* compliant, if not collaborative—

which is not to say that they were happy or satisfied with their lives. They organized, in the end, to be able to leave East Germany, not to reform or remake it.

No one knows anymore how many East Germans actually did inform for the Stasi—which was huge without them, proportionately many times bigger than the Gestapo. A lot of informers had more than one code name, and so far only about three thousand of the Stasi's victims have been able to see their files and match those code names to the man or woman who came over, say, on the night of February 12, 1979, for a game of checkers and a beer. The estimates now are up to three hundred thousand informers—which means that at any one moment over the last forty years as many as one East German in every fifty may have been informing on the rest. They produced eighty-eight million pages of microfilm, and the files themselves are enormous. The people at Geiger's commission—Germans call it the Stasi Commission—say that there are more than thirty-six thousand pages of files on Biermann alone (and they leak a lot of stories about what's in them, like the story about the two Stasi who spent their time monitoring a bug in Biermann's Hamburg apartment, and complained in their reports that he was always listening to the "Goldstein Variations"). Geiger says that the literary informers may have been considered less reliable than, say, the hospital informers or the factory informers—more imaginative, perhaps, more given to exaggeration—because so many of them seem to have been reporting on the same people. There are apparently six hundred names in the files on the novelist Christa Wolf, which means that virtually everyone Mrs. Wolf knew either was watched by informers or was an informer himself.

Sascha Anderson got his code names when he was starting out, in Dresden, and they were not very exciting. David Menzer was the first name, and then there was Fritz Müller and eventually Peters—and, as far as anyone knows, those were the names he kept. The most interesting thing about Anderson's arrangements with the Stasi in Dresden is that he and his controls—a major named Heimann and a colonel named Reuter—left their messages glued under the slot of a condom machine in the bathroom of a local café that Anderson and his friends on the Dresden arts scene frequented. Anderson may have been making a point about collaboration by choosing ordinary German names like Müller and Peters, but some of the names that informers chose, or their controls chose for them, were inspired. Leitz watched everybody. Pegasus flew, because he was watching people in the peace movement, and they traveled to meetings. Matisse watched painters. Hölderlin, of course, watched Prenzlauer Berg poets—which gives a measure of credibility to the theory that the Stasi knew exactly what they were doing when they chose the books that informers like Anderson circulated.

Some people think that the Stasi knew exactly what they were doing up to the moment the Wall fell—that not only Prenzlauer Berg but the revolution itself was, if not a Stasi plot, then, in a manner of speaking, a Stasi co-production, because the Stasi saw better than anyone else the changes coming, and wanted to play a profitable part in those changes. A writer named Henryk Broder is generally credited with the "Stasi revolution theory." Broder is a Polish-born Jew who lives and works in Germany, and it is his thesis that in 1986, when the Stasi produced a white paper setting the protocol for the end of a Communist G.D.R., they helped set the "revolution" in motion. "They jumped on the train and became the conductors" is the way he puts it. They became "progressive." They put their informers in place in the revolution, if not to avert it, then to control it, or co-opt it, or maybe just to launder themselves (like mafiosi with new names and new faces) into respectable and influential new German citizens. Three years later, they were heading the election lists, and running the companies in line for management buyouts, and even—or obviously—leading the burgher committees that "protected" the famous files at Stasi headquarters until the two Germanys voted to unite. Broder's field is not the Stasi. (Lately, it has been the history of the Jewish Cultural Federation in Germany between 1933 and 1941.) But he was caught up in the excitement of German unification, and then bothered by what he calls the "theology" of the discussions about unification. He discovered that many Germans had a biblical notion of history and thought of the division of Germany as "a kind of divine punishment for Auschwitz"—Günter Grass, for one, kept repeating his dictum that there could be no "Germany" after Auschwitz—and Broder doesn't believe in either divine punishment or collective guilt. He thought if you were German and started using the Holocaust as a measuring rod, you would have to divide Germany into an infinite number of "Germanys," and Germans would start thinking of themselves as victims again, and blaming Jews again—which was in fact what was happening in some of those discussions. So he started thinking about the Stasi, who made everyone a victim, and discovered that a good number of the victims were Stasi.

Of course, with three hundred thousand informers, the Stasi was not so much a mirror of East Germany; to a large extent, it *was* East Germany. It employed or involved so many East Germans that it is reasonable to assume that those Germans were various and disputatious, and that many of them were looking forward to democracy or to capitalism, or even to the possibility of not being Stasi. The Stasi were everywhere, and, for all practical purposes, they were everybody. Every church had Stasi, and so did every farm, factory, hospital, school, and housing project, and every political party with honorary access to the Communist parliament. You knew who the Stasi agents and officers were, and very often you knew, or suspected, who the informers were, and you accepted them—or, more accurately, made a marriage of convenience and followed the rules of that sort of marriage, and got used to having them around, and even felt that the problem of marriage was settled. I have met the "house Stasi" at pig cooperatives and chemical factories and pretty brick Lutheran churches, and last month I had a pleasant dinner with a philosopher from Humboldt University who had been informing on his department chairman. He confessed after the Wall came down, and was fired, and then he was reinstated when it turned out that nearly everybody else at Humboldt had been spying too. Now he was looking forward to a semester teaching in America, where he had heard there were still Marxist philosophers like him to talk to.

No one in Germany knows, really, what to do with so many informers. A lot of informers insist that they did no harm. They argue that with everybody spying on everybody else, there was really no such thing as privileged information, or even very secret information, in East Germany; that from the point of view of security or intimidation, a Stasi with "all the information" was no more useful to the state than a Stasi with no information—that "all the information" amounted to a kind of disinformation. The argument against them is, obviously, that for all their meaninglessly logged and catalogued facts and speculations and psychological profiles on the shelves in Normannenstrasse, there was the reality of the deportations and the damaged lives and the mysteriously failed careers and, of course, the political prisons where people were brutalized and tortured, and where many people died. Everyone knew the reality, and certainly the informers knew, whatever they say now about never hurting anybody or never doing anything "bad," or about "protecting" their friends by informing against them instead of leaving them to the surveillance of strangers. Obviously, not every Stasi liked the reality. The opposition was filled with Stasi who said they were going to build a Germany *without* Stasi. But whether or not they believed their lies, as people who lie professionally often do, the fact is that they were active in the revolution, and it is not surprising that some people concluded that they planned it.

∞

Ralf Kerbach is a thirty-six-year-old Berlin painter. He came West from Dresden, by way of East Berlin, in 1982, and now he lives in a Wedding loft, and his shows sell at the Eva Poll Gallery, in Tiergarten. He is what Germans call a "West person," by which they mean that he is easy and confident and open to the world. In Berlin, it is easy to tell a West person like Kerbach. He wears crewneck sweaters and faded T-shirts with his black jeans. His motorcycle jacket is authentic. It is a thick, worn, comfortable brown leather jacket—nothing like the slick black jackets with pleats and studs and too many zippers that East people trying to look like West people wear. He keeps his brown hair cut, and he shaves in the morning, and has a chipmunk smile and a high, narrow nose that seems to be sniffing something and makes him look like a young, dark Bobby Kennedy. East painters, with their serious shaggy mustaches, tend to look like Lech Walesa. People admire Kerbach. They admire his painting and his charm and his nice, fresh, friendly face. When he eats at Florian, which is down the street from Savignyplatz and one of the places to go in West Berlin, the women at the next table smile at him. The waiters ask him to draw on the tablecloth. And he often does, because he is an accommodating sort of person, quite unspoiled by the fact that he is famous. He says he always felt like a stranger in East Germany, but he likes the West, and the people around him and the art around him, and the fact that when he hangs a show, nobody from the police comes to take it down.

The worst thing that happened to Kerbach since he came West was the news about Sascha Anderson. Anderson was one of his oldest friends. They go back to Dresden—Kerbach was in the tenth grade and running in a track meet, and Anderson turned up, running next to him. "It was very crazy," Kerbach used to say when he talked about meeting Anderson. "Sascha knew me, and I didn't know him, and so it began." Now he shakes his head and laughs and says, "It began *and* ended that way," because in January this year the anchorman from *Brennpunkt* came to his loft with a camera crew, and asked to film him, and presented him with papers proving that Sascha Anderson had been spying on him, in East Germany and probably in West Germany, for nearly twenty years.

Kerbach has not been called to see his files, although he applied in January to see them, just after several million Germans saw *him,* on television, disbelieving and confused and staring at the anchorman's papers, telling no one in particular that he couldn't absorb such terrible information. It takes time for someone like Kerbach—someone "undamaged"—to see his files. They have to be processed, which means that somebody at the Stasi Commission has to go through them first and black out the damaging things in them about *other* people, the medical records they supplied or the fact that a friend's wife was sleeping with his next-door neighbor. Then, there is the question of priority. The people who get to see their files first are people who have been in prison because of the Stasi, or have lost their homes because of the Stasi, or have been deported and lost their East German citizenship, or have suffered in their education or their careers, or are over seventy-five and have less time than other people to wait in line. And then there is the question of logistics, because the files have to be transferred from the "archives" at Normannenstrasse to "reading rooms" in the old Interior Ministry, on Glinkastrasse, where members of the Stasi

Commission work, and the rule is that no more than thirty people can share a reading room.

Kerbach is not in a hurry, but he knows now that other people besides Anderson informed on him, and he wonders which of his friends used the code name Max Beckmann, because he assumes that Beckmann was another painter, and he says it's "awful" to think of painters informing on each other. He's interested in his files, but his files are not his life or his *Lebensinhalt*—his "life's contents"—the way they seem to be for Biermann, who comes to Berlin all the time to look at his thirty-six thousand pages. Kerbach thinks that maybe this is because the work of painters is painting, whereas the work of East German writers is necessarily the exploration and explication of what went wrong in the G.D.R. He says that the argument between East and West, left and right, Dada and Dylan, has been recast as an argument between the people who want to forget the Stasi and the people who want to remember, and that he puts himself somewhere in the middle—"somewhere free"—like the actress Katharina Thalbach, from the Schiller Theater, who applied for her files, discovered that they ran to twelve thousand pages, and told the Stasi Commission to throw them out, because she had no intention of spending the second half of her life reading about the first half.

At the beginning, Kerbach was "paralyzed" by the news about Anderson. He would think about Sascha Anderson and say to himself that "as a man, as a friend, I can't imagine doing this to anybody." He tried to paint, and couldn't. He tried to go out and get on with his life, and couldn't. He was looking around for something to do, something clean, when it occurred to him that his loft was in terrible condition. The roof and the walls needed insulating. He had had the loft for seven noisy years, and had managed, but he decided that he could not stay in a noisy loft thinking about Sascha Anderson, so he started fixing it. It took him a month, working every day and most evenings, and somehow while he was working "it all cleared up—the whole thing went up in smoke." He says that now he can look at Sascha Anderson "from the outside." It is what he means by being free.

Kerbach thinks that maybe the difference between him and Sascha Anderson is a matter of family. East Germans talk a lot

about family when they are describing informers—describing the
kind of people who informed, and the kind of people who were
supposed to be "above" informing. Anderson came from a good
family—a *gutes Haus*—but it was not nearly as good as the Kerbach family, in the class hierarchy of the classless G.D.R. Anderson's mother had an architect's degree and worked at making
animated cartoons, and Anderson's father was a dramaturge at the
opera, but they were apparatchiks, really—culture bureaucrats—
and fought about everything but the Communist Party, and did not
much care that Sascha Anderson stopped studying and took up
typesetting, or that he married in his teens and lived with his wife
and babies in one room with a sink down the hall, or that he went
to prison for forging checks. The children of bureaucrats married
young in East Germany, like workers' children, and divorced
young, and the girls got money from the state and raised their babies alone.

Kerbach says that Anderson's was the "normal" East German
background—that Anderson learned from his parents that "if you
do something for the system, then the system does something for
you." Kerbach's own parents were good German burghers, the
kind of parents you saw in Cologne and Düsseldorf but rarely in
Dresden, and what he learned from them was that the system was
terrible. His father owned a metals factory and had a hundred and
fifty people working for him, and when Ralf was a boy and started
talking about becoming a painter, his father behaved like any West
parent and wanted to know what was wrong with staying home
and taking over the business. He died when Ralf was ten, but the
factory stayed in the family until the East German "economic re-
forms" of 1972, when the state seized it, and it made them "different." It meant that the Kerbachs had capital, and were not
Communists—that they did not identify with the system any more
than the system identified with them. Ralf was always in trouble
with his teachers. They thought he was contradictory, and one of
them thought it would be better for Ralf if the school where he was
studying art dropped him—which is what happened. "I liked that
one," Kerbach says. "He was straight—not problematic, like my
'friend' Sascha—and maybe he was even trying to help me, because
there was no way a painter could be educated in Dresden then.
You never saw an original. You got your art—your Matisse, your

Picasso, your Expressionists—from books, from reproductions. And East Germany was like a filter. What you got—in philosophy, or literature, or painting—was not necessarily what was good. It was what came through. Rock came through. I never knew why, but now I know it was a Stasi business. Anything new I got from Sascha Anderson. He would come over and throw things on the table. Biermann's songs. The French structuralists. The books from Wagenbach. When I got the catalogue from the Müller Gallery, in Cologne, that introduced the Neue Wilde painters, Sascha saw it at my house and said, 'Hey, Ralf, they're doing what *we're* doing!' "

Kerbach got his first studio at seventeen. He discovered a village near Dresden where an old lady had a family winery, and rented a huge room in the winery for a hundred and twenty marks a month, and started drawing. He liked the countryside, and so did his friends, who started coming out from Dresden to visit and eventually put together a show of new Dresden painters in an old barn. One of the painters, Helge Leiberg, invited Sascha Anderson to read his poetry at the show. Having poetry at art shows was something East Germans did, Kerbach says, but usually those shows were private and took place in artists' houses, and only people you knew were "safe" were invited. They were less about painting than about getting people together and "doing something *against*"— doing something forbidden—whereas Kerbach and Leiberg and the other young Dresden painters wanted *their* show to be a big public spectacle. They hung posters and mailed invitations, and then, one weekend in May, when the weather was wonderful and people were driving out with their families, they called everybody over and said, "Come on, there's a happening in the barn." Nearly everybody they called did come, and some of them stayed and listened to Sascha Anderson read poems. The police came afterward, and shut the exhibit down.

"Looking back, I think it was all planned, everything that happened," Kerbach says now. "Because when the old lady with the winery died I had to move, and suddenly I was offered a small storefront space in Neustadt, which was the center of the Dresden scene, and it turned out that Sascha Anderson was living across the street. He came to my place and just started talking. He showed me his rejection slips. He told me, 'Ach, we're in the fight together.' He introduced me to poets like him—Bert Papenfuss-Gorek and Stefan Döring—who came through Dresden and were having the same experience. They couldn't get published, couldn't get their writing to the public, whereas all *I* had to do with a painting was frame it. I wanted to help. I knew that if we worked together on a book—if we did it by hand and there were only eighteen or twenty copies—we could publish. So in 1980 I made some drawings for the poems Sascha called 'Jeder Satellit Hat Einen Killer Satelliten' "—"Every Satellite Has a Killer Satellite." "We made the book ourselves, and it was wonderful. I felt like Blake making woodcuts."

Kerbach considered Anderson "a very modern person"—meaning that Anderson had no strong or debilitating convictions. ("A spy without conviction is the first socialist businessman" is how Iris Radisch, at *Die Zeit,* described him.) Anderson hustled all the time. He and Kerbach put out four books of their poems and drawings over the next eight years, and Anderson saw to it that they got around and always got West, to a publisher called Rotbuch, and made a reputation for them both. He was a kind of agent for Kerbach. Kerbach never asked Anderson how he did it, or if he took a cut, or if he had to give the Stasi a cut. He never suspected anything, though he says that he should have suspected—not because their books were successful but because Anderson was so guarded about everything except being successful. Anderson never talked about himself to Kerbach. He never "burdened" Kerbach with his problems; he never even "shared" his problems. He never talked about *Innerlichkeit* or about deep German feelings or deep German angst or about any of the other things that Germans talk about to friends. Kerbach counted Anderson as his best friend, and he had everything he could ask of a friend and collaborator except real conversation, which he was scared to demand, because Anderson had made it clear that confidences were "not cool." Kerbach remembers one day when the two of them were working together in his apartment, and he happened to go to the window and see the whole sky darkening for a storm. He called Anderson. He said, "Look at this. Look what's happening. Look at the incredible sky." And Anderson looked at the sky and said, "The sky doesn't move me at all." Anderson was twenty-three then, and

Kerbach was impressed. "I couldn't imagine that at twenty-three this much cool was possible," Kerbach says.

Kerbach applied to emigrate in 1980, when he was asked to contribute to an exhibit of drawings in Hamburg, and the government refused to let him go. He was often in Prenzlauer Berg after that, staying with Sascha Anderson and his girlfriend—a potter by the name of Wilfriede Maass, who had left her husband for Anderson and lived in a studio on Schönfliesserstrasse that was big enough for Anderson's friends and Anderson's famous evenings. Anderson didn't think much of Kerbach's plan—it was considered "not cool" to want the West, Kerbach says—but he never tried to persuade him to stay. In a way, he brought the West to Kerbach, in Prenzlauer Berg, because people visiting West Berlin who were interested in art or literature or rock or theater heard, sooner or later, about the studio across the Wall where poets were "discovering subjectivity" and "dismantling language" and "alienating language from itself," and even "purging language from the text," and those people got visas and bought their obligatory twenty-five Ostmarks at the checkpoints and spent an evening at Wilfriede and Sascha's and saw the nice work that Kerbach was doing. A lot of Americans came—by the time the Wall fell, Wilfriede's guest book included Grace Paley, Donald Barthelme, William Gaddis, and Walter Abish—but Kerbach thinks the best moment must have been when Allen Ginsberg and Peter Orlovsky appeared, at Sascha's invitation, and they painted a phallus on one of Wilfriede's vases. Anderson has the vase, along with a fine collection of bowls and pitchers and pots that other "friends of Prenzlauer Berg" painted. It was his idea that every artist who wanted to exhibit at the studio on Schönfliesserstrasse reciprocate by painting Wilfriede's pottery, and he kept the best pottery for himself.

Kerbach spent the next few years waiting for permission to go. He worked on his books with Anderson and painted two or three teacups and a whimsical teapot—he puts it somewhere between de Kooning and de Stael—but he never thought of staying. As soon as his exit visa came, Anderson threw him a goodbye party—"more of a wake," Kerbach says—and he crossed at Friedrichstrasse with a suitcase of drawing paper and black ink and the telephone number of someone Anderson knew who worked at Rotbuch and had promised him a bed. "I wasn't a celebrity then," he says. "That was it, that was all I had." He didn't see Anderson again for four years. He started painting in a subsidized loft at the Künstlerhaus Bethanien, in Kreuzberg, and got to know what he calls the "out-of-the-establishment people," and eventually the establishment people got to know *him,* and he ended up as one of the five "new" German artists in a landmark exhibit called "Malstrom," along with his old Dresden friends Cornelia Schleime and Helge Leiberg, who had managed to get to West Berlin too. He made new friends. He moved to Wedding. People started collecting Kerbachs. Those years were very good for him, he says. "I had to test myself in the world, in the market, but I didn't promote myself as a dissident. It was a big business—being a dissident, saying what people in the West wanted to hear. It was a way to get attention, and sometimes the only way to get accepted. But it was not *my* way. I don't think I changed in the West. If anybody changed, it was Sascha. He came West, and we became—there is a word for it in German, *Bekannte,* which means 'acquaintances.' We became a little 'less than friends.' Sascha was under a strange pressure in the West, always thinking about business, and not acting free anymore—maybe because here everybody else *was* free. There were quarrels between us. He would come to my studio and say, 'You paint too heavy, you have to change your colors, you have to change your style.' " It turned out to be mainly East Germany that had bound them. After a while, they stopped working together. In 1988, they published their last book.

The year Sascha Anderson came West, Kerbach made a series of paintings and drawings about their friendship. He doesn't know what inspired them, since it was long before he knew that their friendship was over, and certainly before he knew that Anderson had betrayed him. He thinks that maybe it was a reaction to see-ing Anderson again, from a "West perspective." One of the paint-ings is called "The Friendship Takes a Bath," and it involves a play on the word *baden,* because in the painting Kerbach and Anderson go bathing—*gehen baden*—away from each other in the Wannsee. One of the drawings is called "Sascha," and in it Sascha Anderson has what looks like a clubfoot, and he is running with a briefcase, and ugly, shadowy black birds are pecking at his head and his feet and tearing his jacket apart. Not many people know the painting, but the drawing is famous. *Die Zeit* printed it on January 24 this year—when Iris Radisch came back from the Stasi Commission and filed the story that Biermann's accusations against Anderson were true. Kerbach says that art critics come to him now and ask, "Did you know what you were doing in 1986? The foot, the birds, the briefcase—did they mean something to you then?" And he doesn't know what to tell them. All he knows is that the "Sascha Anderson" most Germans will remember is a picture by a less than friend who might never have got started without him.

"I heard the first rumors about Sascha in October," Kerbach said one night this spring, after he had spent a day working on his loft and was having a schnitzel at Florian. "I had been in France, and when I got home a sculptor I know said, 'Kerbach, watch out! There's going to be a Stasi bomb exploding in your life.' Well, I went back to my studio and thought and thought. I asked myself, Who could it be, in *my* life? I had my guesses, but I wasn't sure, so I asked Sascha who *he* thought the Stasi was, and Sascha said, 'It was me.' This was before the Büchner speech, and it never occurred to me then that it really was Sascha. I thought that when Sascha said 'me' he meant it was just rumors about him that Biermann was spreading. Biermann's a very tactical person, and his tactic has always been to keep the process going—the process of clarifying what happened to artists in the G.D.R. But then I read his speech, and there was also the arrogance of his judging everybody, of his calling Sascha an asshole. I thought, This is not part of the discussion. This almighty, omnipotent attitude of Biermann's is his Stalinist background showing, and he shouldn't forget how it marked him. Not everyone who lived through the shit in East Germany had the chance to move to Hamburg, the way he did, and who has he really helped, with all his talk about victims and oppressors? The people who gave the orders are free, and the informers like Sascha are sacrificed. I don't know—Sascha lied to me. I read one writer's files, and those reports of Sascha's—they went from simple description to deeply private things. I begged Sascha to talk about them, but he refused. The East German furtiveness was still there.

"Sascha had a chance to say no to the Stasi. They all did. A guy

I know was approached in Dresden years ago. He was asked about my work, my private life, and he said no. He said, 'I won't tell you anything, and if I do talk I'll repeat it all to Ralf anyway.' Someone who calls himself a writer has a duty to tell the truth about what happened to him and what he did. That's the minimum—that a writer stand up and tell the truth. I would have liked it if Sascha had stood up and said, 'That's what I did,' and then gone back to his life. I tried to convince him, from the very first day. I wanted him to say, 'Ralf, I told people about your private life.' Not 'I didn't do it.' So I let them film me. I thought that if I did, maybe people would understand what was happening a little better. It's not easy to break a friendship that's as old as my friendship with Sascha, but when Sascha didn't understand, it finally was a break. I saw him several times after that, but now he's stopped coming. I guess I was waiting for him to show up at my house and say something before it was too late—before I read my files. I don't think he will come anymore."

∾

The distress in Germany right now is about something called *Hausfriedensbruch*—an assault, in the deepest, most intimate sense, on home. It is no longer about Erich Mielke, who was arguably the second most powerful man in East Germany when he ran the Stasi, or even about Erich Honecker, who was the most powerful, and is safe in Moscow, demanding his "right" to a tranquil old age. East Germans are angry about Honecker and his friends, and probably most East Germans would be happy if those men died, but they do not frighten East Germans anymore—not the way the idea of being surrounded by informers still frightens them. Jürg Laederach, the Swiss novelist, says that the oddest thing about the G.D.R. is that "once it was over everyone looked like harmless old men, and it was hard to keep the idea, or even the language, of terror alive once the terror was gone." Wolf Biermann sounds crazed lately when he tries to describe a Stasi general like Wolfgang Schwanitz, who in fact beggars description. Schwanitz went on television and said that East Germans never knew that anything was wrong in their lives, or suffered at all, until they read their files and decided to be "victims," and afterward Biermann wrote about kicking in his television screen and dragging Schwanitz through the broken glass into his living room to beat him. But Biermann can be heartbreaking when he writes about people he knew, and especially about writers he knew, like Sascha Anderson. It may be simply that wounds inflicted by friends are the most intolerable wounds. I have heard Biermann described as "a man with his skin peeled off by experience."

At the beginning, it was mainly East Germans who wanted the files opened. It was West Germans who talked about forgiveness, or reconciliation, or tolerance, and pointed out that no one could ever say for sure what he would have done in any East German informer's place. East Germans wanted to know whether it was a friend or a neighbor or a relative or a colleague who had informed the Stasi that they were enemies of socialism, and who that friend was—the friend who wanted their job, or the friend who wanted their apartment, or the friend who simply didn't like them—and what, specifically, he accused them of, or what the Stasi said he accused them of, and if he got what he wanted, or ever even knew what he wanted. They wanted to learn why the black Passat was parked outside their house for a year, or why they were put on trial and sent to prison for ten years as subversives, or ended up exiled in Hamburg, like Wolf Biermann. They assumed that in the process they would come to understand a little more about their own lives. They never anticipated the number of informers. They never thought of how they were going to get along afterward in an "opposition" neighborhood like Prenzlauer Berg—of what the reactions would be, or whether the fragile community they had would disappear when they knew the worst about each other, and how casual most of the betrayals had been. Most East Germans wanted the fate of the Stasi files left to East Germany. They thought that only East Germans could know what those files had meant, and how hurtful or damaging they would be. They said that victims and informers had to come to terms with each other alone, and decide for themselves whether to burn the files or lock them away in vaults, or even ignore them, the way the Poles had ignored the crimes of their secret police. They were frightened for themselves, because so many people had been betrayed, and wanted vengeance now.

West Germans had always believed that the Stasi operation was a "triumph of statism"—the end product of some demented bureaucratic German impulse—but when they opened the doors on Normannenstrasse there was more dementia than bureaucracy in what they found. The most important files were of course gone—lost to the deal between the Stasi and the "revolutionaries" by which the Stasi got to destroy their personnel files in exchange for opening the files with the master codes for everything else. And the most spectacular files were already circulating. Those files began to surface in the spring of 1990, during the first free East German elections, when the famous Rostock civil-rights lawyer Wolfgang Schnur was accused of informing and dropped out of the elections. After that it was clear that the trade in Stasi files was political big business. It was a seller's market, and in those days mainly a Stasi seller's market. Bonn wanted the information, and usually got it free. The press paid for it. The press spent hundreds of thousands of marks on files that were being offered up by everyone from outraged burghers to old Stasi looking out for their retirement to the "information brokers" who are a curious fixture of the West German news business and run a kind of legal black market in other people's secrets. The conservative press, which expected the left to win, bought files on left-wing candidates. The liberal press, which expected the right to win, bought files on right-wing candidates. *Der Spiegel,* which had the money, bought files on everybody. Rudolf Augstein, who publishes *Der Spiegel,* supposedly paid a hundred thousand marks for the Stasi payroll—a list of the names of ninety-six thousand Stasi agents and officers. That list went on the black market a couple of days before Augstein could print it, and for less than a third the price that Augstein paid. People were amused, but not many of them said anything about the ethics of trafficking in information in the first place, and the only person who seemed to do anything about it was the Erfurt painter—his name was Matthias Büchner—who had disappeared with the Erfurt files, occasionally sending word that he was keeping them safe until the Stasi's victims were free to read them first. Now *he* is accused of being Stasi.

A lot of opposition politicians followed Wolfgang Schnur into obscurity. Ibrahim Böhme, the leader of the East German Social Democrats, never returned to politics after the accusations against him. Lothar de Maizière, the leader of the East German Christian Democrats, left politics too. Once the files were opened, in January this year, the leaks became "legal." By then, some of them involved people at the heart of the "revolution"—people from Neues Forum, people who for practical purposes had run East Germany for the first months after the Wall fell. Some of them involved the few Communists everybody trusted. Gerhard Riege, who was a Communist deputy in the Bundestag, hanged himself in February after someone accused him of informing. His suicide note—he said, "I fear public opinion . . . shaped by the media and against which I cannot defend myself"—was read into the record by his Party leader, Gregor Gysi, who had just been accused of informing himself. Wolfgang Berghofer, the last Communist mayor of Dresden, worked with the Stasi. Two of the five new presidents of the East German *Länder* were Stasi. The only East German *Land* president left in office today is a Lutheran lawyer named Manfred Stolpe, who is the president of Brandenburg. Stolpe used to be the liaison between the Lutheran Church and the Communist state. He talked to the Stasi all the time, and sometimes, he says, he "saved" a dissident from the East Germans by suggesting that he be sent away to West Germany. Now he is accused of informing under the code name Secretary. He says, "I would have met with the Devil if he would have helped us." He is still much loved among old East German dissidents. He was like Sascha Anderson—the last person anyone suspected. He did not fit any of the stereotypes Germans had about informers, or seem to have anything to do with Sartre's famous definition of collaboration as *"hégélianisme mal compris."* Sartre thought that informers were either marginal without the courage to dissent or idealistic without the courage to believe or individualistic without the courage to be free, but he did say that what all informers had in common was the illusion that they were "realists." Stolpe was a realist. Anderson may have thought he was a realist too.

∞

Wilfriede Maass still has the studio on Schönfliesserstrasse. It is a big, rambling place, with two potter's wheels, and a couple of kilns, and drying and display rooms, and closets stacked with pots that some of the artists she knows have painted. It is hidden at the back of the courtyard of an old Prenzlauer Berg building, and it used to be that the only way to find it the first time you visited was by the poster beside the door. The poster was a blown-up, upside-down photograph of a naked man in a bathtub. Wilfriede is forty-one, and she is what most Germans would call an East person. She is mild and artisanal, and unadorned except for a silver earring hanging from her right ear, and she is determinedly "natural." One of her friends—a Prenzlauer Berg writer—told me that Wilfriede is like an "organic tomato" that does not fit into the crate with the sleek, accommodating, commercial tomatoes and has to be taken on its own terms.

Wilfriede sits at her potter's wheel in old jeans and mountain boots and a clay-stained denim workshirt, and keeps warm in the wintertime with homemade leg warmers and the heat from two electric stoves. She wears her brown hair short and straight, parted on the side and combed back behind her ears, and she never wears makeup. There are deep furrows between her eyes, and her eyebrows are fierce. They make her look like she is concentrating hard, or even scowling, but the fact is she is a gentle, even placid, person, who never expected anything except a "quiet marginal life" in the German Democratic Republic, a life without much money or ambition, and certainly without the pressures of that mysterious, stressful West phenomenon called "the market." She built her life the way she built her studio, arranging and rearranging and accommodating herself to the things that happened. When Sascha Anderson moved in, and she divorced her husband, Ekkehard, she carried her clothes to an apartment across the hall and kept the family—they had a son and a daughter—together. When she needed room to display her pots, she appropriated the apartment next door, and tore out the toilet, and sometimes sprinkled the floor with sand and rocks, like a Japanese garden. When the Wall fell and she became a "business," she turned her bedroom into a display room and moved into a couple of vacant rooms down the hall. Her rent was two hundred and forty marks a month in November of 1989, and her living was guaranteed, because she was an official "private handcraft industry" of the city of East Berlin. Now the rent is over fourteen hundred marks, and she depends on a yearly stipend from the Berlin Senat—which decided that Wilfriede Maass was "culturally important" to the new

Berlin, and made the gallery a *Werkstatt*—and on selling the pottery her painters decorate when they have a show at the studio, and taking a percentage for herself.

Wilfriede never expected the Wall to fall, although she always dreamed of traveling, and even applied to leave for a month in 1987, when an uncle in West Germany turned seventy-five, and was disappointed when the state said no. She never expected Sascha Anderson to betray her, either, although she was not surprised when she learned he had, because, even after five years of living together in Prenzlauer Berg, "we really knew nothing about each other." Ralf Kerbach, who stayed with Ekkehard Maass on Schönfliesserstrasse while he was insulating his loft, says that Wilfriede was a victim of Sascha Anderson's system *and* East Germany's system. He thinks that the "different experiences" that have made him a West person and Wilfriede an East person are as much of a wall between them as the real Wall ever was—that as far as "mentality" goes, the Wall is very high in Germany, and will still be high in ten or twenty years.

Wilfriede's studio was famous. It was kitcheny and comfortable. It had lumpy old velvet couches and platters of cookies and pot warmers and stray cats and homely spider plants and a nice clutter of cups and books and toys and extra sweaters, and plenty of heat—and it is not so different now, except that now there is a show of Mikael Eriksson oils where Wilfriede used to keep the washing machine and hang the sheets. The painters and poets who came to Wilfriede's from their squats thought of it as the underground, and Anderson sometimes called it "a salon in the French tradition," but it was really just the comforts of an eccentric home that pleased them. They would sit at the big round table that Wilfriede always referred to as her "living room" and watch Wilfriede and her friends placidly glazing pots, and feel taken care of by busy, agreeable, obliging women. There were always women around, working, at Wilfriede's studio. Wilfriede's friend Petra Schramm, who is one of her partners now, was typing the manuscript of *Kassandra* for Christa Wolf the year Sascha Anderson moved in, and Petra says that until she finished typing and *Kassandra* came out, the closest the Prenzlauer Berg women got to feminism was a contraband copy of Marilyn French's novel *The Women's Room* that someone had smuggled in from West Germany.

Ekkehard Maass was a *Liedermacher,* like Wolf Biermann. The men were very good friends. Biermann had taught Ekkehard how to sing and how to play a guitar, and Wilfriede says he worshiped Biermann. He was always disappearing with Biermann. They would go off with their guitars to think up songs about the true socialism, and she would be left at home with the babies, and it was not much different, she says, from being left at home when Sascha Anderson got one of his mysterious telegrams signed "David" and disappeared with his Stasi control. Wilfriede is not a sophisticated person. She comes from a village called Ahrenshoop, on the Baltic coast, and stopped school after the tenth grade and started apprenticing. She wanted to leave the countryside, and maybe even go to college, but when she came to Berlin she met Ekkehard and got pregnant right away, and that, she says, ended her education. Ekkehard was a student. He studied theology and then philosophy and then Russian, and by all accounts he is still studying something. Once, he was expelled from Humboldt for protesting in the Biermann affair. People have said that when Anderson arrived at the studio on Schönfliesserstrasse it marked a succession from the Prenzlauer Berg folksingers to the Prenzlauer Berg avant-garde.

Officially, Sascha Anderson worked for Wilfriede. She always had three or four people working at the studio—the limit for a "private handcraft industry" was ten—and when Anderson arrived she took him on. It wasn't for the work but to give Anderson a paper status, because the capital was closed to people without what the state considered respectable, productive, Communist callings. They were de facto dissidents. (The word the Communists used was "asocial.") They could be picked up and sent home or put in jail or, sometimes, given a choice between the Stasi and home or jail. The official explanation was that people who lived their lives outside the productive purview of the state were stealing from the state. Officially they were criminals, but in Prenzlauer Berg they were only "a little marginal," like everyone else who came, and they depended on friends like Wilfriede, who was marginal herself but, officially speaking, harmless. Anderson had no interest in making pots. He was "more of a patriarch than a potter," Wilfriede says. He settled in and made his calls—Wilfriede had a telephone, which was rare for Prenzlauer Berg—and organized his evenings, and people in the scene were delighted, because at last someone was running things, someone was giving orders and telling them what to do. Wilfriede says now that the system had made them passive.

In January, Wilfriede applied for her Stasi files. She doesn't know what to expect when she gets them, but she still sees Anderson. She says, like Kerbach, that it's hard to break a friendship that is as old as their friendship, and as close, and has survived a long love affair and three years on opposite sides of the Berlin Wall. "About Sascha—you have to revise your opinion with every conversation" is the way she puts it. Sometimes she laughs and says, "Do I feel betrayed? Angry? No. I find it relatively fascinating. It makes him interesting." She keeps a stubborn, skeptical sense of humor when it comes to Anderson. And she is tolerant—more like a mother than a lover he left for the good life in West Berlin and an apartment in Schöneberg, near the Café M, and a girlfriend with better West connections. He was like the system—you didn't expect much and you certainly didn't expect confidence, and Wilfriede says it is pointless anyway to spend your time thinking about one informer when the market is at your door and your rent is fourteen hundred marks and strangers arrive from Cologne and look covetously at your two front rooms, which they tell you used to belong to a butcher in their family. Wilfriede's life was better when Anderson was there. The people she knows, the contacts she made, the fun she had "in this shitty G.D.R.," she owes to Anderson. She says that she always thought there was something wrong, but she was "concentrating on other women"—which, apparently, he was too.

"Biermann says now that Prenzlauer Berg was a vegetable garden of the Stasi, but I suspected nothing," Wilfriede says. "There were rumors in Dresden about Sascha being Stasi, but people laughed. There were always rumors about this guy or that guy working for the Stasi. You treated those people warily, you tried to keep your eyes open, but for every rumor there was another rumor to contradict it, and the rumors were systemic anyway, and usually it was the Stasi who produced them. My husband was once thrown out of a meeting because people thought that *he* was Stasi, but the real Stasi were sent to prison for a couple of days to throw suspicion off them. I never suspected Sascha. I never read the telegrams he got here, because they were not addressed to me. Sometimes he showed one to me. It was always something like 'Come to rehearsal,' and it was always signed 'David.' Sascha was always organizing music, so there was nothing odd about the telegrams. The only thing that made me suspicious was the signature. I didn't know anyone named David. But I never asked him. Sascha had a very intense life, and I had two children to raise, I had my work, my life, and there was not much time to ask about *his* life. I think for Sascha I was like a receptionist, or maybe an executive secretary. There were always calls, messages coming in. My mother's house was like that. *She* was like that. East Germany was like that. You could say I did it for the underground in Prenzlauer Berg."

Wilfriede thinks a lot, lately, about Prenzlauer Berg men. She says that they did not "support our self-awareness," and that even the Russian women who sometimes visited the studio were more skeptical about the lives they led. The Russian women would describe a typical day—working and cooking and standing in lines and trying to look after the children—and they would always end up shrieking with laughter, saying, "And then I had to carry the drunkard home." The only woman Sascha Anderson ever "organized" something for was the painter Cornelia Schleime, who was an old Dresden friend, and then a Prenzlauer Berg friend, and then, when they both went West, a girlfriend. Wilfriede admires Cornelia Schleime—she keeps a painting by Schleime above her potter's bench—but she says, a little ruefully, that Cornelia was the exception. Most of the women in Prenzlauer Berg were not considered very important, unless they were older women—like the painter Angela Hampel, who illustrated a book for Anderson—and already had their reputations, and were married to men who had their reputations. When Wilfriede talks about regret, she talks about the parties at the studio that she missed—like the party in 1984, when Allen Ginsberg came, and she was on vacation with the children—because Anderson never thought to include her. After Anderson left, she started a women's group at the studio. She and Petra opened the living-room table and invited twenty women to come and talk and read their own poems, and show their own paintings, and maybe discuss why so many of them had married young and raised their children alone—which was something they had never talked about before. There were problems among them, not the least being that the Prenzlauer Berg poets they lived with were having "bad reactions" to the idea of women meeting alone and discussing *them*. Some of the women wanted to talk about literature, because *Kassandra* was finally out and the vibrant, bitter, female voice of the oracle stunned and impressed them, and some wanted to talk about consciousness, because of the personal problems they were having in spite of the free day-care and the legal abortions and all of the other benefits offered to women in the G.D.R. and notably not offered to women in "progressive" West Germany. Wilfriede says that it never occurred to them to talk about literature and consciousness together. They met for less than a year, and then they "died," she says, from *Kultur Tourismus*— meaning that people in the West discovered them and they became famous. A feminist press in West Berlin decided to make a book of their conversations and readings. The editors told Wilfriede that she had the first radical feminist group in East Germany, and started coming to Schönfliesserstrasse with their tape recorders, and the Prenzlauer Berg women felt embarrassed and clumsy and uninformed. "History went too fast" is how Petra Schramm describes it. Wilfriede says, "The group broke, like a difficult friendship."

This winter, Wilfriede got a letter from the company that manages her building. It is the company that always managed the building, and the people are the same, but the name is different. The company used to have a typical East German name—a set of initials standing for something bureaucratic and severe. Now it is called Wohnen im Prenzlauer Berg—Living in Prenzlauer Berg. The problem was that one of the neighbors was spying on Wilfriede. "A *real* East German," Wilfriede says. "A man who hates gays, artists, foreigners, everything abnormal—and especially me." He had already spied on the Russian homosexual in the apartment next to his, and on the Jewish family upstairs, and after he looked in Wilfriede's window and saw the sand and the rocks on the floor of her spare room he was able to report to the people at Living in Prenzlauer Berg that Frau Maass was not using the room for "living," and the company wanted it back. Wilfriede says that the only difference between the company today and the company seven years ago, when she rented the room and broke through to her studio, is that today the company has to make the building pay. She blames the fact that a West German has claimed it. It has not occurred to her yet that, with Sascha Anderson organizing an underground there, her spare room was under Stasi protection, though sometimes she wonders if the woman who gave her permission to take the room—it is a big square room, with plenty of sun and height—was Stasi, because whenever Wilfriede calls the company, the company says that she is "out of town."

Living in Prenzlauer Berg invented a word for Wilfriede. Her problem was *Zweckentfremdungsverbotsverordnung*, which means that she was not "correct" when she tore out the toilet and built display racks instead of buying a bed and a chest of drawers. Two housing inspectors arrived one day when Wilfriede and I were having tea and cookies, and they were clearly not West people, because they sat down and one of them said, "I will stay and listen to your very interesting talk." Wilfriede has applied for status as a nonprofit workshop. She has two partners besides Petra, and they think that being officially "nonprofit" might help them keep the studio together. Wilfriede has already let her assistants go. There is no money to pay them now, and it makes her nostalgic for "the old days," when everybody worked together at the studio, and nobody needed money, and life was "quieter." "My life is totally different now," she says. "Prenzlauer Berg is different. People still come when there's an opening—people from here, people from the West who are easy about the past. Coming back depends on how you deal with the past—those who can't deal with it stay away. We have music for them, food, something to drink. But we don't meet privately that much anymore. There are cafés and bars now, and you know exactly where everybody in Prenzlauer Berg is, you know where to find them. The kids go to clubs, but it's different for them. For me—for forty years I lived with the East system, and I was shaped by the system, so I'm lonelier in my daily life. Everybody seems lonelier."

In the old Prenzlauer Berg days, Wilfriede Maass and Sascha Anderson were known for their goodbye parties. Their friends were always leaving for the West, and whenever a friend got permission to go—it was usually after the Stasi came and took his G.D.R. passport and replaced it with a one-way exit visa—they opened the studio and had a party. Kerbach left the night of *his* party, and then some other painters left. At the beginning of 1984, a group of dissidents walked into the American embassy in East Berlin, demanding asylum, and after that a lot of people were able to leave quietly. Women sometimes got out by marrying West men. One of Wilfriede's friends—a painter named Christine Schlegel, who was good at teacups—married a Dutchman, and Wilfriede and Sascha gave her a wedding that lasted three days. It was easy to leave if you found an American to marry, Wilfriede says, because the farther from East Germany you were going to live, the easier it was to get permission.

In 1984, Wilfriede and Anderson began to talk about leaving together. Nothing came of it. Wilfriede didn't want to leave her mother, in Ahrenshoop, or her son, next door—she had custody of her daughter, but her son was with Ekkehard—or, she says, the freedom to live off her pots without worrying about having to sell them. By the time Anderson did go, in 1986, so many people on the scene were leaving Prenzlauer Berg that no one noticed that his permission came quickly, or that he was actually able to put off leaving for a few weeks to "clear things up." Troublesome poets like Sascha Anderson were usually given twenty-four hours to pack their bags and disappear. He and Wilfriede met for a year on trips to Budapest and Prague. After that, he had his West girlfriend, and it was two years before Wilfriede saw him again.

They met at Cornelia Schleime's studio in West Berlin a few nights after the Wall fell. "In all that chaos, Sascha had got on the phone and organized a poetry reading for the old group, and of course I went," Wilfriede says. "There was such an old connection between us." Anderson wanted to be friends. He presented Wilfriede with her first West car—an old Mercedes—and from time to time they met at readings or parties or got together for a cup of coffee. He always came back to the studio for exhibits. He came one night right after the Frankfurt Book Fair, which is where the rumors about him started, and told Wilfriede that none of the rumors were true, and Wilfriede says she believed him. She believed him after the Büchner speech, and after Biermann confronted him on a television show that everyone in Germany saw. The next time he came to Prenzlauer Berg, he took Wilfriede for a drink at the Kiryl (which is *lyrik* spelled backward, and stands for lyric poetry). They sat under a ceiling papered with blown-up pictures and poems from *Every Satellite Has a Killer Satellite*, and Anderson had a lot to drink and kept repeating that everything in his life was wrong—that everything *he* had done was wrong. Wilfriede says that he got so drunk he couldn't walk, and she had to put him in his car and drive him home.

Anderson still came back to Prenzlauer Berg. In January, the old group met in Wilfriede's kitchen, and he assured them he had never informed, and then, according to *Die Zeit,* everybody got sentimental about "community" and the good old "dark times" in East Germany. Wilfriede asked him once more about his meetings with "David"—the mysterious meetings he had when they were still lovers—but she says she didn't have the courage to say "You're lying" when he kept denying everything. The last time he came to the studio—it was a couple of months ago, for a Holger Stark opening—she didn't mention the Stasi at all. No one did. The feeling at Wilfriede's was that people who blamed Sascha Anderson were either West people, who were lucky enough to have been born in the right country and didn't understand anything, or East people like Cornelia Schleime, who had spent a year in New York and got to be a West person, and had pinned up poems on her studio wall "wishing Anderson dead."

"I basically knew the truth," Wilfriede says. "Maybe I always knew. But I couldn't get it out of him, and I thought, Well, give him another six months and then he'll say something. Now I think the time to talk is really past. I think of his double life—organizing exhibits and readings and then sitting down and writing reports—and I think either he's extremely schizophrenic or else he's cool, calculating, and extremely smart. A top agent. Someone you could advertise in the United States. He was always a better organizer than a poet. He wrote like he was—very guarded, with some fantastic lines in between."

∞

East Germans sometimes complain about "paying for the Third Reich," and in a way they did pay. They ended up on the wrong side of the Allied line while the West Germans got "rehabilitated" and then rewarded, and prospered. The fact that some East Germans accepted the Communist regime—and even believed that it was keeping them "safe" from fascists—does not alter the fact that those East Germans believed the moral victory was theirs. They believed that they were sacrificing, while West Germany was not— that "history" was against them. It has to be said that their crimes were minor next to the crime of the Holocaust—that Germany is not going to exorcise the Third Reich with the spectacle of East Germans' exorcising Stasi. Yet the spectacle is inevitably about Nazism. It raises questions that should have been raised in 1945, and were put off and forgotten for a generation, and often for more than a generation. How was this possible? And how German is it?

Michael Naumann, who runs the publishing house Rowohlt and was a writer himself, likes to say that the Stasi were a "sociological miracle," but he thinks it is too easy to say they were a "typically German sociological miracle," even if this is what a lot of Germans believe. He prefers to say that the real precedent for the Stasi was the Saint-Simon cult, where everybody's clothes buttoned in the back, and people always needed someone to dress them, and could never be alone. What interests him is "how people adapt to circumstances of such extreme humiliation." Naumann publishes Biermann, and he is fierce on the subject of East Germany. He was born in the East himself, in 1941, and twelve years later had to leave, with his family, for "class reasons." He says that the people who stayed "lost their history." Some of them came to believe that they were Hitler's "victims." They were "uncivilized in the deepest sense, because they had suffered a disappearance of everyday memory." Memory is at the heart of what Naumann calls his "West German resentment" of East Germans. He says it comes from the experience of having learned about "Germany"—an experience many West Germans of his generation fought their parents to have—and a determination to break the silence about what Germany had been during the twelve Nazi years, and what Germans had done, and how enthusiastic they had been about Hitler. He thinks it separates his West German generation profoundly from East Germans of the same age, because those East

Germans were raised on a rhetoric of anti-fascism that never implicated them, as Germans, at all. East Germans never knew why
they were still goose-stepping past a leader, or even why they had
to continue to live with so many policemen. The ones who "remembered" Germany were usually the East Germans who left and
became West Germans, like Biermann.

Wolfgang Kohlhaase, who is a sixty-one-year-old East Berlin
writer with no connection to the Prenzlauer Berg poets, has a
theory that every country produces its own "cultural intelligence"—which does not mean "culture" but does mean that a
sixty-one-year-old German socialist like him knows something
about how and why East Germany was created, and why it vanished. He says that the writers of his generation who left, like Biermann, and the writers who stayed, as he did, often had the same
reasons for their different choices: they wanted to heal their country and make "socialism" possible. He thinks that the real quarrel
between writers like Biermann and the writers in East Germany
now has to do with which of them are the authentic revolutionaries. He says that maybe, as the century ends, the questions for Germany are "Where are we now? And are we back where we
started?" He does not think those questions are about Prenzlauer
Berg, where the attentions of the West "encouraged the dilettante
to crowd out the genius."

There are people in West Germany who made their careers as
specialists in Prenzlauer Berg literature, although the fall of the
Wall produced its own literary remorse, and the West Germans
who promoted Prenzlauer Berg are engaged in a kind of revisionism, and some of them now say that the West has only itself to
blame for so many inflated reputations. The few East German writers of spectacular talent—writers like Christa Wolf and Heiner
Müller, who won their Büchner Prizes long before Biermann—
helped the Prenzlauer Berg poets, and gave them money and went
to the readings Sascha Anderson arranged, but they did not depend
on Prenzlauer Berg. They depended on Erich Honecker, who let
them publish, and travel, and make the reputations that saved
them. They were an elite in East Germany. "Well, I admit, I never
thought 'the people' were right" is how the writer Stefan Hermlin

explained it. Müller himself has said that he never considered "not traveling because no one else could travel." He is a cynical man, and the fact that the greatest privilege in the G.D.R. was the freedom to leave it does not seem to have disturbed him. He used to tell his friends in West Germany that he lived in "the other dictatorship." He told the filmmaker Marcel Ophuls that he may even have needed the pressure of dictatorship, "because I know how to deal with dictatorship, and democracy bores me."

Bert Papenfuss-Gorek, who is one of the Prenzlauer Berg poets, says that whenever he and his friends were in trouble, Christa Wolf or Heiner Müller would "pick up the phone and call Honecker," and it did not occur to them to ask what Christa Wolf and Heiner Müller were doing, calling up Honecker. Wolf was a socialist and a believer, and she even applied a couple of times for a seat on the Politburo, and was disappointed when she was rejected. She wanted East Germany to stay East Germany. After the Wall fell, she begged East Germans not to leave. She tried to persuade people to resist West Germany, to demonstrate for a "purer" G.D.R., but very few people came to her demonstration, and after that she withdrew and said she was suffering too much because of "history" to take part in discussions about Sascha Anderson or Wolf Biermann, who had always defended her when she was called an apologist for the regime. Her only contribution to the debate about the Stasi, and the awkward presence of Stasi in East German literary life, was her novel *Was Bleibt?*—the novel she wrote in 1979 about a day in the life of a writer who discovers that she is under surveillance; the novel she locked in a drawer for ten years because, as she put it, too much talent had already been wasted in prison, and a writer's duty was not to heroics but to work that endured. She talked about Galileo, but she did not talk about Cervantes or Dostoyevsky, or even Havel. After the Wall fell, she mourned the death of socialism and accepted an invitation to spend a year in Santa Monica, at the Getty Center.

It may be that the "credentials" of writers like Christa Wolf and Heiner Müller—and maybe their courage—depended on their passports, and even that the part they played as East Germany's most celebrated literary dissidents gave them what I have heard described as "the extra aesthetic gratification that made life interesting." Hansjörg Geiger, at the Stasi Commission, calls it—a little harshly—"the gross self-deception of people with advantages in the system thinking they were negotiating 'preventatively' with the system, when in fact they were participating in the system." West Berliners who saw their plays and read their books remarked that they were full of bite and criticism and pain, and even panic. In East Berlin, the bite and certainly the criticism were cut from the text—if it was criticism of home. Müller and Wolf were a kind of model, in that they took a long view, and cycled their work through the West, and made themselves "indispensable" as East German geniuses. The kids writing Dada in Prenzlauer Berg tried to emulate them. One poet told me about his friends' waiting five years to get an anthology published. "The Stasi said no, and then it was published in the West, and *then* the Stasi said O.K., so we finally did it!" By then, nine of the poets in the anthology were living in exile.

The etiquette in Prenzlauer Berg was that you did not complain, and, especially, you did not complain to the media in West Germany—not even after the Wall came down. You were not craven. And you did not play hero. The poet Jan Faktor—who is married to Christa Wolf's daughter—wrote an angry article last year about East German literary dissidents and said, "To play the great warrior was no problem. . . . For that reason, people of refinement have refrained from it." That was before the Büchner speech, but he was talking about Biermann. "Refinement" was what a socialist gentleman depended on in adversity. Wolfgang Kohlhaase says it was a way of telling the West, "If you think I'm going to stand up and say I'm sorry for my life—forget it!" He was a dissident himself, but he thinks that human nature puts most people somewhere in between "dissidence and shameless opportunism"—that maybe human nature is what defeated Sascha Anderson when he started informing. In Communist East Germany, it took what he calls "a spectacularly egocentric talent like Wolf Biermann's" to be able to write lines like "Those who once stood up courageously before machine guns are afraid of my guitar/Panic spreads when I open my mouth," and believe them, and make them come true.

No one knows why people like Sascha Anderson informed—

weakness, pressure, pathology, adventurism, blackmail, or a very German game of "identity," or admiration for the system, or even contempt for the system. No one knows why the Stasi were so successful with those people—whether the Stasi were good policemen or good psychologists or simply good Marxists, spreading the "surplus value" of French thought through Prenzlauer Berg. Michael Naumann suspects that they had read their Marx, or knew, at least, that the highly sophisticated theories of a Derrida or a Barthes were really luxury goods—"the Gucci loafers of Western intellectual life"—and had nothing to do with the kinds of critical discourse that encourage revolution. But no one really knows, any more than anyone knows whether exposing the Stasi now is going to help Germans think seriously about their past or help them ignore the fact that they are not thinking about their past. No one knows who the first "victims" were, or even what the word "victim" means in a country where Stefan Hermlin, who is a Jew, can say that Wolf Biermann's denouncing Sascha Anderson was "only comparable to the denunciation of Jews during Nazism."

The West Berlin novelist Peter Schneider says that listening to writers argue this year he came to agree with Ralf Kerbach that "the Wall between intellectuals has never been so high, or worked so well, or made everyone so crazy." He had never believed that writers in the East and writers in the West were "connected," and it interests him now that most of the writers he knew and admired in East Germany eventually ended up in West Germany, not because of privilege but because the Stasi decided they had to go. He knew Anderson, too. He says that Anderson was "somehow too cool," and that he took it for shyness, and even felt a little sorry for Anderson, because once Anderson was in the West, and hustling for himself, no one seemed to want him. He was like his poetry: he didn't seem remarkable once he was competing for attention. Now he is hiding, and in some Prenzlauer Berg circles he is thought to be more of a "victim" than his victims. It comes back to the question of "victims." Ralf Kerbach thinks that being a "victim" is even victimizing Biermann. He says that Biermann is suffering from what Germans call the Kohlhaas syndrome, meaning that Biermann is behaving like Heinrich von Kleist's horse trader, Michael Kohlhaas, who lost his horses to a wicked Junker, and got obsessed with the crime, and proceeded to ruin his life in the pursuit of "justice."

∞

Rainer Schedlinski was one of the Prenzlauer Berg informers. He is also a Prenzlauer Berg poet and a Prenzlauer Berg critic and a partner in Galrev, a Prenzlauer Berg poetry press that he and Sascha Anderson and some of their friends started, but it is probably accurate to say that being a Prenzlauer Berg informer is what has made him famous in Germany. Schedlinski is thirty-five, and arrived on the scene in Prenzlauer Berg two or three years after Anderson. He had a troubled past, and never courted the attention Anderson did, although he put out an important underground journal called *ariadnefabrik* and was admired in radical poetry circles in the West for his *explications de texte*. When the people at *Sulfur*—"a literary biannual of the whole art," in Ypsilanti, Michigan—wanted to talk about the Prenzlauer Berg poets, it was Rainer Schedlinski they quoted. It was Schedlinski who described how Bert Papenfuss-Gorek dismantled language into "mnemonic unities which, mutually purged from the text, then permit a new arrangement," and how Stefan Döring produced "digitalized, dialectical chain reactions . . . by which one word destroys the one next to it." When people read Schedlinski, they understood why Wolf Biermann was boring—not because Biermann wrote boring poems, which was often true, but because Biermann *believed* in socialism, whereas the new Prenzlauer Berg poets were into "subjectivity" and didn't believe in anything.

Schedlinski didn't seem to believe in much himself. He wrote poetry about "domes of nothingness" and "inner barrenness" and "heavy coffins of emptiness." He says now that he believed so much in the Prenzlauer Berg writers that he took money from the Stasi to be able to publish them in his journal—that he was really helping the people he spied on, because every time he wanted to put out an issue of *ariadnefabrik* the Stasi gave him four hundred marks to pay for the paper. Schedlinski always lived a proper, poor, Prenzlauer Berg life. He says he never got the kind of money the opposition politicians did for informing, which was something like five hundred marks every time they made a report. When

Schedlinski started out informing, the most he got was bags of coffee, and then he got a table, because a "friendly" Stasi who came to his house one day to talk noticed that his old table was wobbly. Schedlinski still lives in Prenzlauer Berg, in a sixth-floor walkup he discovered empty, in 1985, and appropriated. The old bathtub he brought to the squat still sits in the middle of the living room, though now it is part of a "wall" of industrial shelves where he keeps some books and one of his computers, and the room is heated now, and he has a car. He never operated at Anderson's level. There were always four or five informers at a party or reading or meeting of the Prenzlauer Berg scene, and Schedlinski started out in Prenzlauer Berg as one of the writers who informed on writers who were informing on them. Anderson supposedly informed on Schedlinski. They covered the same territory. They had the same friends.

Schedlinski's style was different, though he seems to have modeled his Prenzlauer Berg persona on the Anderson look: he has the same three-day stubble and little round glasses and short, spiky hair. He says that he never really liked Anderson as a writer—that he preferred the language of poets like Papenfuss-Gorek and Jan Faktor. Anderson was wry as an informer. He played to the Stasi's obsession with detail. When he went to exhibits, say, to spy on painters, he would always report on the height of the guests, and the size of the canvases, and even the dimensions of the gallery, whereas Schedlinski, at exhibits, would report on whether or not he liked the paintings. It was said later that if Anderson had "bad consciousness," Schedlinski had no consciousness. He is quite proud of the fact that "ninety percent of my talks with the Stasi were about what *I* thought," as if bad impressions were less damaging than harmful information. He informed on the writer Lutz Rathenow, and told the Stasi how pushy Rathenow was and how terrible his writing was, but not, he says, how Rathenow got his manuscripts to the West, or how much money he made—which might have been because he didn't know. Rathenow was picked up a couple of times and spent a couple of nights in prison, but Schedlinski says that *he* wasn't the reason Rathenow went to prison. He says he did Rathenow no more harm than the critics today who simply quote from Rathenow's German—"Shabby, blooming-cloud factory / Spray-can that will not be emptied / Phono-disk with a crack / Smells tattoo the city"—and demolish him that way. He never went into the kind of detail Anderson did, informing on poets. Anderson once informed on a poet named Uwe Kolbe (who was one of the writers at the Villa Massimo this winter) and supplied the Stasi with the bewildering news that Kolbe was "relieving the noun of its burden . . . with phonetic adjectival exaggerations."

Schedlinski comes from Magdeburg, and he likes to talk about the "close East German feeling" at his favorite Magdeburg café and the people he knew there. He liked those people. They were down-and-out theologians, who came in the morning with their Bibles, and unemployed physics professors, who were using the tables to write a book about Einstein, and one "mystical" graphic artist, who was old and uncompromised and utterly poor. The artist's name was Rudi Thiele. He had a car, but there was no engine in the car, and whenever he found an odd job—restoring paintings in a church, say, or painting a kiosk—he would sit behind the steering wheel and Schedlinski would push him to work. Schedlinski talks about him as a kind of father. "When Rudi died, we all asked, What was it about him? He never had money. We had to get him shoes in the winter. He lived by drawing people in the café and trading the drawings for coffee. He had a purity, and we were his disciples. We were so different, but we shared his values."

Schedlinski has written a novel about his old café. He thinks he might still be there, drinking coffee with his friends, if it hadn't been for his brother Wolfgang's "problem." Wolfgang was a merchant marine with a West car, an appendix scar from Hawaii, and seven espionage trials to his credit by the time the Stasi sold him to West Germany, where he went into business and made a lot of money and got active in a neo-Nazi party. Schedlinski describes him as "the closest to me, the one who went West, the only one who got something done." He suspects that his brother's best business was helping people escape from East Germany, because when Rainer was nineteen he received an envelope from a town near Düsseldorf—Wolfgang was living near Düsseldorf—with two letters for him to deliver in Magdeburg, and that was when his own problem with the Stasi started. He never met the people who got the letters, and he doesn't know whether they went to prison, or whether they ever got to West Germany. He thought that if he delivered the letters, then maybe someday Wolfgang would help him leave too, so he followed Wolfgang's instructions and dropped them off and went home. Four weeks later, the Stasi took him in to their Magdeburg station. They made him sign a paper swearing that he had never been at the station. (It was the peculiar logic at Stasi offices to collect disclaimers from people who wouldn't have had to sign them if they hadn't been there to sign them.) They showed him his brother's letters. They said that as Wolfgang's courier he was facing ten years in prison, and a ban on publishing anything when he got out. A "tough Stasi" did the threatening. A "sweet Stasi" offered him a deal. The sweet Stasi—his name was Joachim—told Schedlinski to think over their offer, because Schedlinski's future was not very promising to begin with, and he would certainly be ruining his life if he refused. Sometimes Schedlinski says that Joachim offered him "help and structure." Sometimes he says, "I signed to get out of there." On his third visit—sometimes he says his fourth or fifth visit—to the Magdeburg Stasi headquarters, he put his name on a *Verpflichtungserklärung,* which was a confession that amounted to a contract to inform.

The Stasi promised to leave Schedlinski alone, and for a while they did, though every now and then they brought some coffee— good coffee—and he got used to the coffee. He says that the first time he "did anything" for the Stasi was when Joachim used his apartment to watch people watching Erich Honecker, who was coming to Magdeburg for a parade. Schedlinski lived at the time on Otto von Guerickestrasse. The police had complained because he didn't have curtains, and the street was a "protocol street," and had to have curtains. But the view was perfect for Joachim. He watched the parade, and Schedlinski got to keep on doing what he liked, which was writing reviews for local papers, and writing poems.

Schedlinski was a "cold agent," which means he was in cold storage—"young and available if they needed me later." His life changed when his controls changed. It happened around the time Sascha Anderson brought Heiner Müller to Magdeburg for a reading, and also arranged for Ralf Winkler, who paints under the pseudonym A. R. Penck, to have a show there. The Stasi wanted information on their local contacts, and they asked Schedlinski. "It wasn't that bad," Schedlinski says. "No one was at risk. No one was ever sentenced for giving a reading or hanging a picture." It would be more accurate to say that artists like Müller and Penck were too important to sentence—that celebrity protected them. The artists the Stasi preyed on were people like Rainer Schedlinski, who had great longings and no currency—either in cash or in status—abroad. They chose Schedlinski because in 1983 Schedlinski would not be missed in the West, or even in the East, if he went to jail.

Schedlinski claims to have been a reluctant spy—"I said to myself that I could tell them what Heiner Müller read but not who was there, or that it was subversive." He says the Stasi punished him by killing his reviews, but his real punishment was being drafted at twenty-five—the age limit for the East German draft was twenty-six—and put to work as a doorman at an army officers' mess near Bad Sarow, where the officers arrived in the middle of the night waving loaded guns and demanding schnapps. Four weeks into Schedlinski's tour, one of those officers shot another officer's ear off, and Schedlinski, who was on medicine for a heart murmur, broke down and took an overdose and ended up in a mental hospital with a pacemaker in his chest—insisting that the Stasi were coming to get him. "It was the pressure of the Stasi, the military, the crazy people that got me," he told me one day, over a beer and eggrolls at the Kaiser von China, a Prenzlauer Berg restaurant he likes. "At the clinic, the really crazy people were the doctors. They kept saying, 'It's your imagination, it's run wild.' I wrote a speech for them called 'Aesthetics of the Military,' and after I read it for an hour they just locked me up, with a diagnosis of paranoia, which is what I wanted. Then they sent me to another clinic, where everybody was crazy. I had to stay inside, but, like everywhere, you find people you want to talk to. There was this one guy who was always running by my window in a jogging suit. One day, he saw me. He called to me, 'Hey, what club are you in?' I said, 'I'm not in any club.' And he gave me some advice. He said, 'I had the same problem yesterday, but today I'm a maniac.' "

Schedlinski wove rugs at the asylum, and cleaned the library. He read Albert Camus, Walter Benjamin, Flann O'Brien, Lars Gustafsson, and a lot of medical books, and decided that he already knew everything those "smart books" said. After six months, the doctors let him go, and he headed for Prenzlauer Berg, where he knew a girl with an apartment. When he talks about his breakdown now, he says either that "pressure" from the Stasi caused it or that the Stasi were "no big deal" and never did anything terrible. The Stasi used to come to his Magdeburg café, and he says that everybody knew who they were, and that "we didn't take them seriously"—that he and his friends sent them notes and joked about it afterward. He says that even the man who organized all the underground exhibits in Magdeburg knew he was talking to Stasi. "It was a conflict for him," Schedlinski says. "But in the end he hired me and another Stasi to install his heating."

The Stasi traced Schedlinski to Prenzlauer Berg when he went to the dentist and had to register an address to get insurance papers. Two Stasi came to his squat and took him in—sometimes he says that it was "prison for a few months," and sometimes that it was "not prison in the ordinary sense but interrogation." The charges this time were "asocial behavior" and "illegal residence," and then the Stasi added "possession of foreign currency," because Schedlinski had just got five hundred marks for his first West publication. The name of his story was "Berlin Simultan." It came out in an anthology of twelve "new German storytellers" and was considered opposition fiction, and the West Berliners who had come to Prenzlauer Berg for "culture tourism" and carried the manuscript out thought that Schedlinski was very courageous, like Sascha Anderson.

"I clarified in my own mind what I could tell the Stasi, and after that it was no problem," Schedlinski told me. "They'd ask me, 'Where did you go on New Year's Eve?' and I'd say, 'Lutz Rathenow's place, and we played Monopoly.' I thought they'd expel me, or offer me something. They knew I was untrustworthy, but they were fairly friendly. They had to report to their own bosses—had to keep them happy—and I had no scruples about that. I thought, If the Stasi want to finance the underground—fine. People knew I was Stasi anyway."

Actually, nobody but the Stasi knew that Rainer Schedlinski was Stasi. There were rumors about his being Stasi, the way there were rumors about Anderson, and, in a way, the rumors protected him.

And then, too, it is unlikely that any of his friends—except, maybe, friends like Anderson, who were informing on him—followed him to the parking lot where he met his control or to the house in the country where he made his reports. By all accounts, his friends were happy when he started editing *ariadnefabrik*. He told them it was "a new concept"—critical essays about "the Prenzlauer Berg thought"—and people like the opposition pastor Wolfgang Ull-mann, who sits in the Bundestag now, and the poet Elke Erb, and Anderson himself sent manuscripts. Schedlinski didn't know Anderson was Stasi, and it is hard to believe that Anderson knew *he* was Stasi, though some people claim to have "proof" that Anderson was so valuable to the Stasi that when he went West he was given the names of all the other Prenzlauer Berg contacts. Mainly, what Schedlinski knew about Anderson was that Anderson had come to Magdeburg with Heiner Müller, and had written for *ariadnefabrik*, and had even sent him a photocopy machine.

The first issue of *ariadnefabrik* came out in 1986—fifty pages of computer printout bound in grainy black construction paper—and after that Schedlinski managed to publish every second month. "I told the Stasi about my new concept," he says. "I told them, 'I'm going to put out this review,' and it was no problem, because the Stasi were basically organizing everything." He insists that the four hundred marks an issue was their only "contribution." He doesn't say where he got eight or nine thousand Deutsche marks for a Japanese computer, or a thousand marks to pay his friend Andreas Koziol to do the typing. Most issues ran to fifty or seventy copies— the law in East Germany was that you could publish up to ninety-nine copies of a newspaper or a review without the government's permission—and Schedlinski sold them for forty marks in the underground. Occasionally, he put together an anthology of stories and poems and ran off a thousand copies on a wax-process mimeo-graph and sold them, too. Eventually, he bought a photo-offset printer, but then the Wall came down and he never got to use it.

Years ago, Schedlinski thought about moving West. He got a visa in 1988, and started crossing into West Berlin, and once he talked to Anderson about simply staying. Anderson tried to talk him out of it, and eventually the girl he was seeing did talk him out of it. He says he is glad now that he stayed at home. "The West German mentality is not convenient for me" is how he puts it.

"The West is not much better than the East—only brighter. That was the first thing I discovered there. The second was that in a bar you always paid for your own drink. It isn't as social as over here. There's not so much solidarity. In the West, there are cafés for artists with silk scarves, cafés for artists with dogs, but no cafés for just artists together. People in the West want to be different. To be 'different' here, you always had to form a group and step out of society together—or else you were the only loser."

Schedlinski went to work at Galrev the day it opened, two years ago. He takes a proprietary interest in the press, although it was in many ways Anderson's project. Anderson organized it. He put in money, and designed a nice house-signature cover—a diagonal slash of color separating the Futura graphics from the illustration—and bought the word processors and the copiers, and even a Heidelberger Druckmaschinen printer, which Schedlinski says is the Ferrari of printers and costs about seventy thousand marks. But the press is run as a cooperative, and today it may be one of the few places left in Prenzlauer Berg where Schedlinski can get a job—though Prenzlauer Berg people tend to think that it's hypocritical and "Christian" to get too angry about informers like Schedlinski, that it's something people pandering to the West do, and this gives him a kind of protection. Most of the people he wounded in Prenzlauer Berg leave him alone so that no one will mistake them for strident, moralistic West people. Or they treat him like a victim himself, which, in a way, he is. Or they get together with him and discuss the ironies of "German identity." The novelist Detlef Opitz—"I could have got him in trouble, but I didn't, I told the Stasi regular, normal things," Schedlinski says—invited him to the beach for a couple of days this winter "to talk it out and clear up the friendship and also to learn more about informers for a novel he's writing." They spent two quiet days at Ahrenshoop, and taped two hundred and fifty pages of conversation that Schedlinski prefers to call "essays and short poems," and got the *Süddeutsche Zeitung* to pay for the hotel.

After the Stasi files were opened, people in Prenzlauer Berg heard that A. R. Penck—who had given several hundred thousand marks to Galrev and had even paid for some of the equipment Anderson ordered—was threatening to take his money out of the business if Schedlinski and Anderson stayed. Penck has been a kind of paterfamilias of the Prenzlauer Berg scene. He is the best-known painter to come out of East Germany, and he has studios now in Düsseldorf, Berlin, and London, but back when he was painting near Dresden the Stasi savaged his studio, and after he was sent West he did what he could for East German artists. He detests the Stasi, but he is close to Anderson, and Anderson and Schedlinski are still around at Galrev. Schedlinski "retired" officially for three months, but he never stopped coming in.

Galrev has a big storefront office, which used to be a marionette factory. Everything in it is painted black or gray to go with the furniture Anderson chose in West Berlin, and there are skinny designer blinds at the window. The blinds are drawn when the seven directors have their Monday meeting, and it may be just as well, since, whatever Schedlinski says about there being "no problem," relations are cool at Galrev now, and the people are suspicious of each other and wary of the strangers Schedlinski brings in. They get their work done, but when strangers visit they are (depending on your point of view) furtive or composed. Nobody looks up, nobody smiles, nobody gets introduced. Wilfriede's friend Petra Schramm, who sometimes goes to Galrev to use the computer, says that Galrev is "a dried-out situation," and that the people who work there are "not clear among themselves." She describes it as "people who work together but don't belong together anymore," and she has a point, because those people are working out of shattered confidence.

∞

Wilfriede thinks that Schedlinski is "a little overvalued" at Galrev—that he got to Galrev because he wanted to be a publisher, and Anderson let him in. Kerbach says no, that the problem at Galrev is not Schedlinski, that nothing would be gained by asking Schedlinski to go. *He* thinks that the problem is strategy, because after the Stasi files were opened, and everybody knew the worst about Schedlinski and Anderson, Galrev never sent a letter reassuring people about its credibility or reliability as a publishing house, not to mention reassuring the banks that loaned it money and thought they were supporting an authentic "alternative" East Germany business. Deutsche Bank gave Galrev eighty thousand marks, at 13 percent, and was negotiating another loan when Schedlinski "retired." (He said it had been decided that "my signature on everything was not good for the publishing house.") Galrev was the first "legitimate" local publisher of the Prenzlauer Berg poets, and it had a kind of celebratory reputation, because it took the poets Sascha Anderson had been publishing in beautiful little typewritten and hand-painted volumes—and selling to the culture tourists for four or five hundred marks as "first editions"—and brought them out of the underground and into the bookstores. It was considered a symbol of the new enterprising spirit among right-thinking East German intellectuals. At first, its only rival in Prenzlauer Berg was a press called Basis Druck, which published nonfiction, and was considered "in Biermann's camp." Basis Druck was "the other side," the West of the East in Prenzlauer Berg terms. It published Rathenow. It published Andreas Sinakowsky, an ex-informer who had written a damning confessional novel called *The Interrogation*. It specialized in essays about complicity and deceit and in exposés of East German corruption, whereas Galrev published Papenfuss-Gorek and Anderson and Schedlinski, and translations of Celtic verse and of contemporary American poets who wrote in the style of early Gregory Corso. It may be that the problem for Galrev now is not its informers *or* its strategy but the reality of the market coming to Prenzlauer Berg. Gerhard Wolf, who is Christa Wolf's husband and an old East Berlin publisher, has just started a poetry series curiously (given the number of Prenzlauer Berg poets who informed) named Janus Press. And the poets themselves are getting restless at their local publishers and are signing up with big West German publishers, who can pay them advances and get them proper "West" distribution and foreign contracts and the publicity they lost with their status as East German dissidents. Anderson publishes mainly in the West now. Schedlinski is dividing his writing between Galrev and Surkampf, the Frankfurt publisher, which put out a book of his poems called *The Ratio of the Yes and the No* a couple of years ago and will probably publish the novel he is working on now. Schedlinski says that he prefers Galrev, because it is "all about authors in the traditional sense—doing their own layout and printing and seeing to everything themselves." He thinks it is Prenzlauer Berg's last link to the old, dark days, "when life was easy-going here, and you didn't have to worry about work or money or apartments or the market, and were freer to write what you wanted." He talks a lot about the market. He seems to believe it was the market, and not the Stasi, that trapped and betrayed him and ruined his reputation and made him uncomfortable in Prenzlauer Berg.

Every morning at about eleven, Schedlinski drives to Galrev. He checks the machines that Anderson bought, and settles down to work on his projects—an American anthology and an anthology of old East German underground papers and a "postmodern-arts magazine" called *Warten: Das Magazin.* Anderson brought the magazine to Galrev; it was supposed to be about "everything from cows to mathematics" but it is really about sex and "anarchy" and has violent, expensive color graphics and pornographic vignettes, and clearly has the market in mind, since some of the text is in English. Anderson comes in sometimes. He is "in and out," Schedlinski says, and does what he has to and doesn't say much to anyone. Anderson rarely calls Schedlinski anymore, but Schedlinski calls him, in West Berlin, when he needs to order supplies or has problems with the machines. Schedlinski thinks that "Anderson doesn't find his position in the whole thing"—meaning that Anderson refuses to talk about why he "belonged" to the Stasi, or even to say that he belonged to the Stasi. Schedlinski says that last fall, after the Frankfurt Book Fair, Anderson bought his own file on the black market. It cost him thirty thousand marks, but presumably it was his "victim's" file, and had to do with the reports other informers had made on *him.* The last three folders of Anderson's "informer's" file—the folders covering his years in the West—are missing, and while informers who operated only in East Germany are not accountable under West German law (which is now Germany's law), there is some question about informers who operated in West Germany, and who could conceivably be brought to trial for espionage. No one knows whether Anderson has those files, or whether those files were destroyed, or were stolen by people who wanted to blackmail Anderson, or protect him, or whether they were part of a deal to keep Anderson from talking. The Stasi recruited Anderson because of the checks he forged in Dresden, and now there are rumors connecting him with other crimes, and people say that the important "West Stasi" who figure in Anderson's missing folders—some of them West Germans in the government—may be using those crimes to "persuade" Anderson not to expose *them.*

There is nothing you learn about any one Stasi that does not implicate dozens of other Germans in the Stasi. And when tourists drive by Galrev on their Prenzlauer Berg "route," or reporters bang on the door to see the place where Sascha Anderson and Rainer Schedlinski print books, Galrev becomes another *point de repère* on an already perplexing moral landscape. Schedlinski lets them in. He tells them the things he didn't do: he didn't tell the Stasi about the *Tageszeitung* plotting to hide newspapers on Polish trucks to get them into East Germany; he didn't tell the Stasi about Lutz Rathenow's money; he didn't tell the Stasi about the really "criminal" things his friend Detlef Opitz did; he didn't tell the Stasi about the politics of his friend Cornelia Jentzsch, who works at Galrev, only about her boyfriend; he didn't tell the Stasi about the plans the peace activist Gerd Poppe had for demonstrating at Russian missile sites, only his "impressions" of dinner at Poppe's house.

Last summer, a producer from Westdeutscher Rundfunk came to Prenzlauer Berg to film a "portrait of the poet Rainer Schedlinski." He returned in January "for additions," carrying pages from Lutz Rathenow's files—Rathenow was passing his files around—and showed Schedlinski a report he had made in 1985 about Rathenow's collecting signatures for a petition about the immigration law, and then he filmed Schedlinski's face. Rathenow said later that with those reports Schedlinski made "my deepest intentions" public, and Schedlinski doesn't know why he felt that way, since Rathenow had published the petition himself in all the underground newspapers, and even in *ariadnefabrik,* and had talked a lot about getting the signatures to the West for publicity. Schedlinski doesn't really see the difference between making your own deepest intentions public and having someone else do it for you—though he knows when the West German press is doing it to him. He denied the rumors about him until the files were opened. He denied them on television until he was handed a copy of his "confession contract."

The first real "evidence" about Schedlinski appeared in *Stern* in

January. It was a copy of his report about playing Monopoly at Rathenow's on New Year's Eve. Then he "confessed" in an article in the *Frankfurter Allgemeine Zeitung.* And after that there were three or four interviews a day, because the Stasi were an ongoing sport—"victims and oppressors," people called it—and the players were expected to confront each other on television and in newspaper columns, and the old Stasi controls, who have good jobs now or are living on pleasant pensions, were paid to follow them, as commentators. Schedlinski got a lot of attention (though he sometimes describes himself as "a victim of press terror"). He wrote articles for all the important German papers, and for a Zurich weekly called *Wochenzeitung,* and for a Dutch news magazine called *Elsevier.* He started a book of essays about "the role of the Stasi in the G.D.R." He was invited to talk about "Germanistics and political science" at Georgetown University, and to read at the Goethe Institute in Chicago. "I'm not nervous," he says. "I never thought I was telling anything important."

∞

People who work at the Stasi Commission have had a common reaction. Many of them thought at first that the files should be closed. They thought that the files would occasion more grief than clarity; that the victims, in their disgust, would become "Stasi," and the Stasi would become "victims," and nothing would be served; that the best thing for East Germany was "forgiveness." The pastor Joachim Gauck was there to remind Germans that the commission was not a court and had nothing to do with judgment or retribution—that it was serving "truth" and a higher justice, and that, whatever the politicians said, the message was, if not "Love thine enemies," then "Know thyself." But it turned out that after studying the files—trying to make sense of millions of pieces of paper full of lunatic speculation about "hostile negative basic attitude" and "enemy behavior" that ran from why Wolf Biermann served cognac to a girlfriend after making love to whether Biermann would leave East Germany if he got the news that his grandmother, in Hamburg, was dying—most people at the Stasi Commission were convinced that the files had to be opened. The intimacy of the files horrified them. Spiros Simitis, the West German adviser to the commission, says it was so horrifying that he decided, reluctantly, that victims *must* have access to their files. Michael Zabel, whose office administers the files, ended up believing that East Germans would have "no future at all" until they confronted their Stasi past and knew the extent of their betrayal. Geiger himself decided that access had to do with the East Germans' "right to control their lives"—with convincing the East Germans that finally they had this right, in "Germany," and could decide for themselves whether someone who had betrayed them "was going to keep on sitting on their couch once a week and drinking their whiskey." I saw Geiger one day after he had read a file involving a sixteen-year-old boy who had told a joke about Honecker to the warden at his church. The joke had to do with Bush, Gorbachev, and Honecker being followed by cannibals, and the cannibals refusing to turn around when Bush offered them money, and even when Gorbachev offered them "paradise," but disappearing immediately when Honecker told them, "In two hundred meters, we'll be in East Germany." The warden repeated the joke to the Stasi, and the boy was thrown into prison for two years. Geiger could not believe what he was reading. He is a mild man, but he gets furious when people say that informers "did no harm," because, he says, the more he reads, the more he understands that the whole of East German society was built on "nightmare, insecurity, and betrayal." The harm haunts him. He told me that one Sunday he was sitting alone in his office, going over a file, "and all of a sudden I heard a cry, and looked around—and then I realized that it was me crying."

Some of the Prenzlauer Berg intellectuals went to a meeting in March and talked about convening a "Russell Tribunal of victims," where informers would be charged with crimes against humanity—and, presumably, a salutary remorse would be their sentence. It was considered a Biermann sort of idea, because very few of the Prenzlauer Berg informers use words like "crimes," or even "right" and "wrong," when they talk about themselves. They say, "I did it for Germany" or "I never did any harm" or "I was frightened" or "I wanted protection"—and turn themselves into victims. The most popular entertainment in East Berlin right now is a weekly consciousness-raising session for victims and informers at a place called the House at Checkpoint Charlie, which an enterprising West Berliner opened years ago at the old crossing. The Stasi who participate call it an "interior investigation." Henryk Broder prefers to calls it an "obsession." He says, "When you see a guy sitting there crying with the neighbor who spied on him, when you see a guy who was persecuted and maybe tortured wanting to talk it over with the Stasi who did it—that's Germany in a nutshell." Some of his German friends say he shouldn't be talking about victims and oppressors, because the Stasi are "a German affair."

My friend Wiglaf Droste is worried about a "cult of victims" taking over Germany. He agrees with Broder (with whom he disagrees on nearly everything else) about what it means when Germans start casting themselves as "victims." When the rumors started about Sascha Anderson, Wiglaf wrote that maybe the scandal would keep Anderson too busy to write "his bad poems," but now, looking at the attention that Biermann and even Rathenow are getting by being such persistent victims, he worries that people are beginning to look at *their* bad poems, and even their bad prose, with something close to reverence—that art is getting to be a matter of politics. He is uneasy about the Stasi Commission "encouraging victims to make themselves interesting, for the press, for their 'art,' for each other." He thinks that right now Germans are indulging a very unhealthy, very German preoccupation with themselves, and that in their search for "identity" they are beginning to sound like Novalis's Heinrich von Ofterdingen, searching for the blue flower, and are making "Germany" the only subject in the world worthy of their attention.

Germans are very complicated when they talk about remorse: they want remorse to be "correct." So they tend to speak in moral metaphors—the Stasi for the Communist state, and the Communist state for the Nazi state, and the Nazi state for "Germany." Sometimes they seem to be saying that they can "solve" their past by resolving their present, that correct consciousness and a correct remorse will cancel past evasions, as if (a Jewish friend in Berlin said this) with enough attention and concentration they will arrive at some "final solution to the Nazi question." The irony escapes them. In difficult times, Germans are not interested in irony. They prefer to talk about the "Germanness" of victims and the "Ger-

manness" of informers and, especially, the Germanness of informers who had some loyalty to the G.D.R. and are left now with only
the evidence of betrayal.

Anderson doesn't want to talk about the "Biermann affair." He
spends most of his time in Jena, where he has a girlfriend, and
keeps an answering machine on his Berlin phone. Biermann refuses
to talk about the affair, because he has an agreement with the people at *Der Spiegel,* and he talks exclusively for them. He has a lot
of grievances. The Stasi devoted itself to collecting evidence of his
"destructive character," and the Politburo met repeatedly to plot
his ruin, and he is alarmed now when East German writers like Stefan Heym talk about Joachim Gauck's being "blinded by hate . . .
and worse than the Stasi ever was" or accuse the painter Bärbel
Bohley of "McCarthyism" because she wants to discover the people who betrayed her. Some writers think Biermann has claimed,
by grievance, the role of arbiter. He tells reporters who call him
what he told me—that "the subject is closed"—and two weeks
later he takes up the subject again on the pages of *Der Spiegel,* and
makes a lot of money, and people read him and say that Wolf Biermann has never suffered so profoundly or written so well.

The real Stasi, of course, are still around. It is easy to spot them
in Berlin. The agents who have not retired on pensions are driving
taxis. The officers are television stars, advising their talk-show
hosts as to the credibility of victims who complain, and the
authenticity of their files, and the moral qualities of the people
who spied on them. The generals are enjoying the good life on
the Bavarian lakes, waiting for trials they will almost certainly
win. Even Alexander Schalck-Golodkowski—who was the official
money launderer for the G.D.R., with a state holding company,
and billions of marks invested in companies all over the West—has
retired to a villa on the Tegernsee, which he learned to love on
business visits to Franz Josef Strauss and other old leaders of the
West German right who were making a lot of money out of Willy
Brandt's socialist *Ostpolitik.* Legally, they are no more accountable than most informers are accountable. Legally, they were
salaried functionaries of the East German state, and they were responsible for "order" in that state. ("But I loved you all," Erich
Mielke says now.)

In January, two conscript soldiers were sentenced for a shooting at the Berlin Wall—but not their general, who had given the orders about shooting anyone who tried to flee. It was not so different from Sascha Anderson and Rainer Schedlinski's getting exposed, while their controls hired literary agents and sold themselves as "historians." The files that might have implicated any of those Stasi in "actionable" crimes disappeared in the deal between the Stasi and the Berlin burghers who couldn't work their software and never thought to call up BASF or ask a West German to do it for them, and this is why informers complain about being "victims," and say that *they* are being ruined while the "system" goes free.

By now, even some of the people who created the system are blaming Stasi informers for the system—a situation I have heard compared to the Nazis' blaming the Gestapo. It makes life simpler, for East Germans and even for some West Germans—West Germans who in one way or another supported the Communist regime, because they made money from it, or because they spied for it themselves, or because they were ingenuous or deluded about it or sympathetic to it out of "socialist" principles, or because they feared fascism in West Germany more than Communism in East Germany, or because the division of Germany was comfortable, or even because the Cold War was a satisfying and convenient distraction from their own history. If the judgment of Nazi crimes (and German complicity) begun at Nuremberg stopped because of East Germany, it stopped in time to keep a generation of West Germans from having to account for themselves, to each other and to their victims and to "history." The Cold War "rehabilitated" that generation faster, and much more successfully, than it could ever have rehabilitated itself, and some of that generation is still running West Germany. It does not have much of an appetite for accountability. It considers itself a generation of realists and is more comfortable, in the end, doing business with apparatchiks of the old East German elite than with any of the messy, moralizing "sixties radicals in Earth shoes" on either side of the invisible Wall. It understands that protecting the men who once ran East Germany is really a kind of self-protection. Geiger says that the people who want to avoid a discussion of the Stasi now, in the interest of "unity" or "healing" or "stability," are keeping not only East Germans from understanding what happened to them but all Germans from understanding.

∞

A couple of months ago, the editors at *Tageszeitung* took some bits and pieces of Prenzlauer Berg poetry, strung them together, and published them as a "poem" by the Prenzlauer Berg writer "Rebecca Goldblum." (They said later that it had been a parody, though not many people in Prenzlauer Berg knew the difference.) Bert Papenfuss-Gorek is not, to my knowledge, in "Rebecca Goldblum's" poem. Most people consider him the best of the Prenzlauer Berg poets, the one who will survive Prenzlauer Berg and have a "German" reputation—despite the fact that he has been living in Prenzlauer Berg since 1976, as long as any of the poets, and has no intention of leaving. The Stasi tried to recruit him in 1972, when he was sixteen and still living with his mother in a town called Greifswald, on the Baltic coast. It was the year he got thrown out of high school and started writing poetry and broke with his father and was sent to work in a factory. His father was an army scientist—an important scientist who had once been able to move the family to Leningrad for a year, and who directed an institute near Dresden, and wanted Papenfuss-Gorek to study medicine. His father was "indispensable," which may have been why Papenfuss-Gorek was able to refuse the Stasi and suffer nothing worse than a couple of years in a factory. He was *débrouillard,* like his friend Sascha Anderson. He says that he grew up reading contraband books on "fundamental anarchy," that he was one of the "Greifswald intellectuals" who managed to get their literature from West Germany, and that for every Hermann Hesse he had to read at school he read a book by Max Frisch, or a book on the German baroque or Russian futurism or Dada sound poetry. He was reading Schwitters long before Anderson introduced Schwitters to Prenzlauer Berg. He was reading the Celtic poets and Albert Camus. "Real literature," he says. He was smart enough to send his own poems to a publisher in East Berlin called Neues Leben, and good enough to get six of them published in *Temperamenta,* which was the best underground East German literary magazine. It wasn't surprising that he moved to Prenzlauer Berg—"It was the boredom that made me come," he says now—or that by 1978 he was forbidden to publish, or to read at the Literaturhaus, like the other Prenzlauer Berg poets, or to keep the job he had managed to get as a lighting and sound engineer at a small experimental theater. He read privately, in people's houses or in churches. The ban was "good publicity," he says. He started a punk band called Ornament und Verbrecher—Ornament and Criminals—and read while the band played, and concluded that when it came to audiences in East Berlin, there was "no big difference" between the punks and the literati. He still plays with Ornament und Verbrecher, though he has a new group now, November Club, which he likes to describe as a "post-punk poetry trash band." And he still lives in his Prenzlauer Berg squat, with three black cats and a fiancée from Chicago and a lot of records and black sheets strewn across the floor. The color black is one of the few enthusiasms that "cool" people in the East and the West will admit sharing, and Papenfuss-Gorek is what most of them would call a "black person," meaning that he dresses in black—his particular style is black boots and slinky black leather pants and a black leather jacket decorated with zippers—and surrounds himself with black things. *He* thinks of himself as more of an "East person." He has the short spikey Prenzlauer Berg haircut, and a Prenzlauer Berg attitude about Sascha Anderson. He does not much care if Sascha Anderson informed, or even if Anderson informed on *him*. He says that there were maybe fifteen painters and musicians and poets in their group. They met in 1977 and stuck together, and everybody loved everybody else—and "if I love a person, if someone is my friend, I accept him as what he is, and I'm not suspicious about his character."

Papenfuss-Gorek was drafted the day before his twenty-sixth birthday. He refused to bear arms and was put in a special division where nobody had a weapon or was even instructed in how to use a weapon. The division was for "enemy persons": anarchists, Jehovah's Witnesses, neo-Nazis, punks, homosexuals, Christians, and a few poets. None of the other soldiers were allowed to talk to them—"We were interesting, but we were the scum," Papenfuss-Gorek says—and he got to practice his "solidarity," which he says was a good thing, because by the time he was back in Prenzlauer

Berg, most of the poets he knew were in trouble. There was no work for them, no cash coming in. The Stasi had given the word that they were "poetically negative," and Papenfuss-Gorek, who wanted to work with Ralf Kerbach on portfolios of silk screens and poems, lived on "money and help" from Heiner Müller and Christa Wolf, and depended on Sascha Anderson's West contacts. His first book of poems was called *Harm*. It came out in West Germany in 1985—the year before Anderson left Prenzlauer Berg. The next time he saw Anderson was at a reading in Rotterdam—it was 1988, and he had a visa by then—and then at a reading in the Italian Alps. Now they read together in Germany. Two months ago, they read in the town of Essen, in the Ruhr. They drove to Essen from Berlin and didn't talk about the Stasi, because "Sascha didn't want to and I'm not the person to force it." They were planning to go on to Cologne because an old Prenzlauer Berg poet they knew lives in Cologne, and *he* wanted to talk about the Stasi, but in the end Anderson refused. "There were 'discussions' at the reading," Papenfuss-Gorek says, "and I have to admit that a lot of people were angry at Sascha, and he was just saying the same thing: 'I didn't hurt anybody.' Sascha was amoral—that's what really disturbed them. And in some ways he's collapsed. He tries to vanish. It started happening this fall. There was a reading in Frankfurt, and Sascha came in and read one poem and there was no discussion. He didn't want discussion. He was really nervous. I said, 'Why are you nervous?' And he said, 'There's a campaign against me.' Biermann was writing that Anderson was a spy, and Sascha said he wasn't a spy—he had talked to the Stasi but he never *worked* for the Stasi. Well, I was kind of angry toward Biermann. Some people got angry at Sascha—good friends of Sascha's like Ralf Kerbach and Cornelia Schleime got really angry. Not me, because I didn't want to be in the company of Wolf Biermann. I didn't like the media scene. I thought, We have to work it out together, we have to have time and patience and not this stress. Sometimes I feel betrayed, but I still love Sascha. And I love to work with him on projects. I work on a book, something I like, and I think, We should be doing this book together."

Papenfuss-Gorek has three new books of poetry this year. He spread them around. He has a collection at Galrev, one at Janus, and one at a poetry press in Göttingen, and he is working on a couple of others—a portfolio for the Berlin art publisher Endart and a "book" that is really a compact disk for a record company called Steidl. He is in Sascha Anderson's anthology of Prenzlauer Berg poets, and he earns his living from poetry readings. I don't think that he is much concerned about whether the Prenzlauer Berg poets were "neutralized by French thought," as West Germans like Michael Naumann say, or whether the churches where he used to read were infiltrated by "pastoral Stasi sociologists," or whether the people at Basis Druck, writing their exposés, are going to ruin the neighborhood. He says that those people are in the "Stasi literati business—that's their program, that's their problem." He went on television once this year to defend Anderson. He said he knew a lot of people who talked to the Stasi, and mentioned Rathenow—"Look at Lutz Rathenow," he said. Now he thinks that Rathenow is a bad sport and can't take a joke, because after the show Rathenow hired a "West lawyer" who threatened to sue him for five hundred thousand marks if he mentioned Rathenow in public again. His view of Lutz Rathenow is that Rathenow shouldn't complain, "because he drives a red Saab." Papenfuss-Gorek has other things on his mind now. He is getting married. His fianceé sings with Ornament und Verbrecher, and he is wondering whether to add her name to Papenfuss, which is what he did when he married a woman named Gorek. He wants to go back to Ireland—he went after the Wall fell—and look at more Celtic poetry, and read more of the mythology. He wants to work on his own poems, which he has said are about "crossing a boundary, insolence, or something of that sort." Ralf Kerbach thinks that East Germany has marked him—that "he draws back and is a little closed"—but he is funny and wry and has a very sweet smile. One of his poems begins, "misfortune am i, a ruffian / & anything but devoted / your wallpaper is mottled / & so your coming to terms / overshadows necessity." It is a love poem, but it is also an East German love poem. "Wolf Biermann is no longer of the East," Papenfuss says. "He's the star of this whole thing, but he's no longer of the East. A great many things have happened in the East without him. He had the East as long as he was here."

SKINS

(JUNE 1993)

A couple of months ago, in the west of Germany, Hans Jürgen Ladinek of the Ludwigshafen criminal police called the mother of a skinhead named Gerhard Horn, who had just done time for what the skins call "sidewalk cracking," which means that on New Year's Eve of 1989, two months after the Wall came down, he and a friend had found a foreigner, kicked him to the sidewalk, and jumped on his head with their steel-tipped Doc Martens until they heard the bones crack. Detective Ladinek was checking up, making a friendly, unofficial call to see what life was like at the Horns' house now that Gerhard had served his year and a half and was out of prison and, presumably, in a job. Ladinek runs a special youth unit of the Ludwigshafen police, and he had been in charge of the investigation in the Horn case. It was Ladinek who had coaxed a confession from the "little butcher"—Horn was a butcher, "a rather small guy you wouldn't notice, but very fast, very brutal," Ladinek says—and had got him to name names and places and attacks in such detail that fifteen neo-Nazi skinheads, from as far away as Heidelberg and even Frankfurt, were rounded up and indicted for a series of previously unrelated crimes that ran from assault and battery to attempted murder.

Ladinek had been thinking about Horn that day because the New Year's Eve sidewalk cracking had been the first discernibly neo-Nazi crime in Ludwigshafen's history. He was curious about Horn, who had confessed after four hours of interrogation, saying that Ladinek was "the first person who ever listened to me talk," and, while Ladinek admits that it's hard to sit and listen to a man like Horn unless you're a cop looking for a confession or a Nazi enthusiast yourself, he wondered what Horn was thinking about his life on the skinhead scene after a year and a half in jail. Besides, he took an interest in the foreigner Horn had cracked—a boisterous young Turkish worker named Ender Basaran, who had somehow survived the cracking and was trying to get on with his life, despite the nerve damage to his face and a white scar next to his left eye and a lot of trouble seeing. Ladinek was helping Basaran with a problem of his own, the problem being a German girlfriend who claimed that Basaran had assaulted *her* after she took a job in a local bar where, according to Basaran, the girls were served along with the drinks instead of pretzels. He felt sorry for Basaran, who had lived in Germany since the age of one and still couldn't tell a hooker from a nice, open, loving German girl. He liked Basaran. What he liked most about Basaran was that he spoke the Ludwigshafen dialect—Pfälzisch, people in Rheinland-Pfalz call it—like a native, and, in fact, as well as Ladinek himself. He often said that the two things that helped him most when he dealt with skinheads and their families were his Pfälzisch and his macho manner—the skins, in his opinion, were marginally more intimidated by a big, bearded cop in jeans and boots, a cop with a stud in his ear and an old red sweatshirt on his back, than by a stiff policeman in a suit. He slipped right into Pfälzisch when he got on the phone with Gerhard Horn's mother. He was happy to hear that Gerhard now had hair and a job and normal clothes. "*Alles ist normal!*" Frau Horn told him. "*Wunderbar! Das ist wunderbar!*" he kept saying.

His German was thick. It was booming and coaxing and full of Pfälzisch sentiment. When Frau Horn lied and gave him the wrong address for Gerhard, and the wrong phone number, he called her back, laughing. You could hear him charming Frau Horn up and down the station-house hall. Ladinek does not put much stock in the notion of rehabilitating Nazi skinheads. He may have charmed Frau Horn, but when he got to Gerhard Horn, Gerhard told him, "*Leck mich am Arsch!*"—"Lick my ass!"—and that was one of the mildest things he said. Ladinek knows as much as any cop in Germany about what turns bored or bitter or disappointed boys into killers who crack Turks and set refugees on fire. Admittedly, he says, it is not much, but he does know that "they have chaos in their heads," and the idea of putting a therapist or a social worker, or even a cop, into a room with a skin and trying to solve his problems or raise his consciousness, or even scare him, amuses Detective Ladinek as much as it amuses the other Ludwigshafen detectives, who tend to agree with Ladinek that "there is no way to recover these kids."

People in the west of Germany who are not policemen arresting skinheads or foreigners avoiding skinheads have always assumed that the benign services of the welfare state could be applied successfully to any social problem, including the problem they have now. But the teenage skinheads, with their swastika tattoos and their alarming brutality and a pathology that Ladinek describes as "having no natural moral borders of yes and no," elude them. The skins today have nothing in common with the skins the West Germans thought they knew—the left skins, whom everybody here calls Redskins because the laces on their combat boots are red, for revolution. To a stranger who doesn't know the codes of earrings and insignia and tattoos, the right skins are indistinguishable from Redskins except that *their* shoelaces are white, for "white power." But the fact is that until the right skins discovered foreigners they were interested mainly in attacking Redskins (who are usually less interested in being menacing than in looking menacing) and in attacking punks (who are not menacing at all, unless you consider green hair or purple T-shirts or tipped-over trash cans menacing). Their ideology, if that is the word, is primitive. No one in Ludwigshafen can remember encountering an intelligent right skinhead, or even an articulate right skinhead. The skins say *"Heil Hitler!"* but they know nothing about Hitler, or the war, beyond the fact that Hitler exterminated people who were "different," which is what they like to do themselves. They do not even know about the "ethnic cleansing" going on a few hundred miles away in Bosnia now. They do not read newspapers. They read killer comic books and listen to Oi music, which is a kind of heavy-metal rock about the pleasures of genocide. Some of them think that Oi comes from the British skins, the Paki (for Pakistani) bashers, whom they admire as the first skins; they think that it means "original idea." Some of them think that it comes from "joy." And some of them think that it comes from the "oi" in "Doitschland." They go to Oi concerts. They do not know that other people think of "Oi" as a Yiddish word. They do not know Jews or anything about Jews, but Jews are certainly on their hit list, along with Turks, refugees, and asylum seekers, anybody "foreign." They try to attack Jews when they can find them. The last time skins in Germany attacked a Jew—they killed him—it turned out that the Jew may have been a Christian. They said later that he "looked" Jewish.

∞

Everybody here has a theory about skinheads. The skinheads are scrutinized and analyzed and categorized with what amounts to a touching German faith that with enough money, with enough attention and expertise, you will always arrive at an explanation. The Bundeskriminalamt, Germany's F.B.I., has put together a profile of the skins for policemen in places like Ludwigshafen, and so has the Verfassungsschutz, which is a special federal police for "protection of the constitution," and which investigates crimes against the state—Nazi crimes, terrorist crimes, crimes by groups that want to overthrow the government. Every policeman reads these profiles, except those policemen—there are a lot of them in Germany, but not in Ludwigshafen—who think that the skins are doing something useful. None of the profiles teach you much beyond statistics, because everything you learn from real skinheads contradicts some of the official wisdom. This much is known: there are about six thousand "right extremist" skins in Germany, meaning skins who identify themselves by Nazi jargon and carry Nazi tracts and sport Nazi paraphernalia they order from catalogues in Britain, Canada, and the United States. About thirty-five hundred of these skins live in the five new German states that everyone still calls East Germany, and the twenty-five hundred others live in the eleven states that everyone still calls West Germany. Last year they killed seventeen people; this year they have already killed nine. The government holds them responsible for three thousand attacks— five a day, lately—characterized by what Detective Ladinek and his friends at the Ludwigshafen police station call "extreme brutality." About 40 percent of those attacks took place in East Germany, but there are so few East Germans—a quarter of the number of West Germans—that the majority of skinhead crimes could be said to be East German crimes. For a while, this pleased—or at least appeased—West Germans, who do not like East Germans now that they own East Germany, and who still say—even now, two and a half years past unification—that "the wall in the head" is still much higher than the Wall between them ever was. The Germanys still tend to blame each other for everything terrible that happens, including the violence they are suffering now.

East Germans like to remind West Germans that the violence started in the West, in the nineteen-sixties, when the first Turkish workers were recruited to replace the cheap labor that before the Wall went up had crossed freely into the Federal Republic from East Germany and Poland. But the truth is that the violence that can properly and consistently be called neo-Nazi gang violence dates from the fall of the Wall, in November 1989, and from a virtual flood of refugees through East Germany, which had never really known any foreigners except the requisite Third World students who came for a Marxist-Leninist education and the ninety thousand conscript workers, from places like Cuba and Vietnam and Mozambique, who were quarantined like the slave labor that, in effect, they were. No one anticipated the fall of the Wall, no one anticipated the xenophobia that followed. No one reasoned that if East Germany had never had a "foreigner problem" it was very likely because East Germany had had so few foreigners with whom East Germans might have tried (and failed) to get along.

East Germans had learned in school that their parents and grandparents were never Nazis. They preserved the myth that had held East Germany together for forty years—the myth that East Germans had had nothing to do with Hitler, that East Germans were closer to socialism than to National Socialism. They never had to look at the past as something that involved them, and this may be why, when racism came out of the closet in East Germany, it proved to need nothing but a light dusting to look new. The skinhead style, which was taken up in West Germany as an English fashion, traveled fast to East Germany, where anything Western, and especially anything West German, became the last word in attitude and comportment among children with no sense of who they were or what they wanted to be or why the freedom they had inherited on November 9, 1989, carried such frustrations and disappointments.

It was clear that nearly everyone in East Germany shared those frustrations and disappointments. The skinheads who attacked

Vietnamese and Mozambican workers in a housing project in Hoyerswerda in the fall of 1991 were joined by their parents, their neighbors, and possibly even a few of their policemen, who shouted and cheered while they chased the foreigners through town. The skinheads who attacked Gypsy and Vietnamese refugees in Rostock last summer were cheered by *their* neighbors, and by a lot of people who weren't neighbors—people who had driven to Rostock from towns all over Mecklenburg for the entertainment. Those were daytime spectacles, public spectacles—"a theater of grievance," someone in Rostock called them—and, in fact, the Rostock attack was announced in advance, like theater, in one of the local papers. It was easy for West Germans to explain them—at least, until somebody thought to ask why other East Germans, with the same frustrations and disappointments, hadn't taken to tormenting strangers. The attacks seemed at first to have nothing to do with West Germany, although it was known that right-wing organizers from Hamburg and Berlin had been in Rostock watching the attacks, like talent scouts at a high-school soccer game.

West Germans talked about the malaise in East Germany. They pointed out that the shipyards that used to support Rostock were nearly shut down after the Wall fell, that a third of Rostock was out of work, that the only foreigners the Rostockers had ever seen were students from Providence who arrived each fall for a junior year called Brown in Germany, and that now, suddenly, there were thousands of refugees camped in their back yards and on their sidewalks—Gypsies, mainly, who picked their pockets and stole their groceries and shit in their gardens. They said that East Germany was "unprepared" for foreigners, unenlightened about foreigners, uneducated in democracy. They wrote pamphlets for the Gypsies, telling them not to shit in gardens. They revised their plans for distributing the refugees who were pouring into Germany. They allowed that it was foolish to expect East Germany to take its share of those refugees, especially when those refugees were Gypsies (the official word is "Romanian ethnic minority") whom the West Germans didn't want in *their* gardens. They talked about inadequate infrastructures and inadequate institutions. They made much of the fact that the minister of the interior in Mecklenburg hadn't commandeered the Rostock police until a refugee hostel was bombed and hundreds of foreigners were on the ground, getting oxygen. They said that maybe the minister hadn't known he was in charge of the Rostock police, and when that turned out to be true they said, "What do you expect in East Germany?" They said that it wouldn't have mattered anyway, since when the police did come they arrested the wrong skinheads—Redskins coming down the road to Rostock to defend the refugees.

The West Germans ignored the attacks that were starting at home. They called them isolated crimes, because they happened at night and never involved a cheering crowd, like the crowd in Rostock, or a rear guard, like the Hoyerswerda parents. The crimes in East Germany were deplorable but "understandable," they said, given the trauma of change in East Germany, whereas the crimes in West Germany were aberrant and had nothing to do with West German attitudes. The West Germans were not overly alarmed when a group of teenage skins in a West German village called Hünxe got drunk on the eve of Unity Day—the anniversary of the day the two Germanys voted to unite, and now something of a skinhead holiday—and put together a couple of Molotov cocktails and threw them into the house of a Lebanese family that had been living peacefully in the village for two years. The people in Hünxe pointed out that Hünxe was not a Nazi town. It was not even a Christian Democratic town. The mayor was a Social Democrat; the parents of some of the skinheads were Social Democrats. Hünxe had won a prize as "the nicest village" in Germany— though "nice" is not a word that many people would use for Hünxe if they saw the gentle Lebanese child who was burned in the fire and is horribly disfigured now. No one in Hünxe but the schoolteachers and the social workers thought that there was anything wrong with Hünxe. People said, "The boys were drunk, you know how young people are." Or they said, "Every boy has his own style." Or they said, "The boys were proud to be German. Who isn't?" It turned out that the father of one of the skinheads had decorated his basement bar with Nazi memorabilia and threw a big party every year on Hitler's birthday. "Everybody collects something," the skinhead's mother said. Some people in Hünxe collected teacups. She said, "My husband just collects something else."

∞

Late last year, skinheads in a town called Mölln, thirty miles east of Hamburg, bombed the house of a Turkish woman, and the woman and her niece and her small granddaughter died. The woman had lived in Mölln for thirty years, and her granddaughter was born there—they weren't refugees or asylum seekers or "guest workers" but as close to being "German" as you could get in a country that still practices *jus sanguinis,* and this seems to have shocked West Germans as much as the attack itself. It was after Mölln that people in West Germany started worrying about *their* skinheads. The social workers had a theory that the West skinheads came from what they called "disordered families"—violent, abusive, "collapsed" families—or from broken homes, and had "no positive experience" and "no positive relationships." It was not a theory that accounted entirely for the Gerhard Horns or for the skins whose parents did in fact collect teacups. The economists had a theory that the West skinheads were a Lumpenproletariat, an underclass with no "access" to the society or, indeed, to jobs in the society, and they said that the problem was economic; the truth was that most of the West skins were apprentices out of technical high schools or were workers with salaries. The sociologists came up with a theory that the skinheads were something "new" in Germany—they were "the children of industrialization," and represented "the isolation of the individual in the industrial world" —and then the psychoanalysts said no, the skins were really in "intergenerational conflict" and were identifying with their grandfathers and with the *Heile Welt,* the safe, stable, orderly Germany that those grandfathers, in their dotage, remembered as the Third Reich. A psychoanalyst I know in Frankfurt is treating a teenage skin who dreams about being a hero of the Reich—the skin "goes out and shoots some Russians," and then he sits alone by a campfire with his rifle, feeling heroic—and a psychoanalyst I know in East Berlin is treating a teenage skin who has the same dream, except that in his dream he has been shooting Americans.

The two analysts could count as experts, because not many people besides policemen get to have a conversation with skinheads—except, of course, other skinheads. The skins are not articulate to begin with. "Really stupid" is the consensus at the Ludwigshafen station house. Most of them are not capable of—or interested in—explaining why they find foreign people or homeless people or handicapped people or any of the other people they kill unpleasant, or why they seem to enjoy killing those people; their favorite song is a piece of Oi called "Türken Raus" that goes "Turkish cunt shaved naked, Turkish cunt shaved away." They like to think of themselves as independent, and even the politicians from right-wing parties like the German People's Union and the German National-Democratic Party, which often try to recruit them as bodyguards, have trouble getting more of a response than Detective Ladinek got from Gerhard Horn. No one knows how long they will want to be independent (though it is worth noting that one of the Mölln skinheads had joined the National Democrats, "for the free beer"). The experts keep publishing their theories, and the government keeps publishing its profiles, but no one really knows whether the skins are "Germany" or a lunatic criminal fringe you could find in any Western country—something terrible but "normal." No one knows whether they are aberrant or symptomatic—today's anomaly or tomorrow's Storm Troopers. Germans who had spent the winter marching in *Lichterketten*—candle vigils—to protest the violence never expected that late last week, six months after Mölln, skinheads in Solingen would kill five women and children in another Turkish family, a family that had been living in West Germany for twenty-three years. The German writer Hans Magnus Enzensberger says that the skinheads' ideology, such as it is, is an "effective masquerade," but no one knows what, if anything, lies behind that masquerade. Skinheads are not very interesting.

∞

Ender Basaran didn't know Gerhard Horn or the other skinhead who tried to kill him. The skinheads lived in projects, on the edge of town, and Ender lives in the middle of Ludwigshafen, on a street where the Turks and the Germans get along—a street where people talking about "foreigners" usually mean the Ghanaian refugees camped around the corner in an old barracks. Ender is twenty-five now. He looks no different from most young Germans on his street. He has the latest German haircut—long in back, and short and spiky on top, like his friend Detective Ladinek's haircut—and, with his haircut and his Pfälzisch Deutsch, and his baggy jeans and the pack of Marlboros sticking out of his shirt pocket, it is hard to think of him as "foreign." He says that maybe it is his "Turkish gold" that makes him look foreign to a skinhead. He likes gold. He wears a shiny gold watch and a shiny gold ring and a gold chain around his neck. They represent his capital—all he can afford by way of conspicuous display to let the world know that Ender Basaran is not simply a *Gastarbeiter* living off his German hosts but a prosperous and productive member of the Kehl window-washing company. He describes himself as the man who keeps the windows in Ludwigshafen clean.

Twenty-five thousand of the hundred and seventy thousand people in Ludwigshafen work for BASF, the chemical company. The city courts the company, and in large part *is* the company. When BASF arrived, in 1865, there was not much more to Ludwigshafen than a Rhine fortress and a pub for the soldiers whose job it was to defend the people in Mannheim, just across the river, from the soldiers in a French fortress a couple of miles to the west. BASF built the city. It began with a grid of brown brick workers' houses, hidden, in proper nineteenth-century factory-town fashion, behind a ring road of big white houses for the managers, and eventually it moved north along the river to build a neighborhood called Hemshof, where seven thousand foreigners—nearly a quarter of the foreigners in the city—live now.

Ender rarely goes to Hemshof. It amuses him that Detective Ladinek prefers to meet him in a Hemshof bar—a Turkish bar— rather than in the German bar in Ender's own neighborhood. He thinks that Ladinek has a weakness for "folklore." The Turkish bar has a huge gold watch on the wall, with a clock for a face, which is really an outsized version of Ender's watch. He admires the clock, but he prefers places where men and women drink to-gether—"European places," he calls them. He likes to say that his family is "more of a European family," although his father goes to the mosque every day, and sits with the men after prayers and listens to the gossip. Ender gets *his* gossip from the right-wing tabloid *Bild Zeitung,* which is the journal of record of German workers. "Hey, I'm a worker!" he tells people who wonder what a foreigner like Ender is doing reading a newspaper devoted to the cause of sending foreigners home. He carries a snapshot of his mother, a pale, beautiful woman in a scoop-neck sweater and a strand of pearls who works in the kitchen of one of the Ludwigshafen hospitals. He wants you to know that his mother is nothing at all like the squat, ruddy Turkish women you see on the streets of Hemshof, wrapped in the bulky coats and gabardine head shawls that they brought from Turkey. He likes Turkey, but he doesn't think that either he or his mother belongs in Turkey. It is as hard for Ender to imagine his beautiful mother in a chador as it is for him to imagine his father, who worked for twenty-five years at the Halberg Metalworks, tending sheep in a tribal village near the Bulgarian border—though that in fact is what his father did.

His father never intended to come to Germany. It was his uncle who got the job at Halberg, and the German work papers; his father "borrowed" the name and came instead, and that was the beginning of the Ludwigshafen Basarans. His father is a small, humorous, courtly man, a family man—someone you would call a good German citizen if Turks who had lived and worked in Germany for thirty years were citizens. But Enver Basaran is not a citizen, and neither is Ender or his brother, Osman, who is sixteen and was born in Ludwigshafen; the fact that Germans are citizens by "blood," not birth, means that a boy like Osman, born and raised and living in Germany, will in all likelihood remain a foreigner. The definition is specific. Ender is a foreigner, and not an immigrant, because officially there are no immigrants in Germany—only contract guest workers. There are no laws about immigrants (the word "immigrant" does not appear in the German statutes), although in reality there are six and a half million foreigners here who think of themselves as immigrants. The ethnic illusions of Germany, it must be said, embarrass most Germans. They do not embarrass Ender. Ender likes to say that being a nonperson is "no problem," because people who don't exist can't have problems.

Nearly two million of the foreigners in Germany come from

Turkey, and there are, of course, some ways for some of those Turks to get to be German citizens. The process is so elaborate and so contingent and so long—you have to have worked in Germany for fifteen years before you can even start the process—that only about thirteen thousand of them have managed to "become" German, or even bothered to try. Most of them came here with the understanding that if they lived quietly and demanded nothing, Germany would leave them alone. It was an understanding they passed quickly to their children, who saw Germans diligently making money, and took it to mean that money, and an enthusiasm for money, was another kind of citizenship. That enthusiasm became their most effective camouflage, the quality they thought would make Germans comfortable about them. "Money, I love it," Ender says by way of an introduction, mixing his Pfälzisch with the English he learned at school. "Turkey's fine, but there are nix bucks in Turkey." He says that money is his politics, by which he means that to survive as a *Gastarbeiter* in Germany you leave politics to the Germans.

It upsets Ender to think that the skinheads who attack Turks in towns like Ludwigshafen may be confusing the Turks with refugees. Half a million refugees, from as many as forty countries, entered Germany last year, demanding asylum (a quarter of a million entered the year before), and the state houses them and feeds them and, from the point of view of a young, hardworking Turkish man, indulges them with a life of charity. Ender once read in *Bild Zeitung* that people on the right want a referendum on the question of foreigners, like the referendum the Austrians called. He says that maybe, if he had a vote, he would vote with them, and then he adds, "Of course, if I could vote I wouldn't be a foreigner." He thinks that people on the right vote the way they do as a kind of protection against people they don't know and don't understand, and this is how he feels about the seven hundred refugees camped right now in the Ludwigshafen barracks and in two big riverboats near the old Rhine bridge, guarded by policemen day and night and taking up the time of nine social workers from the mayor's office. He does not feel much solidarity with the refugees. He may not be an "immigrant," or have an immigrant's access to citizenship, but he has an immigrant's suspicion of newer immigrants, and wonders sometimes whether they are giving the "good" foreigners like him a bad reputation, and whether life would be better in Ludwigshafen if they all went home. It is a classic sign of assimilation.

The first skinheads Ender knew were foreigners—Yugoslavs and Africans whose parents worked in Ludwigshafen, and who came to high school in combat boots and bomber jackets, trying to look as tough as the German skins they saw at the Saturday soccer games. There was always trouble after the games in Ludwigshafen, although at first people thought of it as "Mannheim trouble," since it was usually Mannheim's team playing in Ludwigshafen's stadium. Mannheim skins would march through town on their way to the train station, frightening the foreigners they passed. In those days, Ender says, the foreigners ran away. Now—it started when he was cracked—the foreigners jump right in and fight back. "I'm not Hulk Hogan, but come on, if you need a fight, it's an eye for an eye," he likes to say when he is speaking English. When he is speaking German, he quotes an old Turkish proverb: "The snake that doesn't bite me shall live a thousand years."

He does not talk easily about his beating. He must have been in shock when the skins were jumping on his head, because he can't remember the worst of it anymore, or, reasonably, he doesn't want to remember. The family was home celebrating New Year's. "We celebrated a lot and drank a lot of alcohol, and after a while the men got bored," he says now. "They wanted to see something else besides the women in the apartment, so we went out"—to the friendly "European" bar across the street that Ender prefers. There was already trouble on the street. The skins were out, kicking down doors and throwing firecrackers. They were not looking for the Basarans. They were looking for *Aussiedler,* which is the word used here for ethnic Germans from Eastern Europe. They thought of those Germans as just as foreign as the Basarans—which, it could be said, was true. Five of the skins were drinking in a corner of the bar when Ender and his father and one of his uncles got there, but it was dark and the Basarans didn't see the skins. They went straight to the counter and asked for drinks, and when the bartender wouldn't serve them—he said it was too late, but it may be that he was worried about a fight—they left. Ender and his father were crossing the street when the skins came out and started running toward them. Ender screamed. He says that the whole street must have heard him screaming, but no one helped him. He remembers someone slashing at his face, and he remembers running, and after that "it's like a dream, and the next thing I remember is lying in a parking lot, and the police were there and my mother was there, and she kept saying 'Where are your shoes?' and I kept saying 'Where's my father?' " One of the policemen tried to pull him up by the collar. His mother rushed between them, but not before Ender hit the policeman. He managed to stand then. He said to the policeman, "Now, hit me!" and then he collapsed, and woke—he doesn't know how much later—in the hospital where his mother works. Gerhard Horn described it this way: "We thought he was dead, so we left him."

∞

Helmut Kohl, the German chancellor, was born in Ludwigshafen, and he likes to say that the problems in Germany are not so terrible if you look at the rest of Western Europe—if you look at the South of France, where the Front National gets 30 percent of the vote, or the North of England, where there is violence against foreigners all the time. The question, of course, is how "German" is the German version. Eike Geisel, a Berlin writer who has been working on Jewish archives from the nineteen-thirties, is convinced that the real problem in 1933, when Hitler came to power, was not the eight hundred thousand Nazis but the indifference of millions of working-class people to those Nazis—the indifference of people who should have made an opposition. He calls this indifference their *Deutscher Blick*—which means a kind of German gaze, a German regard that is really a disregard. It is something you see on the faces of old people in the Berlin subway—people who have survived the war, and may even have fought in the war—when someone shoves a foreigner aside or starts shouting at a foreigner to stand up and give a "real German" his seat. They watch, and even stare, but the exchange does not concern them and they are not moved. Geisel thinks that what is "different" about Germany is that Germans have had "so little experience in defending the rights of others," and that maybe it makes no difference who those "others" are.

Many Germans do protest the violence. Three hundred thousand people marched in Berlin last year, on the anniversary of Kristallnacht, and the president of Germany, Richard von Weizsäcker, marched with them. He was pelted with eggs and tomatoes, though not by right skinheads. He was pelted by Redskins, who claimed that he was there as the official "good German." Kohl, who has the power, put in an appearance in Berlin (and left fast, for "reasons of security"), but he avoided any promises after Berlin. There were regrets about Mölln from Kohl's office, but not much in the way of reassurance beyond the fact that he instructed the attorney general to "interpret" his jurisdiction broadly—it covers crimes against the state, which are not usually crimes against grandmothers—and send in federal prosecutors to investigate. Kohl is not any more reassuring now. He refused to go to Solingen, or to memorial services for the Turks who died in Solingen, or to their funerals, in Turkey; he even refused to go on television and talk to other Germans about them. He wants Germans to believe that the killings today are "ordinary" crimes, something the police can handle—not something to alarm a German chancellor.

It isn't surprising that the Berlin march had very little effect on policy, but the demonstrations after Berlin had nothing to do with policy. They were candle vigils. Somebody called them "the triumph of the good will," and a lot of Germans shared that sentiment, because the vigils were disturbingly like the peace vigils of the sixties and the disarmament vigils of the seventies. They had less to do with offering practical political solutions than with what one West German described as "middle-aged Christians saying to God, 'Look at us! We're the good Germans, out for a head count.' " The first of the vigils took place in Munich, in December, and a month later Ludwigshafen had its own vigil. People in Ludwigshafen walked east to the old Rhine bridge, and people in Mannheim walked west to the bridge, and they met in the center, and formed a chain of lights across the Rhine. It was by all accounts a beautiful sight, and perhaps for this reason the asylum seekers stayed in their riverboats and watched, instead of lighting candles and marching themselves. Not many of the Ludwigshafen Turks marched, either. Ender Basaran said what many of them said—that the violence in Germany was "Germany's affair." The first time Turks took to the streets in protest was just this week, after the Solingen murders. They marched peacefully at first; then they started rioting. Someone compared their anger to "a dam bursting"—which was accurate, since they are still rioting, six days later, and downtown Solingen is in ruins.

⚬

The principle (if that is the word) of *jus sanguinis* is not something the Nazis slipped into German law (although the Nazis certainly used it). It was there before there was a Germany—when "Germany" was a language and an ethnic stock spread through Europe by peasants working the land that Germans owned. Bismarck, constructing a real Germany for a Prussian king, recognized two ways of being German—*Deutsche,* for people who were German by blood, and *Reichsdeutsche,* for people who were German by virtue of living in the new nation. ("Bismarck was multicultural," the Green politician Joschka Fischer says.) But in 1913, fifteen years after Bismarck died, Germany looked back and instituted *jus sanguinis,* and after the Second World War it looked back even further, and added *Volksdeutsche,* for Germans born or living outside the country, who were guaranteed a "right of return." By then, there was no real notion of Germany as a nation of citizens, like the French notion. Germany was not simply a community bound by common rights. Germany was blood, it was "culture." Fischer calls it "the terrible old idea," and Werner Bohleber, the psychoanalyst with the patient who shoots Russians in his sleep, calls it "the old, romantic, collective fantasma," but it persists today in what the philosopher Jürgen Habermas describes as "the new reference point of the old Bismarckian Reich," by which he means that even in his own circles there are people who talk about the new Germany as the beginning of the recovery of the "greater Germany" of Bismarck's project—a kind of reassembling of the German *Volk* from Poland to Croatia. No one argued in 1949 about incorporating *jus sanguinis* and the right of return into the West German constitution. Liberal Germans wanted Germans everywhere to share in the responsibility for the war, and for the moral recovery from the war, and conservative Germans wanted more Germans for the economic recovery. Twelve million "ethnic Germans" arrived in West Germany between 1945 and 1962, when the Wall effectively stopped any emigration. A million have arrived since the Wall came down, and there are still two and a half million "Germans" outside Germany, about a million and a half of them Germans whose families went east in 1744 with Catherine the Great, and who are waiting now in what used to be the Soviet Union, trying to calculate just how German they will seem to a gang of skinheads out looking for *Aussiedler* on a dark night in Frankfurt or Cologne. The truth is that Germany will not be rid of its blood fantasies as long as those fantasies are part of official definitions of identity—"until the political culture moves from Reich to Republic," as one German writer put it, or, as Habermas says, "until we stop defining ourselves as an ethnic state and start defining nationality in legal terms." The only other democracy with a right of return written into its laws is, of course, Israel. It is an irony lost on most Germans, who also talk solemnly about "the German diaspora" and "the German homeland." A Hamburg comic called this "German Zionism: the theocracy of the blue eyes and the blond braids."

West Germans have lived for forty-five years with a fairly healthy ambivalence about loving Germany. The country of *jus sanguinis,* the country with six and a half million foreigners and no immigrants, was also the country with the most liberal asylum laws in Europe, if not the world. Not anymore. Those laws were changed in the Bundestag this month, under pressure from the right, and Article 16 of the German constitution no longer carries its famous guarantee of the right of asylum to "any politically persecuted person"—which means that Germany will stop taking in anyone who makes it to the German border and demands asylum, and giving him the right to stay until his status is decided. Now Germany will do what most Geneva Convention countries do: instruct its border guards to turn back refugees who come through other Convention countries, or from border countries, or from "safe" countries, or, indeed, from countries other than their own.

The idea of Germany as an asylum country was part of the project of a moral recovery—though practically (and propagandistically) speaking it was a function of the Cold War, and was not much of a problem for West Germans as long as there were Communists in the East who could be counted on to keep refugees from leaving. There was always a certain amount of refugee dumping by the East into West Germany, but it never seriously upset the balance of East-West provocation. And not many refugees got to Germany through Western Europe. The countries they stopped in either let them stay or (more likely) sent them home, and West Germany went on with its recovery and got to be unimaginably rich, and, slowly, people in Pakistan or Sri Lanka or Nigeria thinking about a safer (or a better or a more lucrative) place to settle stopped thinking about Los Angeles and Paris and started thinking about Munich and Cologne.

Last year, two hundred and thirty thousand *Aussiedler* came "home" to Germany. Two hundred thousand Bosnians came, and a hundred thousand Romanian Gypsies. They found Germany in the middle of the recession that is usually referred to here as "unification blues." There was no money to pay for East Germany and at the same time absorb so many people (or so the government said). There was nowhere to put so many people. Thousands of refugees went into old American army barracks (a hundred thousand American troops in Germany had gone to the Gulf to fight, and never came back), and the rest were scattered, city by city, *Land* by *Land,* throughout the country, at the expense of whatever town happened to (the official word) "receive" them. They lived in boats like the Ludwigshafen riverboats, or in tents or containers or defunct hotels that were sold, at a huge profit, to town councils with a refugee-housing problem. They were given food, shelter, and minimal welfare. The asylum seekers I met at the Gelnhausen barracks got eighty-one marks a month, which is worth, at most, five beers and a carton of cigarettes.

Kohl had never told the Germans, East or West, how cruel and costly unifying Germany would be. He was happy to let the foreigners take the blame for the unemployment and the special taxes and the impossible resentments—that is, until the killing started, and Germany suddenly looked like "Germany" to the rest of the world. Germans complained, with reason, that they were getting more than their fair share of refugees—they like to point out that while four hundred and fifty thousand refugees applied for asylum here last year, four hundred and fifty refugees applied in Poland—but the fact remains that refugees don't want to go to Poland.

There is no way for Germany to avoid its reputation as a prosperous country, or a free country, or a country where the hospitals work and the schools are open and nobody starves, without turning into Poland. Some of the German Greens think that the problem has been words like "foreigner." They never use them. They use the Green term "world person." They are sure that once Germans start thinking in terms of world people they will love the world people, and pretty soon everybody in the world will love everybody else. Maybe. Right now, Germany's refugee problem can't really be separated from its problem with all the foreigners who live here. Germany has to admit, finally, that they *are* here. Spiros Simitis, who worked for months to keep Article 16 from being dismantled, says that now that it *is* dismantled it is more important than ever for Germany to develop an immigration policy and draft immigration laws and let a certain number of people enter each year as immigrants, with reasonable access to citizenship—and, especially, to acknowledge children born and living in Germany as German. The cracking of Ender Basaran began with the fiction that Germany was "German"—and the conviction that Germany should be "German"—and ended with a young man lying in a parking lot on the main street in Ludwigshafen with his head cracked open while the neighbors who heard him screaming opened their holiday champagne.

∞

The mayor of Ludwigshafen is a Social Democrat from Westphalia. His name is Wolfgang Schulte, and the Party sent him to Ludwigshafen in 1985, to run for the city council and become a deputy to the old mayor, who was getting on, and then to take over when the mayor retired. His job in Ludwigshafen was Social Affairs—which meant that, for all practical purposes, any problem having to do with skinheads or foreigners was going to be *his* problem. He remembers 1985 as the year the third big wave of foreigners (the Turks came first, and then the Vietnamese) began to hit Ludwigshafen. He likes to say that he arrived "in time for" the Iranians, the Afghans, the Kurds, and the Somalis—for refugees fleeing from wars and revolutions and regimes that some people in Ludwigshafen had never heard of. All told, eleven hundred refugees came to Ludwigshafen in the next five years. The city housed them and fed them, and paid for more German classes and more sewing circles and social workers, and, eventually, it rented the riverboats. They were hotel boats, and easier to guard than an asylum house on a busy street, or a Turkish store. The only time anyone tried to attack the riverboats—it was "a spontaneous attack by a group of young people," Schulte says—the guards stationed at the boats were able to stop them by brandishing a couple of ordinary water hoses.

Schulte is proud of the Ludwigshafen police. He knows that most of them are progressive and humane, and look at Ludwigshafen's "foreigner problem" as a problem having mainly to do with the people who want the foreigners to go. Two years ago, when thirty very young skinheads stoned an asylum house that Schulte had built for some new refugees, the police invited the skinheads' parents to the station on Wittelsbachstrasse, and they say that now only four or five of those skins are active. They are the hard core, the ones Detective Ladinek describes as having "chaos in their heads." Ladinek himself thinks they would be in trouble with or without the foreigners, and this is probably true, since one of them went to the World Cup soccer games in Italy in 1990 and was arrested and deported within a few hours. The skins who stoned the asylum house had actually set out looking for Redskins; they couldn't find any Redskins, but they were worked up and boozed up and seem to have needed to attack somebody, and the refugees were "visible"—they knew where refugees lived, because refugees usually lived together. Schulte says, "It's not just a problem of violence against foreigners, it's a problem of violence against everything," and in many ways that problem is the same all over Germany. The skins in Mölln were on their way to an asylum house when they killed the Turkish family. The skins in Hünxe, one of them told Esther Schapira, a young Frankfurt television journalist who made a remarkable movie about the village, were looking "for Jews, for anybody not German."

Ludwigshafen has always been a fairly open, tolerant town. There are no old Ludwigshafen families talking about maintaining traditional "German" values, for the obvious reason that there are no old Ludwigshafen families. Schulte says that being a foreigner and a worker is probably the only "old" Ludwigshafen tradition. The town is still solidly a workers' town, where everybody belongs to the Gewerkschaftsbund, and the Social Democrats never get less than 50 percent of the votes, and even the cops will go out on a candle vigil against racism. It is not a beautiful city, or a city with the money or the clout to choose its refugees, the way some West German cities can. (I know a rich town near Frankfurt that negotiates for Asian and European refugees, and then "invites" them for a two-week trial.) But it is a city that lives easily with foreigners. There was never much violence against anybody in Ludwigshafen. Seven or eight homicides a year—fewer than in most German cities. Schulte says that until this year his work was mainly to "create a balance" between the demands of the foreigners who came and the needs of the people who were there before them.

Now, suddenly, that balance is in question. Schulte thinks that two things are changing Ludwigshafen: the number of refugees, which has doubled in the last few years, and, more important, the arrival in Ludwigshafen of fundamentalist Islam. The mayor does not have much political patience with orthodoxies. He thinks they get in the way of assimilation, and Social Democrats like Schulte believe in assimilation. When he came to Ludwigshafen, the problems between the local kids and the Turkish kids were mainly what he calls "males going off." The German kids and the Turkish kids would meet at the youth clubs and insult each other and occasionally fight each other. "They were both minorities, in a way," Schulte says. They were scrambling for the same housing and the same jobs, and the only time they really got together was when an institution—a kindergarten, a classroom, a soccer club—got them together. But they were not scrambling to be different. Schulte worries that what he calls the "Islamization of Ludwigshafen" is going to complicate the very ordinary problem of there not being enough to go around. He is a realist and knows, as he puts it, that "some Germans do not deal well with other cultures." He thinks that when Turkish families start sending their girls to the market in chadors and their sons to Koranic schools, they feed the fear that the skinheads enact so brutally and the right exploits.

The asylum laws and the politics of the Middle East have opened cities like Ludwigshafen to all kinds of militants and fundamentalists, who come to recruit the Muslim workers already there as a kind of vanguard—visible and vocal. "We don't know who's in the city," Schulte says. "There are Turks, Kurds, Pakistanis. People come and go. It's the price of an open society." Now he is not so sure it's a price that the city can pay. He says sometimes, "What will happen to Ludwigshafen when the whole Red Army comes, and asks us to support it?" He worries that fantasies like that are giving the parties on the right their issues.

Four years ago, two German nationalists were elected to the city council on a platform having mainly to do with foreigners. One was expelled for hitting a local punk on the head with a baseball bat because he didn't like his hair, and the other eventually resigned, but Schulte assumes that right-wing politicians like them will be back after the next elections. People in Ludwigshafen are learning to blame the foreigners for whatever crime they have. They know all about the Turkish mafia and the Kurdish mafia. They know all about the African who was caught collecting welfare from eight Rheinland-Pfalz villages, and about the local Thais who have been importing Asian children as prostitutes. But they tend to ignore the German crime, a lot of which is linked to the neo-Nazis. The bar where the skins who cracked Ender Basaran had their headquarters—it's called the Crazy Corner, and it's painted with black, red, and yellow stripes, like the German flag—was owned by a local criminal who sold drugs and had a houseful of Nazi paraphernalia. He turned up, murdered, in Luxembourg last year, and maybe because of this the skins have not been much in evidence in Ludwigshafen lately. Ladinek saw a group of them not so long ago, hanging out at a demonstration, and he sent them packing. He says, "I'm not a law-and-order person, but they have to know you mean it."

The word is out that the Ludwigshafen police "mean it." The master sergeant of the uniformed police is a chubby paterfamilias named Jakob Falk, but his cops refer to him now in English as "the skin hunter." He is deceptively benign when he says, "When the skins attack, it hurts me personally." He has made it clear that "here they are not welcome," but he is not under the illusion that they have disappeared. The fifteen skins who were rounded up after the attack on Ender have, if not an organization, then a network. They know hundreds of other skins from Oi concerts and soccer games, and they get together with those skins to "celebrate" on holidays like New Year's Eve and Unity Day. They are what Ladinek calls "actively connected."

The Crazy Corner skinheads moved on after the attack. They tried meeting in a Saarland bar, and when the bartender threw them out they went to a bar in Kaiserslautern. Now they have their meetings in Frankenthal, ten miles from Ludwigshafen. Falk, who tracks them, says that it's always the same skins, the same bars, the same concerts, the same soccer games, the same pattern. There is not much more he can say, because there is no overall government file on skinheads. The government claims, with reason, that a file on people with shaved heads and bomber jackets would violate its data-protection laws, but this makes it almost impossible for local police to trace a skinhead meeting to the kinds of crimes that often follow those meetings. A couple of months ago, eighty skinheads met in Cottbus, in East Germany, near the Polish border. Five nights later, there were skinhead attacks all over Germany—four attacks on refugees, three on Jewish cemeteries, one on a Turkish restaurant in an asylum center—and no one knows, or presumably will ever know, whether they were random attacks or attacks planned at that Cottbus meeting. The closest thing to a skinhead file that Germany has (besides a Verfassungsschutz file on "right extremists") is a record of hooligan crimes in the data bank at the Bundeskriminalamt, in Wiesbaden. It tells them a lot about the people who start fights at soccer matches—one of the Solingen skins was one. But those are not always (or necessarily) the people who listen to Oi and get drunk and then go out and try to murder foreigners.

∞

Late last year, the leader of an Oi band called the Böhse Onkelz—which, if it were spelled right, would mean the "Bad Uncles"—got in touch with Daniel Cohn-Bendit about performing at a Frankfurt concert called Rock Against the Right. Most people do not think of Daniel Cohn-Bendit as someone involved with concerts. They think of him as Danny the Red, the Paris student with the curly red hair and the Little Red Book who led the occupation of the Sorbonne in May of 1968 and was expelled to Germany (the rumor was that he made the trip in Jacques Lacan's Jaguar). But Cohn-Bendit is German, and Jewish, and when he came home to Frankfurt he worked in a bookshop and started a radical review and got into German politics. He was a Sponti (for "spontaneous"), and then a Green, and four years ago he ran for office and ended up as a deputy mayor of Frankfurt, in charge of a bureau of his own creation called the Office of Multicultural Affairs. Frankfurt has more foreigners for its size (and apparently fewer skins) than any other German city, and it was considered a typically "Frankfurt" idea to try to court the boys and girls who might otherwise go to Oi concerts with a great concert about loving foreigners.

The problem was that it is almost impossible to have a great rock concert in Germany. Apart from a couple of Hamburg groups, German rock is terrible. The Onkelz, who were responsible for the song about shaving away Turkish girls, were no worse, musically speaking, than the groups like Tote Hosen (Dead Trousers), whose heart was in the "right left place"—only the Onkelz' message was hateful, and maybe because of this they had always had a certain celebrity in Frankfurt, which was where they lived. The murders in Mölln changed that. Their record "Heilige Lieder"—an ambiguous piece of Oi about Germany conquering the world with a "holy-appearing song"—had been fifth on the charts for months in 1991, after Germany united, and was still popular with kids in East Germany, but it was considerably less popular in West Germany after the murders in Mölln, with millions of people lighting candles and going on vigils in memory of the Turks who died. The Onkelz were nearly thirty years old and hurting. No one would rent them a hall or book them a concert, or even stock their records in a store. It was said that with "Heilige Lieder" they had written the hymn for the violence—hundreds of attacks on foreigners—that the skinheads claimed as their personal celebration of German unification on the eve of October 3 last year.

The Onkelz said they had "changed." They said they were not racists anymore and had never been Nazis, but they did not persuade the impresarios who were putting together the Rock Against the Right concert to let them into the Frankfurt fairgrounds to perform, and so they called Cohn-Bendit and complained, and Cohn-Bendit threw them a press conference and announced that the Onkelz were going to give their own concert and raise money for asylum seekers and "star" in the city's ad campaign—"Don't give the right wing a chance."

To a lot of Germans, the idea of the Böhse Onkelz helping refugees was as ludicrous as the idea of the Ludwigshafen skinheads showing up for counseling. People said it was clear that Cohn-Bendit had never in his life been to a heavy-metal concert, let alone an Oi concert, and knew nothing about the violence of that sort of occasion—that he came from a generation of sixties and seventies people who were "stuck in the culture of radical bookshops and natural food and had no instinct for 'the culture of culture.' " (He said, "I won't say the Onkelz are clean, but the kids listen to these people, so I thought it was worth a try.") But the discussions in Frankfurt were instructive, because what *was* clear was that while middle-aged, middle-class Germans like Cohn-Bendit, Germans who had "made their 1968," knew a great deal about kids on the left, and even violence on the left, they knew very little about kids on the right and *their* violence, and where that violence came from—that the lessons of Weimar they had learned so earnestly at school might just as well have been the lessons of some other country. Some of them looked at the skinheads as a kind of mirror image of the left-wing terrorists in groups like the Red Army Faction. They assumed that the skinheads were organized and efficient, that they had some sort of global master plan, that they chose their victims cold-bloodedly and carefully, the way the Red Army Faction had chosen *its* victims, who were always the bankers and politicians and industrialists, the people with the economic and political power. They didn't understand the "chaos in the heads" of the East skins—or, for that matter, of their own skins—or why the chaos in the music of groups like the Böhse Onkelz was familiar, almost soothing, to the skins, or even that it was chaos.

The skins in Ludwigshafen liked to listen to the Onkelz, and to a group from Cologne called Störkraft, and a group called Endsieg, and one called Kahlschlag (which describes, say, what a field would look like after a couple of days of napalm). The stores may boycott those groups, but their tapes circulate in the skinhead underground and are the more desirable for being boycotted. Skinheads follow the news about police raids on Oi studios and Oi producers—it's the only news they do follow, except the news on television about themselves. They know when "Türken Raus" was banned, although it's probably safe to say they do not know that the Onkelz started as a punk band, and that their own particular violence had nothing to do with Turks; it involved a mild amount of hippie bashing in the local flea markets. Klaus Walter, who writes about rock and produces the rock program at Hessischer Rundfunk, says that the Onkelz were "dumb kids who maybe got into the right without really wanting to." He means that the more abusive they were, the more they sold, and that the more they sold, the more attention they got—and they were not the kind of people to reflect about what kind of attention that was.

The lead Onkel—his name is Stephan Weidner, and he is the group "spokesman," being by all accounts the only Onkel capable of putting a sentence together—went off to India after his meeting with Cohn-Bendit and the Frankfurt press. No one knew if he went to find his Aryan roots, or what he would do in a country with nine hundred million people at least as dark as the Turks he wanted to shave away, but Walter, who doesn't think that groups like Weidner's should be allowed to perform in Germany, said when he left, "He's out of it. He's gone from dishwasher to millionaire, and now he's in India, chilling out, smoking grass, while people here are getting murdered."

In the end, it probably doesn't matter whether the Oi business is cynical or stupid or angry, or even ideological. What matters is that it is big business—business for the masses—and that it links the neo-Nazis surfacing in Germany now to millions of latchkey children looking for something to do, someone to blame, some way to pass the time in towns or projects with a parking lot, a pizzeria, a public phone booth, and not much else. The business belongs, in large part, to a man named Herbert Egoldt, who lives near Cologne and puts out an underground label called Rock-O-Rama. Egoldt used to have a record store. He specialized in punk music, and the Cologne punks would meet on Saturdays at the store and talk about what was wrong with Germany, and eventually they started fighting about what was wrong with Germany. "The scene split, left punks and right punks," Walter says. Egoldt went with the right and liked it.

Nazi language is illegal in Germany. It falls under the category of *Volksverhetzung,* which includes incitement by "negative propaganda," and is the reason you don't find Oi in the big chain stores in cities like Frankfurt and Cologne. You find it in little record shops in towns in East Germany which nobody bothers to monitor—or, perhaps, wants to monitor. East Germany is Herbert Egoldt's best market. The Onkelz' most vicious tapes are still sold openly there, although the Onkelz themselves claim that they wanted to sue Egoldt to get those tapes out of circulation. They recorded "Heilige Lieder" not with Egoldt but with a small Frankfurt company, and tried to persuade the critics that they were ironists at heart, and that their lyrics were really a "double message," something on the order of Bruce Springsteen's "Born in the U.S.A." Groups like the Onkelz are not an easy subject for a young rock critic like Klaus Walter, because the subject of censorship is not easy for him. He says it's a question of weighing your feelings about freedom of expression against your feelings about protecting innocent people from hate. When his friends on the rock scene say that censoring Oi groups contradicts their basic principles, he tells them, "What about us? The Nazis are against *our* basic principles." It's a question of where you draw the line and start saying no. Do you say no to the Onkelz? And, if you do, do you also say no to the old Nazis in Berlin who are now out of the closet and all dressed up as "volunteer policemen"? And to the men in Hünxe who put on *their* "uniforms" and sit on their horses at parade rest while the king of their yearly hunt drones on about the German race (and says, later, that he was moved by thoughts of the brave young Hünxe men who fought and died in the war, and the brave young Hünxe women who had to leave their beautiful houses, but that he never thought of Zeinab, the little girl whom the skinheads in Hünxe burned)? People say, sometimes, that the skins and their music are a kind of revolt, because they break "the Hitler taboo," which is the only taboo left in Germany. Esther Schapira, after a year in Hünxe, doesn't think it's a revolt at all. It is no coincidence that Solingen skinheads set the fire that killed a Turkish family

only three days after "respectable" German politicians had re-
voked asylum laws that to many people were the symbol of a new
morality and a new responsibility and a new tolerance; their fire
was a reflection, almost an acting out, of the mood around them,
and Esther Schapira says that this was true of the fire in Hünxe,
too. She says the most puzzling thing about Hünxe was that "if
you were young and full of energy you couldn't love this village,
these terrible people," and yet the skinheads who threw the fire
bomb into Zeinab's house thought they loved the village—they
thought they were just like their fathers and grandfathers, dressed
up for the *Schützenfest* and making patriotic speeches. They talked
like their parents, who referred to May 8 as "the day we lost the
war," and not "the day Germany was free." They used the same
language.

∞

There were elections in Hesse this spring. They were the first important elections since the violence in Rostock and Mölln—since
the left went out on its candle vigils and the right mobilized around
a "foreigner problem"—and people in Ludwigshafen followed
them as a bellwether for the elections in 1994, when Ludwigshafen and the rest of Germany would be voting. They were interested in how the Republican Party—which is Germany's latest
"legitimate" right-wing party, something on the order of the National Front in France, or the Freedom Party in Austria—would
do, and especially how it would do in Frankfurt, which, like
Ludwigshafen, had always voted Social Democrat, and was even
nicknamed "red-green Frankfurt," because a coalition of Social
Democrats and Greens ran it. People were right to be interested.
The Republicans got almost 9 percent of the vote in Hesse, and if
it hadn't been for a big Green vote, red-green Frankfurt could have
fallen to a Christian Democrat who once remarked that she would
not dismiss the idea of a coalition with the Republicans—at least,
with the Republicans she knew. One of them was the Republicans'
local leader. His name is Heinrich Frank, and he used to sell insurance. Today, he sits on the Frankfurt city council, along with
nine other Republicans who won their seats in the election.

Heinrich Frank is fifty years old, a war baby who never saw his father, a self-made salesman with bad manners who doesn't shake hands with women and who thinks that refugees should be isolated in barracks, away from Germans, and get their allowance in coupons, to keep them out of German stores, and be sent home as fast as possible. "We want to help them and then it's 'Out!'," he likes to say. "We don't want a Florida in Germany." He means by Florida "someplace where the Puerto Ricans move in and the whites move out, and it leads to multiculturalism and problems." He knows Florida because his sister is married to an American. His sister lives in a "nice German neighborhood" in Mobile, Alabama, a neighborhood where everybody speaks German, but he doesn't think of Mobile as "multicultural" because there are Germans there, living together and never speaking English. He describes himself as a "national conservative," by which he means a Christian Democrat who saw the light when the party of Helmut Kohl was "subverted by radicals." It puzzles him that the press treats Franz Schönhuber, the Republican Party chairman, as if he were a fascist when he is just another concerned, patriotic, democratic national conservative, someone who wants a clean, Christian Europe, with no minarets to spoil the scenery. Republicans are well advised, and most of them are careful to talk the way Frank does—about being democrats, being patriots, being Christians. They are never racist, only alarmist; never angry, only concerned; never right-wing nationalists, only national conservatives. They have built a following by avoiding the rhetoric of the National Democrats and the German People's Union and the handful of other right-wing parties that are legal in Germany but are often in trouble for "propaganda against democracy."

There are twenty-four thousand people in the German People's Union (a thousand fewer than the Republicans have) and about six thousand in the German National-Democratic Party, and the police believe that many of those people use the parties as a kind of cover, a way of staying in contact and staying legal when the real Nazi groups they belong to are raided and have to disband. There are a lot of groups like that—seventy-seven is the official count. Most of the groups are small. Some have fewer than fifty or a hundred members, though Alexander von Stahl, the German attorney general, told me there were five thousand people in the three neo-

Nazi parties he investigated, and banned, this year. Often, the groups are armed. They buy their guns from Russian soldiers who have been left behind in East Germany, and never get paid, and live by selling off whatever arms they can. The groups usually last until the police find them, and then they reappear under other names. Michael Kühnen, who lived near Ludwigshafen and founded two of the biggest neo-Nazi parties, is said to have thrown together a dozen other groups in the odd years when he was not in prison. His followers slipped into and out of clandestinity, and now they are busy recruiting in towns in East Germany, where the police are disorganized (if not members themselves) and the population impressionable and the symbols of salutes and swastikas appealing. They have been less successful lately in West Germany. The problem in West Germany is not old Nazis so much as young, educated people organizing on the fringes of the right, people who make money and live well and take their politics not from Nazi folklore but from the pages of a slick review out of Freiburg called *Junge Freiheit*—people like the twenty-two-year-old Düsseldorfer who managed Oi groups like Störkraft and became a millionaire and went into politics. "He's the future," Esther Schapira says. "He's much more dangerous than a crackpot shouting '*Heil Hitler!*' "

The Republicans make a point of having nothing to do with the neo-Nazis. They screen their militants for "Nazi affiliations" and "Nazi tendencies." They "purge" the party every year. They like to say that they are not interested in the past, or in the problems of the past—they are interested in the problems of the people now. They try to sound like a Social Democratic mayor in Ludwigshafen, joking about what will happen when the Red Army arrives at his back door demanding asylum and jobs and beds. The big red hearts on their posters mean "I love Germany." They say, like Heinrich Frank in Frankfurt, that "you don't have to learn about your past in a humiliating way." They try to explain this to people they say might "misunderstand" them. (Ignatz Bubis, the head of the Jewish community in Germany, told me that Frank, whom he doesn't know, calls him on the phone, "speaking like an old friend," and asks to get together.) They lift their slogans as easily from the left as from the right when it serves their purpose. Their flyers in Frankfurt are out of Rosa Luxemburg—"Freedom is the freedom of people who think differently," the flyers say—though they do not, of course, credit Rosa Luxemburg. They say that National Socialism was a "mistake" for Germany. They concentrate on the "victims of Stalingrad." They never make the kind of mistake the National Democrats did when they tried to start a private army, or when they invited an American named Fred Leuchter to speak at a party congress and present his "proof" that the Auschwitz gas chambers had been built by the Allies in 1945 to discredit Germans. The Republicans denounce the Holocaust. They say their models are not Hitler but Jean-Marie Le Pen and Franz Haider and Umberto Bossi, the man who wants to take Lombardy out of Italy, although they stay away from any official alliance, suspecting, rightly, that the other nationalists would give them a bad name. Right now, Schönhuber, in Munich, is the closest thing to a leader they have, and he is seventy years old, and the man he seems to want to succeed him is a Stuttgart intellectual who does better with the liberals who watch him debate on television than with the shopkeepers and salesmen who vote Republican because Schönhuber is a *Bier und Heimat* kind of person, just like them. Schönhuber, in fact, started out with the Waffen S.S. After the war, he became a journalist. He was a Communist journalist, and then a Social Democratic journalist, and, finally, a television talk-show journalist, promoting Franz-Josef Strauss (whom he knew from a Munich drinking club for people called Franz) and his Christian Social Union. Hans Sarkowicz, a young Frankfurt historian who has written a book about Schönhuber, says he will probably go down as one of the great opportunists of German postwar politics, but at home in Bavaria he is much admired for his opportunism and, of course, his guile. He likes to talk about "ethno-pluralism." He means, by ethno-pluralism, that it is cruel to take Turks out of their country and put them in Germany, where they lose their culture and become unhappy. He loves the Turks too much to see them unhappy. He says that his politics are about making Turks happy by encouraging them to stay at home. He has a summer house on the Turkish coast, and evidently it was the presence of so many happy Turks at home in Turkey that shaped his politics. He uses words like *Volksgemeinschaft*. He says, "No violence against foreigners. Vote Republican," and unless you knew the code you might easily think it was Abraham Lincoln saying that ballots are better than bullets.

It may be that the racism here *is* different—different from the racism you see across the Rhine, in France, or even in Switzerland, where the xenophobia is so exaggerated that some of the foreign workers are cycled in and out of the country every nine months, and few of them ever have a chance to call it home. Certainly the arguments about foreigners and economics now—about Germany not being able to afford its foreigners—are as suspect as the arguments about Weimar economics "causing" Hitler, and maybe they are just as bogus, too, since in the end the foreigners here are not very expensive. Most of them work, and Germany needs them, and sometimes needs more of them than it has: German farmers have to import two hundred thousand migrant workers a year just to keep up with their own labor shortages. And the refugees who don't work—most of them are forbidden by law to work—cost the country a fraction of what it costs to support the three and a half million Germans who are unemployed. They certainly cost less than the seventy-six million dollars that Germany is going to pay Poland over the next two years to take a few thousand of them back, and to build the fences to keep them from leaving.

Manfred Schiedermair, a Frankfurt business lawyer active in civil rights circles, thinks that part of the problem is that Germany never really had to pay for anything until the Wall fell. "Democracy didn't cost so much," he says. "It was a present from the Allies, a box of candy, and there was always a honeymoon feeling about it." He means that as long as Germany was rich most Germans believed they were good democrats—that German democracy is much more fragile than any of those Germans thought, because the old Germany was always there, radical in its fantasies and not really very safe in its shiny new institutions and commitments. In the end, it doesn't matter if you trace those fantasies to Heine or Hitler, to the Black Forest or the blond pigtail. *Blut und Boden*—Blood and Soil—is not about jobs or public housing or food coupons. It is in the language, in the poetry, in the images of Germany received in childhood. It has to do with a kind of ethnic exaltation, located in race and place. It runs through the German canon from *Parzifal* to the fascist popular poets like Agnes Miegel, who were kept in the schoolbooks long after the war was over (while Bertolt Brecht was still excluded), to the playwright Botho Strauss, who has been publishing polemics on the collapse of "German" values of the sort that used to inspire Germans to give their lives for "identity." It even extends, sometimes, to the Greens. It is where left meets right, where the "good" Germans and the "bad" Germans still sometimes come together. It is comfortable with words like "purity" and "defilement," and, while the Greens and the racists mean very different things when they use these words, they are not words you usually expect to find in Western politics. This is why a lawyer like Schiedermair, talking about the democracy, or a professor like Spiros Simitis, talking about the constitution, or a philosopher like Jürgen Habermas, talking about the social contract, can sound like a voice from some other country, while Botho Strauss, talking about German values and German identity, sounds "German."

∞

At six-twenty on the morning of February 14, the phones in the pink stone police station in Ludwigshafen started ringing. People on Schulstrasse, about a mile from the station house, were calling to report that the Turkish grocery on their street—the store called Baskent—was burning. The firemen came, and evacuated the building. Then the ambulances came. Ten people who lived directly above the store—Germans, mainly, and a few Turks—were taken to the hospital. One child, who had inhaled a lot of smoke, was kept in the hospital. It was a Sunday morning, but the fire seemed to have awakened everyone on Schulstrasse. One woman said that the Baskent "exploded." Another woman said she was sure that she had seen two men running out of the burning store, and that one of the men had turned and thrown what looked like a "burning object" back inside, but she told the police that that was all she saw.

The Baskent was still smoking when the police found Nigar Ergeldi, the young grocer who owned the store, sleeping at his parents' house in Hemshof. By the time he arrived, the Baskent was gone. The sidewalk was piled with smoldering bedsprings and antennas from the apartments upstairs, and with twisted pieces of frame from Nigar's awning, and a television crew was down from Frankfurt, filming for the midday news, but all that remained of the Baskent was a little safe in what had been the back room, where Nigar kept some money, for change, and his receipts. The site was sealed, and Nigar worried about his safe. He kept telling the police, the reporters, the neighbors, "I don't have enemies, I have mostly friends"—which is what the police expected him to say. "Our experience is that Turks and Kurds don't give information to official people" is how Mayor Schulte puts it. "They think it's dangerous."

The fire on Schulstrasse was the second fire set in a Turkish grocery store in Ludwigshafen in as many months, and it embarrassed the city. The mayor pointed out that the two fires were the only serious incidents involving foreigners since the sidewalk cracking of Ender Basaran, three years earlier, and the police complained that it was hard to proceed calmly, looking for real clues to those relatively minor crimes, when everybody else seemed to be looking to Ludwigshafen for clues to the German crisis. They had, in fact, a couple of clues to the first fire bombing: they had a glass bottleneck with a homemade detonator inside it, and they had pieces of three hammerheads, which in all likelihood had been used to smash the grocery's plate-glass window. There was a fragment of a price tag left on one hammerhead. No one knew how it had survived the fire, but it was just big enough for the police to trace the hammers to a local hardware store and to get a description of the man who bought them. They ordered a portrait drawn—a mockup face from the Landeskriminalamt computers—and ended up with a picture of a dark, heavily bearded, "foreign-looking" man. It was not anyone's idea of a picture of a skinhead.

Detective Ladinek thinks it's possible that the man at the hardware store was wrong, or that skins had persuaded a friend with a beard to buy their hammers, but he also thinks it's possible that the Turk with the grocery had refused to pay the local Turkish mafia, which collects "protection" against the local Kurds, or, indeed, the local Kurds, who collect "taxes" for "the Kurdish state in exile," or even the Italians, who collect their own protection in the area. Ender Basaran agrees with Ladinek that almost anything is possible, even an insurance scam. He was not much interested in either

fire—"My pain was so much greater" is the way he explains it—
but when he thinks about the fires now, they puzzle him. He says
that his father "hears things at the mosque" about protection rack-
ets and the Turkish mafia, although the things his father hears usually have to do with gambling clubs, not grocery stores. Thinking
about the fires, he is not convinced that skinheads set them. The
cops on Nigar Ergeldi's case—four policemen from a special
"terrorism and extremism" squad, three policemen from the
organized-crime squad, and one policeman who is an expert on
arson—say there are similarities between the two crimes. There
were none of the usual skinhead signs at either fire—no Nazi graffiti, no swastikas scribbled on a wall or a sidewalk, only a "wrong
way" swastika on a building next to the first grocery, which the
neighbors said had been there for days. This puzzles the police, and
so does the fact that the fires seemed planned, and that they were
set at dawn, which is the time most skinheads have finished ma-
rauding and are home in bed, drunk and sleeping. But what puzzles them most is that the stores were empty, and they know by
now that skinheads are not much interested in stores. Skinheads
are interested, if that is the word, in people. "A skinhead goes for
people, not property," Mayor Schulte says. "He goes for homes
and bars and train stations and asylum centers, for places with foreigners around. He is not looking for tomatoes."

The mayor would obviously like to see the fire bombings solved.
"We used to have fights between skins and foreigners, but this violence is a new violence," he says. "We're careful not to speculate:
Is it right extremists? Is it foreign terrorists? What's important for
us is to learn what the *purpose* of these burnings was, and what in-
fluences were at play." It makes him uneasy, even now, to suggest
that an act of violence against foreigners might involve foreigners,
and in some way feed the racism he is trying to discourage. He
knows that at this moment in Germany there are bound to be protection crimes, and insurance crimes, and even political crimes,
dressed up to look like the crimes everyone sees on television and
identifies as skin crimes. But it is difficult to look at the rubble of
what was once a prosperous Turkish store and say that Turks or
Kurds did this, because that is what people on the right say whenever there is a fire bombing. The right maintained that Turks from

a Hamburg mafia were responsible for the killings in Mölln. They kept saying it—even after two skinheads were charged and one confessed—though they were hard put to it to explain what the Turkish mafia had to do with a fifty-one-year-old grandmother and two girls. Only about a third of the skinhead crimes get to trial. The police may know it was skinheads, and, in many cases, know which skinheads, but often they lack the evidence they need for a conviction; and when there *is* a conviction the terms are apt to be remarkably light, either because the skins were minors at the time or because they were drunk, or both. German law incorporates the curious notion that Germans getting drunk and committing "spontaneous" crimes is something inevitable and extenuating. Most skinheads are like Gerhard Horn—they are out of jail within a few years.

Detective Ladinek says that there are fifty right skins active in and around Ludwigshafen now. Sergeant Falk has men following them all, and men (and fences and phones) at the big asylum houses. He knows in general when to expect trouble, and he never expected trouble at a couple of Turkish grocery stores. The rule of thumb at the Ludwigshafen station house is still that skinheads are stupid, and Falk and his cops agree with the mayor when he says, "To buy hammers, break windows—that's too organized for a skinhead." The problem is that after three thousand skinhead attacks in Germany, it is difficult to say that a skinhead is simply someone with a shaved skull and a couple of tattoos. Violence spreads, and the pretext for violence spreads, and in the end there may be no real definition of a skinhead crime. A skin who grows his hair and settles down, and maybe even joins a respectable right-wing party, isn't apt to like foreigners any more than he did at the age of seventeen. He is apt to resent the five million marks it costs the city to keep nine social workers assigned to the Ludwigshafen refugees, and the money it takes to maintain the boats and containers and sports centers where the refugees live. Once he has a job, and a little more hair, he is apt to resent it as a taxpayer and (by his lights) a citizen.

∾

Nigar Ergeldi had a schedule. Every morning except Sunday, Nigar got up at exactly four o'clock, shook off sleep with a glass of Turkish coffee, and drove his used Ford Transit van to the wholesale Turkish market in Mannheim to buy produce for his store. Sunday mornings, he slept, which is the only reason he was home in bed in Hemshof, and not in his store, unloading vegetables, when the fire at the Baskent started. Nigar called his store Baskent because *"baskent"* means "capital" in Turkish, and Nigar had spent the first eight years of his life in Ankara. The name reminded him of home, and, besides, it sounded important. He says, "It sounded serious." Nigar himself is serious. He is soft-spoken, polite, and very guarded, very shy, and he looks like a student. He has a delicate face and small, delicate hands that you do not usually associate with someone who is up at four in the morning loading and unloading crates of food, and the truth is he does not much like loading and unloading crates of food. He does not like being a grocer, even a grocer on a prosperous pedestrian street with a "French" dry cleaner and a unisex "coiffeur" for the neighbors. He wants to have a "profession." He used to work at BASF, at the photocopy machines. Once, he apprenticed with a mason. Early last summer, he went back to high school. He says he wanted "a quiet, anonymous life." He never imagined that on a Sunday morning in February this year he would be walking into the Ludwigshafen police station, past the "Wanted" signs and the pictures of murderers and rapists and the framed photographs of retired police chiefs, to answer questions about why somebody would want to hurt him.

The Baskent used to belong to Nigar's brother. His brother found the storefront in March last year, got himself a partner, and registered the business at the Rathaus. Now he is "retired" from the business, and gets his sleep, and has a nine-to-five job at the window-washing company where Ender Basaran works. Nigar's father took over the lease in August. The store was doing well, and he wanted to keep it in the family. Nigar left school and signed some papers and, at twenty-two, he became a grocer, with a fourteen-and-a-half-hour day and a monthly rent that amounted to twenty-eight hundred dollars. "It's natural," he says. "It was to please my father." He is a dutiful son—a Turkish son—and it is hard to imagine him having a beer with a German cop, the way Ender Basaran does, or, like Ender, courting a German girl, or even approaching a German girl. It is hard to imagine Nigar with Germans at all. Germans make him uneasy. It would not have occurred to him to walk in the Ludwigshafen candle vigil. He says, "It was too cold for walking around with candles, and anyway, it had nothing to do with me."

The Germans Nigar sees are mainly the Germans on his street, who come to the store to market and to try his Turkish specialties. When he was a boy, he sometimes played with the German boys at school, but they never went home together. The Germans liked rock, and Nigar hates rock. They liked soccer, and Nigar hates soccer. "I think it's stupid, running after a ball," he likes to say. "I get my sports every morning at the market." Now, whenever he has some time to himself, he takes a walk with his Turkish friends and they stop at a café and talk, and that accounts for his entertainment. He never reads—not even the paper—unless he has to. He never travels unless he has to. He has been to Munich, Heidelberg, Mainz, Frankfurt, and Cologne, and he says that they looked the same. He used to go to movies. This winter, he saw *The Silence of the Lambs,* and it scared him; he wanted to leave, but the friend he was with said, "We paid, we stay." He has not been back to the movies since.

When Nigar goes to Turkey, he never says that he's from Germany. He tells people that he's from Ankara. He doesn't want to be "looked at differently," like the *Gastarbeiter* he knows who visit their fathers' villages and have trouble with the people who stayed behind and think that all the Turks in Germany are millionaires. "I don't like it when people say, 'You live in Germany, you make money and never have to work, and here we are—we're poor and we work hard, all the time.' " The people in his own village always say this, because Nigar's father was the mayor there, years before he came to Germany, and the villagers thought that he was very smart, getting so many votes, and would certainly be rich anywhere but Turkey. They have forgotten by now that everyone in the village was his cousin.

Nigar's father worked for sixteen years at a John Deere factory in Mannheim. It was hard physical work, and a couple of years ago he had a heart attack, and the factory let him go. He has nothing to do now. He used to help, sometimes, at the store—he called himself "the comptroller"—but his German is nonexistent, and he couldn't understand the customers. Mainly, he stood around "seeing that everything was in order," making sure that Nigar kept busy and didn't get into bad German habits, like lunch or coffee. He said that the longer Nigar worked, the better it was for the business—which Nigar admits was true. Nigar says he was beginning to like his store when someone burned it. He says that the more the money came in, the more he liked it. He knows that all of his father's hopes were in the Baskent, because so much else in his father's life had changed. The family used to live together— "the way Turkish families are supposed to live." Now they do not. Nigar's brother is married and has his own apartment, and it is up to Nigar to make the money for the kind of place that will tempt him back. "I'm here to work," Nigar says. "I don't care if I'm a Turk in Germany. Citizenship here? What for? People know I'm a Turk anyway. I'm allowed to live here, work here. For us, it's not important who's in power. If it doesn't affect me, I don't care."

Nigar says he has been thinking a lot about his life lately. After the fire, he was too frightened to think at all. *"Schreck"* is the word he uses—"shocked and scared." For a while, he talked mainly to reporters—people from Südwestfunk, and from the Frankfurt papers, and even from *Hürriyet,* which is the biggest paper in Turkey and has a Frankfurt office. He didn't really feel like talking, but, being polite, he told them, "It would not be right if you came in vain." His insurance was paid. He wasn't that worried then about the money. Now he worries. He worries about whether his German landlord is going to want a Turkish tenant who gets firebombed and raises his own insurance rates and makes his other tenants nervous. He may even wonder, after the killings in Solingen, if his landlord is going to want a Turkish tenant at all.

"I did everything I had to legally," Nigar says. If he was paying protection to a Turkish mafia or to Kurdish separatists, it is not something he is going to tell you. If he refused to pay, that is not something he is going to tell you either. "In general, I'm not afraid of anyone," he says. "When I see '*Ausländer Raus!*' I think nothing. But I'm a little afraid now. I don't know what happened. It could happen again, with me in the store. I think now, Maybe I have enemies. Anyone can have no hair."

THE POLITICS

OF

MEMORY

(AUGUST 1995)

It could be said that in the fifty years since the German field marshal Wilhelm Keitel laid down his staff and his hat on a Berlin table, and the war in Europe ended, Germans have been trying to talk their way out of an unutterable past and back into what they like to call History. They have been talking mainly to one another. History is a German obsession, a German métier. There are people who claim that, with Hegel and the great nineteenth-century historiographers, Germans actually invented history, and it is certainly true that the country now produces historians the way Italy produces lawyers, or Argentina psychoanalysts—in aggressive, even defiant, disproportion. By history, Germans mean German history. They call it a *Wissenschaft*—a science—though it is arguably more alchemy than science, since it has always had to do with turning the myths, memories, and language of "Germanness" into a kind of collective destiny known as the German nation. It may be history's revenge that today, fifty years after the surrender, Germans are still arguing about what to do with the destiny that they invented.

For practical, political purposes—purposes of state—the negotiation of a new German past began six years ago, when the Wall came down, though some Germans have put it much later, somewhere around the time *Schindler's List* opened in Berlin and the prospect of what could be called "the past of the good Germans" was, suddenly, so evident and so exhilarating. Some say that it was Helmut Kohl's project all along—this new and revised Germany, settled into its history, comfortable, even, in its history. Call it— this is the past of choice—Victim Germany. It is the Germany that Hitler "seized" in 1933 and "occupied" for twelve dark years; the Germany that was "liberated" in 1945, as if it were Holland, or a concentration camp. And it may have been the inevitable Germany, because once the Wall fell in 1989, this Germany turned out to be the only version of themselves that East Germans and West

Germans could be brought to hold in common. The two Germanys do not much like each other now that they are one Germany, or agree on anything beyond a taste in cars, but they share this: They are determined to settle their crimes into "history." They want to resolve a duty to remember and a longing to forget, as if duty and desire were the thesis and antithesis of a dialectic of destiny. They have a stubborn, almost innocent German faith that their past is like their prime rate or their G.N.P.—something that with a good plan and a lot of attention can be adjusted, refreshed, pressed into the service of the new German nation. After fifty years, they have lost patience with the painful plain truths of recapitulation. They prefer the symbolic simplicities of objectification—the monuments, memorials, and "commemorative sites" that take memory and deposit it, so to speak, in the landscape, where it can be visited at appropriate ceremonial moments, but where it does not interfere unduly with the business of life at hand.

The etiquette of commemoration is thorny, at best, in Germany, and this year it has been especially thorny—something the Germans might have learned from their Polish neighbors, who staged the first of Europe's fiftieth-anniversary ceremonies on January 26, the day of the liberation of Auschwitz, and bungled the occasion thoroughly when Lech Walesa delivered a long speech in Kraków without once mentioning Jews. (Fifteen hundred camp survivors who had actually come to Poland for the anniversary boycotted the official ceremony and staged an "alternative ceremony" in a field near the camp.) In any event, not many Germans were in Poland for either ceremony. There was no official commemoration of the liberation of Auschwitz in Berlin, which was busy celebrating the ninetieth birthday of a local actor named Bernhard Minetti, who was one of Hitler's favorite actors; the nearest thing to a ceremony anywhere in Germany was an evening of speeches at the municipal theater in Frankfurt.

The first big anniversary commemoration here took place in Dresden, on February 13, after a day in which thousands of people marched through the city to the ruins of the Frauenkirche, carrying candles, in memory of the Dresden bombings—bombings that the marchers remembered as a savagery visited on the city for reasons most of them were hard put to it to explain. It fell to

Roman Herzog, the German president—whose job it mainly is to appear at ceremonies like Dresden's and administer moral dicta to the crowd—to remind them of London and Coventry, and of the fact that the Second World War was not a war that the people who bombed Dresden started. Dresdeners, anyway, do not necessarily think they were liberated in 1945. Most of them think they were liberated in 1989, when the Wall came down, and the few who do talk about May 8, 1945, as "Liberation Day" share a convenient confusion over whether they were liberated by the Allies or *from* the Allies. No matter. Liberation today is less a no-win than a no-lose concept, and it is certainly not the concept that Richard von Weizsäcker had in mind when *he* was president of the Federal Republic and introduced it in a speech on the fortieth anniversary of the Nazi defeat. Weizsäcker is a decent, complicated, introspective man, the son of a Nazi state secretary and one of the few Christian Democratic politicians to persist, publicly, in addressing the past with anything that could be called appropriate anguish. When he talked in 1985 about "the liberation of Germany," he wanted Germans to understand that 1945 was not the end of Germany— which is what a lot of their parents had told them—but the only possible beginning for Germany. It was an understanding he shared with many German intellectuals (Jürgen Habermas and Hans-Magnus Enzensberger among them), but it has very little to do with the political understanding of "liberation," then and now. The politics of liberation have always been Helmut Kohl's department, and Kohl, through thirteen years as chancellor, has been determined to leave Germans with not only a united country but a heroic one. ("He wants to put Germany on the winning side; it's as simple as that," a young historian in Berlin put it.) You could say that in this he has been the first really successful revisionist of postwar German history.

Kohl's genius was to understand that Germans were not interested in hearing any more explanations—even friendly explanations—of their choices. Germans had had enough of the old historians of the German right, who liked to hypothesize about how National Socialism was a response to Bolshevism, or to Weimar inflation, or the Wall Street crash, or the Treaty of Versailles. Kohl was the new German right. He understood that Germans, like everybody else, want to be exonerated from their choices. You could say they want to be "liberated" from their choices, and if this is true, it is understandable that by now they want that liberation to be comfortable—something on the order of the baggy pants in the Levi Strauss Dockers ad that went up on billboards all over Germany this liberation year. "Try them on," the ad said. "They may even liberate your soul." Germans want their past to have happened to them. They want to have suffered from themselves, the way everybody else suffered from them.

∽

Two years before the Wall fell, a local television talk-show hostess by the name of Lea Rosh announced that Berlin was going to have a memorial to the six million Jews who died in Europe during the Second World War. She collected a list of famous names— among them Willy Brandt, Günter Grass, and Christa Wolf—and launched a celebrity version of what Germans call a "citizens' initiative." In a few years' time, she had a twelve-million-dollar budget for her memorial. She had a promise from Kohl of a hundred and forty million dollars' worth of Berlin real estate on which to build it—five acres of what was once a no-man's-land near the Brandenburg Gate, between the Pariser Platz and the Leipziger Platz, and is now the middle of town. (The land was said to be over the ruins of Hitler's bunker, but after it was announced that "in the place of the perpetrator, the victims shall be remembered" it turned out, to everyone's embarrassment, to be over Hitler's driver's bunker.) Bonn was involved. The Berlin Senat was involved. Despite (or maybe because of) Lea Rosh's own celebrity, and her relentless promotion, there was so much controversy surrounding her Holocaust-memorial project that the project itself turned into a ghoulish public entertainment. By liberation year, five hundred and twenty-eight artists and architects were competing for the chance to build the memorial—"the soul of Germany," Hanns Zischler, the Berlin actor and writer, said, dryly, after he saw their models—and everyone in Berlin was fighting about what the definition of a Holocaust victim should be.

Rosh is a media grande dame of fifty-eight, given to jeweled bifocals, plunging black bustiers, and raspberry suits that match the gold-flecked, kidney-shaped raspberry Lucite table in her Hannover office, where she receives visitors and discusses the Holocaust while sipping white wine, answering mail, and autographing pictures of herself. She is famous in Germany for self-invention, and avid when it comes to her image and her reputation. Sometimes, she says that the idea of a Holocaust memorial came to her when she and a Stuttgart historian named Eberhard Jäckel were working together on a documentary about collaboration. Sometimes, she says it came to her when she was visiting the memorial at Yad Vashem, in Israel. But she is quite clear that the idea was *hers*. People who have followed her career from talk-show hostess to a director of North German Television say that whatever inspiration she claims now, once she had the idea, the project was inevitable.

Rosh is in what her critics call—always in English—"the Shoah business" (as in, regrettably, "There's no business like Shoah business"), although it has to be said that a lot of those critics are in the business themselves, part of a thriving new German industry in books and essays and public art and commemorations devoted to the Holocaust. Germans right now are absorbed in an elaborate exercise in "solidarity," if not identification, with Hitler's victims. (The writer Eike Geisel calls this "Jewish envy.") There are hardly any Jews in Germany. There were only about twenty-eight thousand before the Wall fell; there are sixty thousand now. But there are an astonishing number of Germans who proclaim their solidarity with Jews by speaking in synagogues and inviting their friends to Seders, and even giving their children Hebrew names—showing the Poles, someone here told me, that in a country without Jews it is just as easy to love Jews as it is to hate them. Lea Rosh, as it happened, gave *herself* the Jewish name. She went to the Berlin Registry and renounced "Edith"—and legally became "Lea." She likes to tell people that her best friend is a Jew called Rachel, and that her husband is Jakob. She seems to "feel" Jewish. She feels Jewish not so much because she is partly Jewish herself—her mother's father was a Berlin Jew—as because she has taken up identification with Jewishness as a German duty. Some Germans simply assume she is Jewish—because of her name and because, in the strangled rhetoric of identity that philo-Semites and anti-

Semites share, she "looks" Jewish. She is brassy and a little crude. And she is unnervingly enthusiastic on the subject of Jewish suffering—an enthusiasm that has touched some Jews I know in Berlin and horrified others, many of whom remember the day she interviewed a camp survivor named Cordelia Edvardsson on her talk show, and asked, in a cheery, no-nonsense television voice, "Miss Edvardsson, how did *you* get to Auschwitz?" Miss Edvardsson looked up coolly and said, "By train, Miss Rosh."

I met Rosh late last winter, on the day she finished editing a short film about the liberation of Bergen-Belsen. The film was put together from a famous segment of British Imperial War Museum footage known to movie buffs as the Hitchcock reel, because Alfred Hitchcock helped with the editing. But Rosh didn't mention Hitchcock. She was not much interested in anybody else who could be said to be in the Shoah business. She wanted me to know that because of her the city of Hannover had a Holocaust memorial, near the opera-house square, on which the names of all the Hannover deportees were engraved in stone, and I had already heard rumors in Berlin that she and her husband, Jakob—Jakob Schulze-Rohr is a city planner—were going to build another memorial, a small memorial of their own, and donate it to the Grunewald station, where the trains for the camps once waited. She had had problems in Hannover, where some people didn't want a memorial at all and the people who did want one complained ceaselessly about her being peremptory and heavy-handed. And she was certainly having problems in Berlin. A lot of Berlin intellectuals had been opposed to her project to begin with. They wrote articles in the *Tagesspiegel* and made speeches at the Literaturhaus saying that Germany had no "right" to the memory of its victims. "Other people," they said, "but not Germany." They argued that the memory of the Holocaust belonged to the Jews who survived it— that it was not only a question of identity but, in a way, of property. They tried to persuade Rosh that a Holocaust memorial in Israel meant something very different from a memorial in the middle of what was once Hitler's Reich. They thought that putting a memorial like that in the shadow of the Brandenburg Gate would only add to the confusion about "perpetrators" and "victims" which has marked Kohl's project to settle the past by turning defeat into liberation and Nazi Germany into the Germany that Hitler seized.

Berlin is already full of memorials—although, it has been pointed out, very few that evoke a common or a proud history, or even a real history. The East Berliners built memorials as object lessons in the new East German past, in which "Hitler's victims" meant Hitler's *Communist* victims, and the West Berliners—despite the evidence of the ruined Kaiser Wilhelm Memorial Church, at the top of Kurfürstendamm, and the mountain of rubble in Grunewald that is known to everyone here as the Devil's Mountain—were usually just as reluctant as the East Berliners to accept that the capital of the Third Reich was a ruin of its own making. And, once the Wall went up, the memorials that West Berliners did build were put to a convenient, if ambiguous, political purpose—conflating, simply by being there, the real war and the Cold War, the perpetrator and the victim. It has to be said that if the East Germans hadn't raised a wall the West Germans might have had to raise one for them, because the walled-in West Berlin was less a city in any ordinary urban sense than a theater of politics, a vast performance space where generations of Cold War politicians practiced the rhetoric of division and unification on which they hoped to make their reputations. West Berlin stayed unaccountable—to its past, to its future—for as long as the Allied armies occupied it and Bonn paid for it. People stopped in West Berlin for trial runs of ideology and attitude, at a safe remove from the Federal Republic, where the "real" Germany was located. If you were a West German—a busy, productive, forward-looking West German—the city confirmed not so much your past shame as your present valor as a born-again democrat up against a sinister East that began at your back yard and stretched for five thousand miles to Vladivostok. West Berlin was good for you—uplifting, and even cathartic—but it was not the real world once the Wall went up and John F. Kennedy flew in and compared the West Berliners to citizens of ancient Rome, pronouncing the magic words *"Ich bin ein Berliner"* and, with them, turning the city into an owned and operated symbol of democracy. Now, suddenly, the past has replaced the Wall in the psychic archeology of the city that is once again the German capital, and nobody really knows where to put it, or how to address it, or what to do with so much memory as the people who remember die.

∞

The historian Reinhard Rürup told me once that in his opinion the way to reclaim the real past and confront it was, literally, to dig for it—to dig through the rhetorical ground cover of Cold War Berlin until you reached what was left of Nazi Berlin—and this, in fact, is what he did. He dug into the Kreuzberg lot where the Gestapo, the S.S., and the Nazi state-security police had had their headquarters, and turned the lot into the archive and exhibition center called the Topography of Terror. It was, he says, a "history of the perpetrators" project, by which he means that it was very different from the kind of projects Lea Rosh had in mind.

Rürup came to Berlin, from Westphalia, as a young man. He had just started to write a book on the eighteenth-century emancipation of German Jewry, and he had what he calls a gnawing interest in "how an emancipatory eighteenth century turned into an anti-Semitic twentieth century." His view of "liberation" was that "what Germans needed was to be liberated from themselves." And he thought that the place to start was where Germany's policemen and bureaucrats and S.S. office workers had sat at their desks and done their jobs and issued the orders of the Nazi terror. He wanted Germans to know what "the everyday details of that criminal system" were—who sat next to whom, and who collected the mail, and who ate in the cafeteria. "Not memory but history" is how he describes his project. It was not an easy project. Most of the well-known German historians of the war were interested in what Rürup calls "the processes" of National Socialism, but he was more of a "dig where you stand" person. He wanted to look at "the places" of National Socialism, and the place that particularly interested him was so big that it spread across the Soviet and the American sectors and, in due course, across the Wall. No one then knew precisely where 8 Prinz-Albrecht-Strasse—the address of the headquarters—started. The street had disappeared from the city maps after the East Germans razed it and built a new street, with a proper proletarian name: Niederkirchnerstrasse, they called it, after a seamstress named Käthe Niederkirchner, who had fought in the Communist resistance and been murdered in Ravensbrück eight months before the German defeat. The nearest building on the western side of the Wall was a ruined city museum, the Martin-Gropius-Bau. But Rürup persuaded the city to start digging, and eventually cellars were discovered that turned out to have housed a Gestapo washroom and kitchen. By 1987, he had covered the walls of those cellars with documents and pictures and was able to open a small temporary exhibit about the men and women who had spent their time recruiting death squads and thinking up catchy slogans for a final solution (the order requiring Jewish shopkeepers to pay for the damage of Kristallnacht was called Operation Clean Streets) and inventing new enemies, as in "persons roaming in Gypsy fashion [will] be compelled to submit to a racial-biological examination." It was not what Germans call a memory site, or a *Kranzabwurfstelle*—a "wreath-throwing place." It was, like Rürup himself, pedagogic, formal, and a little severe. But it was on the tourist route, and it was oddly popular, and, once the Germanys united (and Kohl began to demand that Niederkirchnerstrasse and most of the other streets with Communists' names get back their "proper" German historical names), Rürup and his history-of-the-perpetrators staff were able to start planning for a permanent archive, four times as big as the cellars they show in now.

Rürup says that Lea Rosh was "my only controversy." Rosh wanted the site for her Holocaust memorial. She fought him for it. She used her celebrity. She courted German Jews who were also celebrities ("I got her letter and my feeling was Why the hell don't we have a memorial in Berlin?" Hellmut Stern, the old assistant concertmaster of the Berlin Philharmonic, told me), and she courted ordinary German Jews who were not celebrities and, as Rosh put it, "didn't want to attract attention, didn't want to be noticed, [until] we made it clear that this is a *German*, not a Jewish, thing." Rürup had nothing against the idea of a Holocaust memorial in Berlin, but he thought it was "inappropriate" to use the land at 8 Prinz-Albrecht-Strasse for a memorial to one group of victims when "*all* the persecutions originated there." Rosh, on the other hand, was very clear about wanting a Jewish memorial. "Hitler's killing program was *for* Jews, it was *about* the destruction of Jews" is the way she puts it. "All the other killing followed from it." She would not agree to a monument to "all victims." She thought that if you started calling everybody who died because of Hitler a Holocaust victim you would end up with "another Neue Wache," by which she meant the memorial on Unter den Linden, in the east of Berlin, which was built as a guardhouse after the Napoleonic Wars, and over the years has done duty as a First World War memorial, then as a Communist memorial to "the victims of fascism and militarism," and now as Helmut Kohl's memorial to "the victims of war and tyranny." (Kohl added a big bronze cast of a Käthe Kollwitz Pietà and was roundly criticized by the left for "the imposition of Christian symbolism.") Kohl called *his* Neue Wache a monument to "reconciliation," but the result has been that some of the wreaths and flowers left at the base of the Kollwitz bronze are inscribed to the memory of S.S. officers who died in the war, and whose families consider them victims, too.

Lea Rosh told Rürup that once a Jewish memorial was built she would see to it that a memorial was built for other victims. It was not an idea that appealed to the professor, who envisioned the Gypsies, say, complaining because the Jewish memorial was bigger than *their* memorial, and the Jews replying that there were, after all, many more Jewish Holocaust victims than Gypsy victims. He saw the gay community demanding *its* memorial, because the Nazis had tried to exterminate homosexuals, too, and then the Poles demanding *their* memorial, and then the Jehovah's Witnesses, until the new Prinz-Albrecht-Strasse turned into a carpet of monuments—monuments stretching endlessly into the distance, like pyramids in the desert. He thought that memory and mourning would be "lost to the banality of conflicting claims," and lost to politics, and lost even to the Germans, who would shake their heads and say, "Look, the Jews and the Gypsies are fighting. What do you expect?" And it was not hard to imagine that happening, since the leader of the Gypsy community here had already started saying that wherever the Germans decided to put their Holocaust memorial, he wanted "creative and spatial proximity" for *his* memorial, and the leader of the Jewish community was saying no, there had to be twenty-five yards, at least, between them, because for Jews a Holocaust memorial was like a cemetery, and rabbis would want to pray there, and cantors would want to chant the Kaddish, and they would do this only if the memorial was "Jewish ground." In the end, Kohl settled the problem of sites by presenting Rosh with her five prime acres of central Berlin. It was a perfect place, from the point of view of prominence and status. But it did not settle the question of victims, or stop the argument.

∞

There were a hundred and sixty thousand Jews in Berlin in 1933. Today, there are no more than twelve thousand, and Lea Rosh was right when she said that most of those Jews did not want to get caught in the middle of an argument about a Holocaust memorial. Some of them liked the idea of her memorial. Some of them even said that Germany "owed" them the memorial. A few of them claimed that when Kohl put "all the victims in one tomb" at the Neue Wache, and Ignatz Bubis, the head of the Jewish community in Germany, complained, Kohl had actually promised Bubis that the Jews would have one. But it may be that just by being here and being afraid of calling attention to themselves, those Jews gave the lie to the official conviction that the past was "history." A designer named Inge Borck—a Berlin Jew who used to dress Rosh for her television show and is now raising money for her memorial—told me, "They don't want to be advocates for the project. They want to live privately, for their families, for their businesses. That's all they want." (It occurred to me later that she could have been talking in the nineteen-thirties.) Borck said it was much easier to approach the foreigners who could be called "honorary Berlin Jews"—people like Daniel Barenboim, who conducts the Deutsche Oper and had offered to give a benefit concert for the project— than to persuade ordinary Berlin Jewish families to sign a check, or even a petition. "It's very difficult for them to express Jewish feelings on the Jewish experience" is the way she put it. Maybe it's simply that they don't trust Germans. Berlin Jews have always been leery of the sort of people whom the journalist Henryk Broder—who earns his living as a critic in and of the Shoah business—calls "the professionals of redemption," even when those professionals are Jewish themselves, like the blond Frau Borck, who says without a hint of irony that she is better at raising money from Christians "because I look like an ordinary German woman, I don't look Jewish, I am not the stereotype with the long nose."

Only about eight hundred people who could properly be called

Berlin Jews are left now. There are nearly as many Israelis in Berlin, and certainly as many East European Jews, who are either camp survivors or the children and grandchildren of survivors—of Jews who came to Berlin as displaced persons and, out of fascination or determination or fatigue or simply hopelessness, never moved. The great majority of the ten thousand Jews who make up the official Jewish community of Berlin today are recent Russian immigrants, and it is doubtful whether many of them are interested in paying for Lea Rosh's Holocaust memorial, or, for that matter, have even bothered to walk into the back yard of the community center, on Fasanenstrasse, where the Jews of Berlin have built a Holocaust memorial of their own. It is a simple memorial—a small bronze wall, like a wailing wall, with the names of the death camps spread across it. Every year on the anniversary of Kristallnacht the community faithful come to the wall to mourn.

Estrongo Nachama, who is an Auschwitz survivor and the oldest cantor in Berlin, always sings the Kaddish at the center on Kristallnacht, and I remember his son, Andreas, telling me once that after forty years of hearing his father sing he had come to the conclusion that the yard behind the center was the only proper Holocaust memorial for Berlin, "because you enter it through a living Jewish community"—a community of survivors and their children. You acknowledge *them*. Andreas today has strong doubts about Lea Rosh's project. He went to the first public meetings on the memorial, to answer questions about Jewish customs (he is a historian himself and, as it happens, Rürup's deputy at the Topography of Terror), and the artists and architects he talked to called him afterward with Hebrew texts to translate. He was amused that at the beginning all the meetings began on Thursday and lasted through Saturday—in other words, through the Jewish Sabbath. "Amused but not surprised," he says. He suspects that a lot of Germans know more about dead Jews than they know about Jews who are living in their midst, and about what those Jews are like, and about how they celebrate and how they mourn, or even why they are here.

"Why?" is often a matter of generation. The historian Werner Angress, who got out of Berlin in 1937, at seventeen, when a Jewish family with a tobacco farm in Virginia supplied him with a job and a farmworker's visa, and who came back to Berlin to live fifty years later, put it this way: "I'm not a victim. I didn't have Kristallnacht. I don't have roots here anymore, but I have memories, and they are not bad memories." Hellmut Stern, who left Berlin for Harbin twelve days after Kristallnacht and was saved as a "German" because the Japanese commander in Harbin didn't distinguish between "German Jews and German Germans," told me, "Coming out of the subway here, there's a certain smell, and that smell was 'home.' " Inge Marcus, who today is a seventy-three-year-old Berlin grandmother, was "invited out" of Berlin by an Englishwoman she had met at a concert in Marienbad in 1936, and she came back early, in 1951. She says, "Well, there was not much left, but the empty spaces reminded me of what had been, and the air was familiar, and I thought, Yes, I could live here." Younger Jews, of course, have no Berlin to remember. Nicola Galliner, who is forty-four and runs the Jewish community's adult-education program, grew up in London and came to Berlin in the late sixties, and *she* thinks that Jews her age are drawn to Berlin because "the city itself is a memorial." She says that she often wonders if she and her friends have some sort of special, even morbid, attraction to the capital of the Third Reich—if they chose Berlin because Berlin is "the only place where you can live out fully your Holocaust neurosis." Maybe. A lot of Jews are not in Berlin "for the Holocaust," as the saying goes. There are Jews who chose Berlin, quite simply, for the reasons educated, assimilated Jews chose Berlin in the nineteen-twenties—because Berlin was cosmopolitan, it was experimental, it was exactly where they wanted to be.

Those Jews are an elite, not so different from the Weimar elite in their passion for German culture. They are conductors like Barenboim, and novelists like Irene Dische, and curators like Amnon Barzel, who is about to open a Jewish museum that a Jewish architect named Daniel Libeskind designed. Some are German Jews. Some, like the theater directors Thomas and Matthias Langhoff, are distinctively *East* German Jews. (Matthias's daughter, Anna, who is a playwright and director herself, says that her problem growing up in the theater in East Berlin was not being Jewish but being "other," being arty, being bored.) But most came here from other cities, and even from other countries, and, with the exception of Barenboim, they are not involved in the local debates about "memory projects" like Lea Rosh's memorial. They think of Rosh's memorial as an establishment obsession—as something that has very little to do with them. Barzel says the only debate about Jews that interests *them* is "the one between dead Jews and living Jews"—by which he means between that establishment of historians and Shoah-business people and the artists and intellectuals who know that "how we think together now is the future." Barzel, who in his time has put together museums of modern art for Florence and Prato, is already in trouble with the city for announcing that his museum here is going to promote "living" Jewish art instead of the frozen, folkloric stereotypes of Jews and Jewish history which in his opinion are another way of saying that Jewish culture "died" with the Holocaust. His view of a German Holocaust memorial is "I'm not against anyone who makes an effort to remember, but I think that all you can do with this area would be plant some green grass with a small stone in the middle: 'Remember the Holocaust.' " Anything else would be "art," and Barzel believes that Holocaust memorials have very little to do with art—that trying to "express" a holocaust kills any artistic impulse. He says that all an artist can do with the fact of the Holocaust is "to say 'Ah!' and then you have to hide."

∾

Still, when Rosh announced her memorial a lot of German artists started thinking about what Eike Geisel once called "German 'solutions' to the Final Solution." A Kassel artist named Horst Hoheisel started collecting stones—palm-size stones, like the ones that Jews traditionally leave on graves—and a few years later he put a thousand and seven stones in a big glass cart, each one wrapped in a letter to a Kassel Jew who had died in a concentration camp. Schoolchildren wrote the letters. Hoheisel's plan in Kassel had been to involve those schoolchildren in thinking about the Holocaust by assigning each child the responsibility for one victim— making the child get to know that victim as a human being, with a name and a family and a history that was part of Germany's history. The children were given a book called *Names and Fates of the Jews of Kassel,* but it seems that some of them simply copied the euphemisms of the Final Solution. Their letters used words like "verdict" for deportation order, "sent" for deportation to a death camp, "perished" for exterminated in a gas chamber. Hoheisel had originally wanted to keep children collecting stones. He wanted to cover all the Holocaust victims in Europe, and to end up with six million stones. He thought about bringing the stones to Berlin as a Holocaust memorial, but somewhere along the way he must have changed his mind, because he entered Lea Rosh's memorial competition with a project that involved tearing down the Brandenburg Gate and using *those* stones for a memorial. It was a "history of the perpetrators" sort of project, in its suggestion that Germans needed to sacrifice in order to commemorate, and, speaking symbolically, it was not really such a bad idea.

It was Eike Geisel who told me about Hoheisel's stones. Geisel is not Jewish, but many Germans assume he is because he has produced the nearest thing to a chronicle of the Shoah business in the German press—and because, like Henryk Broder, he is mordant in his criticism. He says he is constantly amazed by the ingenuity of the "solutions" to the Final Solution—especially the ones like Hoheisel's, which have to do with the incantatory magic of numbering and naming. He refers to them collectively, and skeptically, as "the adopt-a-Jew movement." He thinks that in their emphasis on "We, as Germans, do this" they have more to do with Germany reinventing itself than with Germany thinking about its victims, and certainly Lea Rosh, whose byword is "We, as Germans, do this," would be hard put to it to contradict him. Himmler once made a famous speech in which he urged Germans not to weaken in their resolve against Jews simply because "everyone knows a decent Jew," and Geisel suspects that some of the projects he writes about now have to do with putting this "decent Jew" back into German lives while leaving the real drama of the Holocaust—of complicity in, and even enthusiasm for, the Holocaust—almost entirely unexplored.

In a way, the decent Jew is the flip side of the coin called "the good German." Werner Angress, the historian, once told me that he wondered whether his father was some good German's decent Jew—whether his father would have returned to Berlin and walked into the bank he ran and opened the door to the same clients and, in time, sent money to Lea Rosh for a Holocaust memorial in the city that sent him to die in Auschwitz. Angress himself thinks that at this late date building memorials to Germany's victims isn't a very healthy or useful occupation. "People get tired," he says. "They want to do something, feel something—but there comes a point where they can't do it any longer." He means that the danger may be less that Germans forget their victims than that they exhaust themselves remembering their victims. It leads to the same denial.

This may have something to do with why so many Berlin Jews worry about Lea Rosh's memorial—about the effect of what Nicola Galliner calls "this ultimate, terrible, forced, ersatz attempt to commemorate officially"—and why, in one way or another, other Berliners worry. They worry that monuments are slowly replacing the real *lieux de mémoire*—the camps themselves. They think that it is only a matter of time before those camps are turned over to developers and supermarket chains. The historians who work at the Ravensbrück and Sachsenhausen camps, which are close to Berlin, have already filed for what amounts to bankruptcy. Their research and operating budgets were cut this year, and Sachsenhausen today has so little money, even for repairs, that some of the buildings are collapsing—which means they are getting too hazardous for visits by the local schoolchildren, who are bused in routinely as part of their German history classes. It distressed Galliner that Rosh's collaborator, Eberhard Jäckel, came back from a visit to Yad Vashem and went on television and said he was "so uplifted." Galliner told me she does not want Germans to feel "uplifted" by Holocaust memorials. She wants them to go to the camps and feel ashamed. She thinks that a huge memorial here in Berlin will give the indignity of the Holocaust a kind of "death dignity," and, like a lot of other Berlin Jews, she is puzzled that Israelis (including the people at Yad Vashem) have, by and large, been enthusiastic about Rosh's project. It may be that the farther you are, as a Jew, from the politics of memory in Germany, the more appealing that project seems, and it is certainly true that few Israelis have made the connection that Berliners make—between the dwindling budgets for places like Sachsenhausen and the promotion of wreath-throwing places in the new capital. Three-quarters of the people in Germany today were born after the war, and the camps are really all that is physically left of the Nazi years for them to learn from. Some, of course, don't learn. A professor I know who volunteered to help with a grade-school trip to Auschwitz told me later how horrified she was to see the children running around the camp, hooting and laughing, and a friend who visited Buchenwald one weekend this spring heard parents telling *their* children, "If you don't behave, we'll leave you here."

Not long ago, two young Berlin artists named Renata Stih and Frieder Schnock came up with a scheme to use the Holocaust-memorial project as a way of getting people to visit the camps. They entered the competition with a model that took the site and bisected it with a one-way street lined with bus stops; their idea was to fill it with big red buses that would leave on schedule for the various camps, and thus turn the memorial into the beginning of what Stih called "a journey to the real thing." She described it to me as an "anti-proposal," because she and Schnock never expected to win—nor, for that matter, did the artist who wanted to fence the site with barbed wire and leave it empty, so that Germans visiting the memorial would be puzzled and uneasy, and would have to start asking each other, "Where do we put these flowers? Why is there nothing here?" Stih and Schnock are not Jewish, and they are not native Berliners—Stih was born in Zagreb—but they share this with a lot of people their age who live in Berlin and *are* Jewish: they are wary of what Stih calls "the Holocaust genre." I know a Berlin Jewish novelist named Marc Svetov who sometimes describes himself by saying, "My grandfather was a Chicago labor racketeer, from Odessa, and he didn't think of himself as a victim." What Svetov means is that fifty years after they *could* have built a Holocaust memorial, most Germans prefer to deal with Jews as a kind of mythic collectivity—"the Jewish victim"—rather than as ordinary people who might even have gangsters as grandparents. (This is a problem that my friend Wiglaf Droste calls the what-happens-if-you're-robbed-and-the-robber-is-Jewish problem.) Svetov came to Berlin the way a lot of Jewish kids come now—more or less by accident. He followed a girl here, and when she left, he stayed. He got a job with the American army through a Jewish colonel whose only requirement was that you had to be

Jewish and you had to show up at an army chapel for Friday-night services. He ended up with a sideline supplying PX peanut butter to rich businessmen at the synagogue where Estrongo Nachama is cantor—making him, he acknowledges, something of a gangster himself. Now he has a German girlfriend. She comes from a village in Bavaria, and it was part of their courtship that they read together "pretty intensively" about the Holocaust and visited some of the concentration camps. She is "cool about the Holocaust," Svetov says, but he doesn't think that most Germans are cool. He thinks that "Germans have something in their heads about Jews," something that compels them to want to build memorials to their own victims. In a way, he agrees with the Jewish writer Rafael Seligmann, in Munich, who has argued against Lea Rosh's memorial, saying that most Jews want to stop seeing themselves as victims—that Auschwitz was not a Jewish invention; that it was Hitler's invention; that when Jews base their identity on Auschwitz they are letting Hitler mediate their relation to themselves. Rosh would say that the memorial is a German thing, and "not their thing."

∞

The year Lea Rosh started collecting signatures, the East German government started wondering what to do with its history museum on Unter den Linden. The museum had been a Prussian arsenal. East Germany had inherited it, along with eight centuries' worth of rifles, cannons, and rusty armor, and over the years had turned it into another kind of arsenal. The museum was a repository of Communist kitsch, with terrible dioramas of what could be called Marxism-Leninism's greatest moments, including a reproduction of Karl Marx's London study. It was not the sort of place likely to draw crowds in the new, liberated East Berlin, or to do much for the image of the born-again democrats running for office during the brief year that a free East Germany actually existed, and no one here was surprised when the East Germans closed it abruptly in September of 1990, "for forty years of lying" about history—as if the objects, and not the East Germans who made those objects, had been doing the lying.

It was well known then that Helmut Kohl wanted a new historical museum in place in Berlin. ("You have to remember, the improvement of Germany's image is on Kohl's mind day and night," a friend in Berlin had said after a story broke about Kohl's offering ten million dollars to the Holocaust Museum in Washington, on the proviso that it devote a section to "the democratic rebirth of Germany." The German government denied it.) Kohl was already building a historical museum in Bonn, but that was a museum devoted mainly to the history of West Germany. In Berlin he wanted a museum that would take the Germany that Bismarck had pieced together in 1871 and give it a coherence and a continuity—a "Germanness," so to speak—that went back centuries. He wanted people to see a Germany that was nobler, and certainly more enduring, than the Germany that in seventy-four years had started two world wars and caused the death of nearly fifty million people. The museum he had originally had in mind was for West Berlin—an extravagant Aldo Rossi complex that was going to cover the public gardens near the Reichstag, at a cost to Bonn of five hundred and fifty million dollars. But with East Germany to pay for, he couldn't afford Rossi. He took over the arsenal instead and gave it a new name, the German Historical Museum, and a new director, a Munich museum director named Christoph Stölzl. Last December, on the eve of the liberation celebrations, Stölzl opened an exhibit called "Witnessing German History." One critic called it "Nationalismus Lite."

Berliners tend to underestimate Kohl, because he is so provincial. He is porky and sentimental and a little befuddled, a little thick, like a postcard peasant sweating it out in a politician's suit—which, in a way, is what he is. They clip Helmut Kohl pictures and print them on T-shirts. (I had one of Kohl's helmeted head sticking out of the top of a NATO tank.) They trade Helmut Kohl jokes, which differ from, say, Polish jokes or North Dakota jokes only in that most of them are true. (It is true, for example, that Kohl clapped to the beat of "Sag Nicht Keinmal," the song of the Warsaw Ghetto uprising, at Simon Wiesenthal's eightieth-birthday party at the New York Marriott Marquis. On the other hand, it is not true that he raised his glass to Wiesenthal with the toast "For us, every night is Crystal Night." An American rabbi who came to the party did that.) "Shrewd" is the most that Berliners usually grant their chancellor—as in "not smart but shrewd"—which may be why he was shrewd enough to avoid anyone on the Berlin scene when he was looking for a curator to decide what images of Germany other Germans were going to see. Stölzl was regarded in history circles as too much of an aesthete for the job, and in art circles as too much of a bureaucrat, but conservatives in the west of Germany found him "culturally inspiring." He told them the good news about German history that they wanted to hear. He was—to quote a historian who has worked with Stölzl—someone for whom the aesthetics of "Germanness" would not be diluted by too much scholarship or too much soul-searching, or even too much accuracy.

Stölzl told Kohl that for him German history began "with Luther sitting down and writing the German Bible." He told *me* he saw Germany "as a mainstream flowing through the history of the West." He saw it "as a river of the Enlightenment." One of the first things he bought for the museum was a 1776 German-language edition of the American Declaration of Independence; it was the original translation, and he spent three-quarters of a million dollars for it. When people wanted to know what the Declaration of Independence had to do with German history—or, for that matter, what the terra-cotta Diderot off the museum's great hall had to do with German history, or the Houdon George Washington that he had announced his intention of buying—Stölzl replied that the "pursuit of happiness" was an Enlightenment goal that Germans and Americans historically shared. (As it happens, Hannah Arendt thought so too.) Stölzl said that the Declaration of Independence was "where we got *our* ideas of independence"; that it was "part of *our* history, like the French Revolution and the Commune, and the Crystal Palace"; that, once the museum had expanded, it would have pride of place between a big movie theater where people could "look at democratic enlightenment in the rest of the world" and a permanent exhibit of masterpieces from Germany's own Enlightenment. Stölzl ignored the critics who said that as far as they were concerned Germany's problems came from its having *missed* the Enlightenment. Stölzl ignored the historians who explained that, in fact, Frederick the Great was so distressed at Germany's having missed it that he summoned Voltaire to instruct him and, having learned his history and practiced his very good French, settled back into his comfortable autocratic ways and sent the philosopher home. Stölzl ignored anyone who tried to remind him that Germany was never like England or France, or even Italy; that Germany had always been an ethnic idea, and only rarely an idea about citizenship; that Germany had never had a successful revolution, or even, until Weimar, a democratic parliamentary system.

Stölzl told me he was reclaiming Germany's "common history," which had almost been lost—to Hitler, to the shame that followed Hitler, to the federalism that followed Hitler. He dismissed Jürgen Habermas, who had pointed out that until the Federal Republic was founded, in 1948, and a proper constitution was written, the only history Germans had in common was, unfortunately, the wrong history. But he was fulsome about Kohl. He said that Kohl "understood" Germany in ways that, say, Richard von Weizsäcker had not. Weizsäcker had had too many "misty, philosophical thoughts" about Germany. Weizsäcker, with his complicated notions about "liberation," had been "a gray-haired man on a throne." What Germany needed was leaders like Kohl— no-nonsense, get-on-with-it, *progressive* leaders, who knew how unhealthy it was to mistake the "tributaries" of Germany's bad moments for the mighty current that had produced the Germany of 1995. Never mind that it was the Allied armies, defeating the old Germany, that produced a new Germany. Stölzl doesn't want his museum to dwell on the "lows" of a century his exhibit flyer describes as "a period with highs and lows that are still a part of many people's experience." He thinks that the camps do that— which is certainly true. "Here you can go next door to a camp and see the authentic object" is the way he puts it. He says, "The Americans did a wonderful job with the Auschwitz thing in Washington, but you have to remember that it's a fake Auschwitz." He talks about "authenticity" like an antique dealer. He wants for his museum "the aesthetic opposition of authentic objects." It is a taste he shares with Kohl, who saw to it that his museum in Bonn displayed the pullover Gorbachev wore and the cardigan Kohl himself wore when the men were walking around Stavropol on a chilly day arguing about how much money Kohl was going to pay Gorbachev for East Germany.

A historian named Hans Wilderotter, who put together three shows for Stölzl before he and Stölzl parted company, says that history at the museum now is history about "gaga leaders and nice people": about how the Kaiser liked big boats, and so you had the German navy; about how Hitler liked power, and so you had National Socialism. He says that any museum that pretends to rep•resent Germany in the twentieth century has to involve an understanding of the choices Germans made, whereas the museum that Stölzl opened for Helmut Kohl refuses to implicate Germans in any choices, or even acknowledge that they had choices. Another historian, who worked for a while on "Witnessing German History," says that for him the problem was not just Stölzl—the problem was "Germans." He thinks that people at the museum never really understood that in arranging art and objects into the aestheticized Germany that Stölzl wanted, they were manipulating political perception, not to mention history. They were given a cheerful, progressive model called the West and were instructed to slip Germany into that model, and in the end it didn't matter whether or not that model was faithful to any real German experience. "A lot of the staff had no competence to weigh the social and political significance of the material," he told me. "To say 'revisionist' is to overestimate their capabilities and their intentions." Wiglaf Droste put it this way: "It shows that if you leave history to these people it's the end of history."

"Witnessing German History" begins in a long great hall, which, from what I could make out on a couple of visits, stands for the long mainstream on which Helmut Kohl is floating German history. The hall is adorned with objects of Light, from Goethe's dining-room chairs to a room-size fantasy of the founding of the Reich at the Palace of Versailles (with the rulers of the world in costume) to a Wilhelm Röntgen X-ray machine. Everything else is, so to speak, a tributary. Stölzl's First World War is a collection of helmets and some posters, and his Second World War opens with a bust of Hitler staring back, through Weimar, at Fritz Erler's famous poster of a helmeted fanatic with burning eyes. Weimar itself is squeezed into a room between them. There is a rack of Communist militia uniforms right next to a rack of Nazi militia uniforms. There is a glass man, which, according to Stölzl, "you can look into from the left and the right, eugenically, symbolically, and psychologically." Visiting Stölzl's Weimar, it is hard to imagine that Weimar was also a flowering of the arts or of politics, or even that it was the first German democracy. Stölzl's Weimar is "balanced" (which is to say that, true to current fashion, it turns Marx into Stalin, on a rampage in an earlier life), and it is "inevitable." It follows "inevitably" from the First World War, and Nazism follows inevitably from it—as if it were History, and not Germans, that set the country on its *Sonderweg* to fascism. Even Stölzl's National Socialism is "balanced": a love letter from a captured German soldier "balances" a letter from the Plötzensee prison; a battlefield picture of a dead soldier "balances" the self-portrait of a Jew on his way to Auschwitz. The twelve dark years of Hitler take place in a small, dark room, and the camps are represented by one military map, which is so small that most people walk through "National Socialism" without noticing it at all.

∞

Berliners have a joke about the three most overcrowded boats in history being Noah's Ark, the Mayflower, and the German Resistance in the Second World War—because, in reality, the German Resistance was pitifully small. It was small because one of the first things Hitler did in 1933 was to start building camps in Germany and filling them with the people who might have made a resistance, and it was small because most Germans who were not in camps shared his views. The meaning of "resistance"—*Widerstand*—is ambiguous, at best, in Germany. There is "resistance" as a kind of immunity, and Germans use it, not always ingenuously, for people who were "immune" to National Socialism, like nuns whose "resistance" was to say "Hail Mary" instead of "Heil Hitler." And there is the real Resistance. In East Germany, the word was used exclusively for the Communist Resistance, which drew on more than a million Communist Party militants and was certainly the only mass resistance in the country during the nineteen-thirties. In West Germany, it was used for everyone else who resisted—for the Social Democrats of the Kreisauer Kreis, for the Lutherans of the "confessing church," and, above all, for the Wehrmacht officers who attempted the only real coup against Hitler, the Officers' Plot of July 20, 1944. But the fact remains that if you are talking about the *Widerstand* in wartime Germany you are talking about no more than ten or twenty thousand people. It is not a figure to inspire young Germans looking for heroes.

And it is complicated by the evidence that very few of the officers arrested after July 20, 1944, were the kind of people those young Germans would want to have running their country now. The officers were not democrats. They did not like Jews. Many of them believed in a "Jewish question"; some of them wanted to empty the camps and ship the Jews to Canada, with the possible exception of the Kaiser Jews—the First World War veterans— who, according to one of the kinder plans, would be offered a limited form of citizenship. Most of the officers had started out as Nazis, and they remained Nazis until Germany began to lose. One of them had commanded a death squad charged with killing captured Russian officers, and the coup leader, Claus Schenk Graf von Stauffenberg—it was Stauffenberg who planted the bomb that was supposed to blow up Hitler—wanted to sabotage the Allied invasion, because the Allies, with whom the group had contacts, had demanded, reasonably, that the Wehrmacht surrender unconditionally before the fighting stop. The officers' cause was "honor"—Germany's honor, their own honor—but it was not always, or necessarily, the pursuit of happiness for the great majority of the German people. There were so many "Graf"s and "von"s among the officers who tried, too late, to kill Hitler that their names and their bland, entitled faces evoke an army of knights— noble and pure, and therefore, in the *Geisteswissenschaft* called German history, mythically "German." Marion Dönhoff, the publisher of *Die Zeit* and a countess herself, called them the people of "our best tradition." It was, at any rate, a tradition that the Third Reich could be said to have betrayed.

There is, of course, a memorial to the officers of July 20. It is a large bronze nude of a young man with his fists clenched and his wrists crossed and bound, and it stands in the courtyard of the Bendlerblock—the Wehrmacht command post, near Tiergarten, where Hitler made his famous speech about Germans needing *Lebensraum* in the east and where, eleven years later, the officers of July 20 plotted their coup against him. Whenever I visited the

Bendlerblock, there was a bunch of tulips at the statue's base. Today, part of the Bendlerblock is given over to an archive called the German Resistance Memorial Center; there are lecture rooms, reading rooms, and nineteen galleries with an ongoing exhibit of five thousand photographs and documents. A Passau historian named Peter Steinbach oversees the center. He is a resistance specialist, and has been working on the archive ever since 1983, when Weizsäcker (who was mayor of West Berlin at the time) brought him to the city to start collecting material. The understanding then was not so much to reinvent the resistance—to make it bigger than it was, or more prominent, or more pervasive—as to look at how, in a country where so few people resisted, certain men and women came to risk their lives, and usually lose them, in defying Hitler. Steinbach's job was to straighten out the record—in part because the Communists, in East Berlin, did not really credit the Officers' Plot—and it may be that he straightened it out too well, because, in the end, the twelve years of most of what could be called the German Resistance became a footnote to the legend of July 20. The impression you get at the Bendlerblock now is that the will of all "good Germans" was expressed entirely in those few young men who tried to salvage a piece of Germany for themselves on July 20; that the meaning of a thousand small acts of resistance was entrusted to them; that they were "Germany." They were in fact simply Germans who, *faute de mieux,* turned out to be the only people close enough to Nazi power to try to replace it.

When the German Resistance Memorial Center opened, in 1989, most of the criticism came from the left. It came from liberal Germans who felt, to quote one of them, "profound pedagogic distress at the distortions of history" taking place as the soldiers of Germany's *Lebensraum*—converts to "liberation" on the eve, and evidence, of Germany's disgrace—became *the* German Resistance, while the men and women whose resistance went back to 1933, and the Reichstag fire, became their acolytes. Now the criticism is from the right, and it comes from the same people who once sent Helmut Kohl to Bitburg with Ronald Reagan, from people like the old Bavarian deputy Alfred Dregger, who thought that 1995 should be a year of mourning—for the defeat of "greater Germany," for the loss of East Prussia, and for his own brother, who died on the Eastern front in the last month of the fighting. The trouble began last year when Stauffenberg's son—a famously dim conservative politician, who is sometimes described as Germany's Randolph Churchill—attacked Steinbach during an anniversary ceremony at the Berlin library. He accused the professor of "defiling" Germany's name, and the Stauffenberg name, by hanging pictures of Communist criminals like Walter Ulbricht on the walls of his father's post. A few days later, the exhibit was sent abroad. It was a stripped-down version of the Bendlerblock show, having mainly to do with the Officers' Plot, and it seemed to people who saw it then that the plot was transformed again, into a revolution—you could say into a declaration of independence—in which the future democratic Germany was prefigured. ("The Old Testament of German democracy," someone called it.) By then, Kohl was involved. It is said that Kohl told his ambassador in Washington to get on the phone, and if the ambassador did, he must have been persuasive, because in short order the German Resistance show was up on the walls of the Library of Congress, which had already turned it down. Then it traveled to Columbia University, where the German army chief of staff spoke at the opening. Steinbach himself did not show up at Columbia. He claimed that his archives were being used "politically," and he was right.

Wiglaf Droste, talking about the exhibit now, says that by the time the year is over, the Communist Resistance will probably cease to have existed at all. It will have been replaced by "Helmut Kohl's resistance." In January of 1995, Kohl carried a wreath to a memorial ceremony in the old French sector of Berlin—a ceremony for, among other resistance heros, Julius Leber, who was a Social Democrat and one of the leaders of the Kreisauer Kreis. Kohl made a short speech and recited the names of "Christians" who had also died resisting. Then he presented his wreath "in the name of the Christian Democratic Party"—*his* party. He called it "the party of the Christian resistance."

∞

Helmut Kohl is having second thoughts about Lea Rosh. By now, he is not so sure that having a Holocaust memorial in the capital is really going to help promote Germany's new image in the world.

When he presented Rosh with a pricey chunk of central Berlin, he may have been thinking about a nice park, with another sentimental Kollwitz statue—something discreet, something to show the world that whatever anyone said about Jews and Germans, their relations were tranquil; they had all been liberated on May 8, 1945, and the rest was "history." But Rosh wanted to build a monument that was, as she once said, "big like the crime." She wanted a big public. A big budget. Big discussions. Big ideas. Her own idea was a vast subterranean Jewish star, which you would enter through gates like the gates of concentration camps—gates that said *"Arbeit Macht Frei."* The architect for her star was a Swiss by the name of Harry Szeemann. It was his plan, and Rosh's, to build a series of rooms in the star, with wailing walls and "symbolic installations," and to commission, for the grounds, a "monumental" piece of sculpture by someone like Richard Serra. The design was, even by monument standards, dreadful. It engendered a lot of protest and a lot of black humor, and in any event it was scrapped as soon as the Berlin Senat got involved in the project, in 1993, by pledging four million dollars. The Senat wanted to hold what could be called a competition as big as the crime, because Berlin has (this is the official term) "a democratic competition culture," and also because the memorial, with a total budget of twelve million dollars, was going to be the most expensive memorial project in Berlin's history, and the city wanted to have a say in whose project it was going to be. Bonn, which had also pledged four million dollars, wanted the same say. And so, of course, did Lea Rosh. The trouble began when it was time to name a jury: Bonn chose five people, Berlin chose five, and Rosh chose five, and their agreement was that no one could veto anyone else's choices. Stefanie Endlich, who writes about public art and describes herself as "the public-art specialist" on the jury, was one of the Berlin jurors. She says that it wasn't a job she wanted. She told the Senat, "A monument is not what we need." She had always thought that the city should be spending its money on a museum, or on a Holocaust-documentation center, or on the camps near Berlin, like Sachsenhausen. "I felt terrible joining that jury," she told me. "I had nightmares." She worried about the memorial turning into an *Ereignisstruktur*—a kind of "happening place," where people would be walked through the experience of victimhood and then go shopping, or go home to a nice lunch. She was skeptical about the project brief: "The power of contemporary art should create a synthesis enabling us to face this subject in sorrow, shock, and respect, and to remember it in shame and guilt. A place should be created where insight can grow." She didn't know what "synthesis" or "insight" meant when you were talking about the Holocaust, and she said so. When Rosh heard that Endlich was on the jury, she wrote her an open letter and sent it to Bonn, to the Jewish community, to the Senat. It said that Endlich was "against memory."

The jury started meeting in January of this year—a mishmash of politicians, bureaucrats, historians, artists, architects, and journalists, with different tastes, different priorities, and different people to report to. Some of those people had wanted to restrict the competition to Germans ("the perpetrators' school"), and some had wanted to open it to anyone in the world who had a design to offer—the idea being, as the poet Durs Grünbein put it, that the meaning of "Holocaust" was not something the Germans owned. They compromised. They said that "participants must have lived or worked in the Federal Republic of Germany for at least six months," and then they chose twelve "international artists" and paid each of them thirty-five thousand dollars to participate too. Rosh told me the designs were "secret," but if you put in a Sunday afternoon at the Paris Bar and listened to the art gossip you eventually heard about Richard Serra's scooped-out granite bunker and Rebecca Horn's "meditation spiral" and Dani Karavan's garden of yellow coreopsis planted in the shape of a Jewish star. And in the end you began to wonder if they shouldn't be *kept* secret. Walter Jens, a Tübingen historian who served as the jury chairman, admitted in March of this year that there was "no aesthetic 'solution'" to the memory of mass death. But, as Henryk Broder wrote later, it was clear that the jurors were determined to find one. They voted in March, and found two, and then they opened a Holocaust-memorial exhibit at an old East Berlin government hall, and Berliners finally got a look at the five hundred and twenty-eight designs that had been placed in competition.

Eike Geisel, writing in *Konkret,* said he was horrified by the exhibit—not least, he told me after his first visit, because he was "the only one not laughing." And Broder, writing in *Der Spiegel,* called it "a field site for anthropologists, psychologists, and behaviorists" and for anyone else interested in the soul of "a confused nation . . . that will enlist its victims to purify itself." Broder put the cost of the memorial, to Germany, at "2.5 marks per victim," but the calculation was wrong. The models were not only grotesque, they were gigantesque. One of them was a kind of silo—"a drum," according to the man who designed it, "for the blood of six million Jews." Another was a field covered by six million glass shards. There was a giant oven, to be fired day and night, like an eternal light; and there was a Ferris wheel hung with deportation freight cars instead of baskets; and there was a salt sea, a sea of tears, with a slowly corroding block of steel floating in it; and there was a huge sealed building shaped like Europe, with twelve million "eye holes" bored into the roof. One of the competitors quoted Heidegger on the "*Existenziell,*" and one thought that the Star of David was "a Jewish symbol of oppression," and one said that he wanted to "engage" visitors in his project by collecting their combs for five to ten years and building a monument with *them.* The competition may have been democratic, but it did not do much for democracy, or for art or memory or Lea Rosh's budget, and it did not even begin to settle the argument about "victims." The two finalists went back to their drawing boards with instructions to elaborate on their "feasibility studies," neither of which were clear, but what *was* clear was that they disagreed about victims. One of the finalists was a Cologne architect named Simon Ungers. His project was big—"monumental, unavoidably present," the jury said. More precisely, it was a seventy-eight-thousand-square-foot quadrangle enclosed by double-T steel girders on cement blocks, with the names of the death camps pierced through them and thus repeated, in sunlight and shadow, on the ground. It was not beautiful, and it was certainly not "uplifting," but it seemed to open up the definition of victims, which the other project did not.

The other project—it was designed by a Berlin group working under a local painter named Christine Jackob-Marks—was very specific to the jury's brief, which had been to create a memorial specifically to "the murdered Jews of Europe." It covered the en-

tire site with a hundred-and-eight-thousand-square-foot tilted concrete slab—a "tombstone bigger than a football field," as Broder
described it—in which the names of four million two hundred
thousand Jewish victims of the Holocaust would eventually be engraved, and on which eighteen stones from Masada, one for each
of the countries that deported Jews to death camps, would be scattered. The problem was that Jackob-Marks's stones were boulders;
Eike Geisel estimated that, given the cost of transporting boulders
from Masada (assuming there *were* boulders left at Masada) and
the cost of pouring ninety thousand square feet of concrete,
Jackob-Marks was talking not twelve million dollars but more like
a hundred and twenty million dollars. He figured that it would
probably take thirty years to engrave the names, and that, if you
were going to be able to read them at all, it would probably take
three football fields. That was how many Jews died in the Holocaust. It was something, he thought, that Germans still had trouble understanding.

Late in June, Lea Rosh announced that she was going to build
the tombstone. She had not recalled her jury. She was not interested in any more encounters with Berlin's "democratic competition culture." She met with the deputy home minister, from Bonn;
with the Berlin senators for building and for culture; and, from
what was described as "Rosh's group," with Edzard Reuter, the
old chairman of Daimler-Benz (which was supposed to contribute
to her project), and the Daimler-Benz public relations director.
And then she chose the tombstone, which seems to be what she had
had in mind to do from the beginning. The minister from Bonn de-
murred—he did not really like the idea of such a big tombstone,
though he said he could live with the tombstone—but Rosh, who
loved the tombstone, didn't care. She said later, "It was the past
that was gigantic, not the memorial slab." She was prepared for
some criticism, but certainly not the barrage she got. It came in-
stantly, and it came from everywhere. It came from a Frankfurt architect named Salomon Korn, who had been the only German Jew
on Rosh's jury, and who hated the tombstone. It came from Ignatz
Bubis, who said that if Lea Rosh started engraving the names of
Holocaust victims—and nothing else—on a tombstone she was
going to end up with a thousand Moses Rabbinowitsches whom

no one could tell apart. It came from Amnon Barzel, at the Jewish Museum, who had challenged the concept early on, saying that Masada was about a fight where everyone died, and had nothing to do with the Holocaust, or with Jews who survived the Holocaust. It came from journalists, who called Rosh "Stepmother Courage" and said that her tombstone was "a big stone covering the past." It came from developers who had plans for putting up public housing on Wilhelmstrasse, near the Pariser Platz, and who wanted their tenants to look down at the statue of Goethe in the Tiergarten, and not on a five-acre concrete slab with the names of dead Jews written on it. And it came from politicians, who knew that, given all the trouble with skinheads in Germany lately, the tombstone would have to be "protected" at night with floodlights and policemen, and maybe even dogs, and who pointed out that floodlights and policemen and dogs had never done much for Germany's "image" in the world. Rosh gave way on some points: no boulders from Masada; more "information" about the victims. But she started insisting that *she* was a victim, too—of the press, of the pols, even of the Jews who complained. She didn't think that Jews had a right to complain. She put it this way: "It's the successors of the perpetrators who are building this memorial, not the Jews." It looked like the beginning of a scandal—which, from Helmut Kohl's point of view, meant a scandal about Jews and Germans that he would soon be reading about on the front pages of *Le Monde* and the *Jerusalem Post* and *The New York Times*. Two days later, he vetoed the tombstone. He said he was looking forward to seeing a Holocaust memorial in Berlin, but he thought that the memorial Lea Rosh had in mind was "monstrous and without dignity." ("Gigantomania" was a word he used.) He called for "a pause for reflection . . . to be followed by a public discussion" to find a new design—one that would inspire "a bigger consensus." Then, of course, the mayor of Berlin said that he was also for things like reflection and discussion and consensus. In a few days' time, the only politician in town who had anything good to say about Christine Jackob-Marks's design was Wolfgang Nagel, the senator for building. Nagel thought that the design should stand; he said he liked "the naming," but his reason seemed mainly to be that he had just spent a million dollars of Berlin's money running the competition to choose it.

Kohl, right now, is holding on to the land he promised Lea Rosh. Rosh, on the other hand, says that the land is hers. She has asked the Berlin Senat to decide. After thirty years in German television, Rosh is thick-skinned and vindictive. The fight excites her. Kohl doesn't intimidate her any more than the historians intimidated her when they said that Lea Rosh was "an amateur of memory" and did memory no real service. Her view of the historians is "They think they own history. They're scared of losing it." And that is probably her view of Kohl. I remember that the day I met her she got on the phone to answer an invitation to a cultural-prize ceremony involving the memorial in Hannover, and demanded that her name be put on the invitation, "like Rita Süssmuth's name." Rita Süssmuth is the president of the Bundestag, and she was presenting the prize. "I have contributed much more than Rita Süssmuth!" Rosh barked into the telephone. She meant more for Germany. She wanted to be on camera. She wanted to make her pitch. ("It's really *her* tombstone," Eike Geisel said later.) I almost admired her.

Rosh used to talk about going to the *Deutsche Volk*—the German people—with her project. She talked her way into free "Holocaust memorial spots" on twenty-one television stations. She persuaded the publisher Bertelsmann to cover the cost of five million flyers. She got free advertising space in most of the German press, and even free forms for her contributors, courtesy of the Landesbank Berlin. She even, as Geisel had predicted, invited every German to adopt a Jewish victim with his check. Her friend and fund-raiser Inge Borck says that she got a lot of envelopes from "ordinary people"—five marks, ten marks, the Christmas-card-sale proceeds from a Catholic church, the collection from a Berlin kindergarten—but no "big money." The chairman of Bosch had promised to contribute, but the money was not forthcoming, and neither was the money from Daimler-Benz, despite the fact that Rosh had been careful to put Reuter on her memorial board and even to include him in the meeting at which she chose the tombstone. (Stefanie Endlich says Rosh should have remembered that after years of putting off paying reparations to survivors who were forced to work in its wartime factories, Daimler-Benz came up with less than fifteen million tax-deductible dollars.) So Rosh counted on the German people. In the end, they gave her two hundred and twenty thousand dollars.

It may be that the German people were never a very promising prospect, because what's left in Germany, after all the revising and reclaiming and renaming and cleaning up, is still the past, and the people who would like to keep it. This spring, a man at the German tourist office in New York unearthed a directive about discouraging "Jews, blacks, Asians, and Hispanics from visiting Germany," and says he was fired for it; an old professor from the technical college in Aachen admitted to being the missing S.S. Hauptsturmführer in charge of supplying equipment for medical experiments at concentration camps; the German security police in Karlsruhe announced that the incidence of anti-Semitic crimes had been rising steadily for a year. The list goes on, and it doesn't take long to understand that the teenage skinheads torching foreigners and bombing synagogues are only one part of Germany's "Nazi problem." The real problem has to do with another kind of list, a list of questions: When will the past be over? Should it be over? What happens to memory then? Wiglaf Droste says that he left the theater after *Schindler's List* with a crowd of people who were blowing their noses and shaking their heads as if they had never heard of the Holocaust until Steven Spielberg thought to tell them about it—and this despite the camp visits and the books and the pictures and the vast and profitable and ambiguous industry of the Shoah business. Droste thinks that if people are blowing their noses and shaking their heads like that all over Germany, a Holocaust memorial is not going to settle the country's "Jewish question" any more than the officers of July 20, 1944, would have settled it with a couple of boats to Canada.

∞

Last winter, I met a professor in Berlin named Gert Mattenklott. He wasn't on Rosh's jury, and he wasn't a historian—he teaches comparative literature at the Free University of Berlin—but, like Rosh, he had a Jewish grandfather, and he told me he had always been interested in what he calls "the culture of remembrance."

Two years ago, he put together an exhibit about memory and monuments that traveled all over Germany. Today, he is by way of being Berlin's "memorial expert," and it is his opinion that "the passion for memorials in Berlin, where everything is symbolic but vitality happens somewhere else," has had a kind of neutralizing effect on the meaning of anything built here.

Mattenklott thinks that most Berlin monuments are destined to become "all-purpose receptacles of guilt," whose meaning changes every couple of years, with the politics of the moment, and even the prejudices of the moment. He likes to say that the only valuable thing about monuments is the discussion they provoke: they give "memory" an airing. "Memory is fluid, like writing," he told me. "You can't put memory into a monument." As a writer himself, and a student of other writers, he looks for memory now "in used-book stores, in the reminiscences of old Jews"—in people who still inhabit the interstices between private memory and public discourse. He says that when he started hearing about a monument to the Holocaust in Berlin his first thought was "Where's the money for Buchenwald?" He told me that thinking about Buchenwald (where the stump of Goethe's beech tree sits in the middle of the camp, and the guides have been known to ask if you're there for the poet or the Holocaust) and then thinking about Lea Rosh's memorial "was like taking one step forward into reality and three steps back into a past expanding like a huge desert." He said, "You can't build a monument to a paradox. You can talk, you can write, but you can't 'create' out of the trauma of the Holocaust." He thinks that only one German artist has even come close to understanding this: a sculptor named Jochen Gerz, who built a memorial in Hamburg, using columns that sank, little by little, into the ground, and materials that disappeared—materials that acknowledged the tragic fact that commemoration, like memory, is fragile and ephemeral, and in no way adequate to the "history" of what happened.

There is a word in German—one of those long compound words that Germans put together to extend a concept. The word is *Vergangenheitsbewältigung,* and it means "management of the past"—but always in the sense of mastering the past, even of manipulating the past. Mattenklott used it when we talked. Earlier,

Werner Angress had used it. He had told me that 1995 was going to be the year of *Vergangenheitsbewältigung,* and that I would find it in everything I looked at here—the liberation celebrations, the resistance archives, the new historical museum, the Holocaust-memorial project itself. Most of my Berlin friends, in one way or another, said this, too. Hansjörg Geiger, at the Stasi archives in East Berlin, used the word *Schlusstrich.* He said he got interested in 1995 because it was like the *Schlusstrich*—the line—that he found at the end of Stasi files. He thought that 1995 was going to "strike a line through history. Finished. Over and done with. Gone." Geiger believes that one of the reasons Germans are so fascinated by what he calls "the Stasi past"—the story of the secret police in East Germany, and its millions of informers, and its tens of millions of pages of reports and accusations and surveillance transcripts—is that the Stasi past has in fact become a metaphor for the Nazi past, and for German complicity in that past. A metaphor, perhaps, that Germans can "manage." A couple of years ago, Geiger went to Israel, and—like Lea Rosh and Eberhard Jäckel—he made a pilgrimage to Yad Vashem. He says that ever since then, when he thinks about being German, about what it means to be a human being with a holocaust in your history, he thinks about what he read on a black panel at the exit of Yad Vashem: "The secret of redemption is remembrance." The sentence is ambiguous, but Geiger suspects that anything written, as this was, by an eighteenth-century Galician rabbi was meant to be ambiguous, because when *he* thinks about a Holocaust memorial here in Berlin he does not think, Redemption. He thinks, A ten- or fifteen-second exculpation.

Jens Reich—the biologist who led the citizens' movement in East Berlin when the Wall was coming down—told me not long ago that Rosh's memorial project had left him "at a loss." He worried about "all this management of the past." He said, "It seems that the more we commemorate, the more we dilute the seriousness of commemoration; the better we describe, the less we mean." Reich is something of an East German Weizsäcker, in that he is an intellectual, like Weizsäcker, and is given to the same sort of "misty, philosophical thoughts." (In fact, he hoped to succeed Weizsäcker; he ran for president last year.) Reich says things that successful politicians in Germany never say. Sometimes he says he's speech-less. He said "I'm speechless" when he first visited a concentration camp and everyone there was waiting to hear him say something. He liked it that Roman Herzog, who got the job he wanted, said *he* was speechless at Auschwitz in February. "To digest Auschwitz, to digest that information, to be able to think of something 'original' to say in such a context—how is that possible?" Reich asked me. He spent the war in Dresden, and he remembers the bombings. He can smell the asphalt melting and the first corpses, and the piles of bodies waiting to be burned, but he says that he can't turn those memories into "commemoration" or else he'd have to talk about who bombed first and "commemorate" Coventry and Len-ingrad, and then he'd have to go on "commemorating"—Sarajevo, Rwanda, Chechnya—and in the end he wouldn't be any closer to the mystery of the Holocaust, or of any holocaust, or to the ques-tion that haunts him: "How did this happen in the middle of Eu-rope in a 'civilized' century?"

∽

When Renata Stih and Frieder Schnock submitted their bus-stop project to Lea Rosh, they had already finished one memorial pro-ject for Berlin—a project that many Berliners think is the only memorial that even begins to approach the experience of being Jewish in Germany under Hitler. It isn't a monument. It consists of eighty silk-screened aluminum signs—outsize street signs, really—that Stih and Schnock have attached to lampposts all over the quiet residential neighborhood called Schöneberg. Schöneberg used to be a *bürgerlich* Jewish neighborhood. It was rich and, as its name says, pretty—Jewish Switzerland, people called it—and in this it was not much different from other rich, pretty Berlin neighbor-hoods, except that sixteen thousand Jews lived there, Jews who thought of themselves as so "German" that a handful of them were still in Schöneberg in 1943, waiting for other Germans to save them. They were on the last train out to Auschwitz. What Stih and Schnock wanted to do in Schöneberg was to trace the small, every-day, "ordinary" discriminations—the orders and prohibitions and decrees—that led to Auschwitz by taking sixteen thousand assimi-lated German Jews and slowly, methodically, placing them outside the pale of German life and German empathy and German compassion. On one side of their signs they printed bright, simple storybook pictures: a stage curtain, a bunch of radishes, a bathing suit, a cat, a pail of milk. On the other side they printed the orders that went with the pictures: Jews are forbidden to act in theaters (March 5, 1934); Jews are forbidden to grow vegetables (March 22, 1938); Jews are forbidden to go swimming (December 3, 1938); Jews are forbidden to own pets (May 15, 1942); Jews are forbidden to buy milk (July 10, 1942).

The first of the signs I saw was right in the middle of Schöneberg, on the Bayerischer Platz, near the town hall. It was a picture of a red bench, and it said, "Jews can sit in the Bayerischer Platz only on benches marked in yellow." I got a map and started walking, and after a while I grew used to the signs. I knew how "normal" it must have seemed to other Germans when, in a few years' time, Jews were forbidden to do anything but die—and how by then nobody but Jews thought much about it. I followed the signs around the neighborhood until I got to a sign with the last Schöneberg deportation order—and, finally, to a sign with what could be called the first official revision of the Holocaust. On one side was a picture of a black file box with a blank label. On the other side was an order issued on February 16, 1945. It said, "All files involving anti-Semitic activity are to be destroyed." People in Schöneberg today live with the signs. They are not "art." They are like small memories, and, in their depth and simplicity, they leave very little to say.

ABOUT THE AUTHOR

JANE KRAMER is *The New Yorker*'s European corre-
spondent and writes the "Letter from Europe" for the
magazine. She is the author of seven books, most re-
cently *Whose Art Is It?*, which in its original form won
the National Magazine Award in 1993. Her book *The
Last Cowboy* won the National Book Award in 1981,
and her book *Europeans* won the Prix Européen de
l'Essai Charles Veillon in 1993 and was nominated
here for the National Book Critics Circle Award. She
is married to the anthropologist Vincent Crapanzano,
and they have a daughter, Aleksandra. Jane Kramer lives
in Paris and New York.

ABOUT THE TYPE

This book was set in Sabon, a typeface designed by the well-known German typographer Jan Tschichold (1902–74). Sabon's design is based upon the original letter forms of Claude Garamond and was created specifically to be used for three sources: foundry type for hand composition, Linotype, and Monotype. Tschichold named his typeface for the famous Frankfurt typefounder Jacques Sabon, who died in 1580.